I WENT TO GDAŃSK W

By Jonny Blair

NORTHERN
IRISHMAN
IN POLAND

I Went To Gdańsk With Somebody:
How A Northern Irishman Ended Up Living In Poland
by Jonny Blair

I Went To Gdańsk With Somebody:
How A Northern Irishman Ended Up Living In Poland
by Jonny Blair

Names and Locations: While most of the names and locations in this book are completely true, some may have been changed to protect the identity of people and places.

Editing and formatting by Jonny Scott Blair.

Logo designed by: Jonny Scott Blair.

Cover designed by Daniel Sidebottom at Frgstn designs: https://www.behance.net/frgstn

Additional editing by: http://www.bookbaby.com/

Additional artwork by Ilona Skladzien: https://www.ilonaskladzien.com/

Author's websites: http://dontstopliving.net and http://www.northernirishmaninpoland.com/

Author Biography

Jonny Blair is a Northern Irish travel writer based in Poland. Jonny was born in Newtownards in 1980 and grew up in Bangor in Northern Ireland. Since leaving his hometown in 2003, Jonny has travelled far and wide, detailing his journeys on his one man travel blog, Don't Stop Living. Jonny has visited over 190 countries across all seven continents including Bangladesh, Lesotho, Belize, Nauru and Iceland. Jonny has also travelled to some lesser known places such as the Kingdom of Romkerhall, Karakalpakstan, Adammia, Sovereign Military Order of Malta, Herm, Antarctica, Gorno Badakhshan, Narnia and Eneko Island. As well as working as a freelance writer, editor, teacher and copywriter, Jonny has also worked in bars, hotels and restaurants as well as on ferries, in farms, in schools and in offices. Jonny writes every day in some capacity and is also a poet and a football fanzine editor. Aside from travel, Jonny is a passionate football supporter of Glentoran FC, AFC Bournemouth, Klub Piłkarski Starogard, Legia Warszawa and Northern Ireland. Jonny aims to inspire other people to get out there and see the world with their own two eyes.

Jonny's Online Presence

Don't Stop Living:
https://dontstopliving.net/
Northern Irishman in Poland / Połnocny Irlandczyk w Polsce:
https://www.northernirishmaninpoland.com/
Jonny Blair on Twitter:
https://www.twitter.com/jonnyblair/
Jonny Blair on Facebook:
https://www.facebook.com/donotstopliving/
https://www.facebook.com/northernirishmaninpoland/
https://www.facebook.com/Jonny-Blair-Poetry-623933877981938/|
Jonny Blair on Instagram:
https://www.instagram.com/jonnydontstopliving/
Jonny Blair on YouTube:
https://www.youtube.com/user/jonnyscottblair/
Jonny Blair on LinkedIn:
https://www.linkedin.com/in/jonny-blair-8378975b/
Jonny Blair on Flickr:
https://www.flickr.com/people/jonnydontstopliving/
Email Jonny Blair:
jonny@dontstopliving.net
jonnyscottblair@hotmail.com

I Went To Gdańsk With Somebody:
How A Northern Irishman Ended Up In Poland

"Lightning strikes everytime she moves" – Calvin Harris.

"I Went To Gdańsk With Somebody" is the story from travel writer Jonny Blair after his epic *"Backpacking Centurion"* series came to a culmination in March 2015.

The story of how Northern Irishman Jonny Blair ended up in Poland is far from straight forward. Even the pages of this book are not enough detail to explain. The journey was long and fateful. It was a golden dream and a blackened nightmare all in one. But it had to be written and released. Not every Bangorian Northern Irelander dreams of a plate of pierogi with śmietana and a glass of grzaniec in a stare miasto. In this world, Jonny seems like the odd one out.

"He's like a man with a fork in a world of soup" – Noel Gallagher.

It all started with a Gerry Taggart brace in 1991. Northern Ireland beat Poland 3-1 in a football match that Jonny attended in Belfast that night. Jonny's journey to Poland took him via an ice cream hut in Bournemouth, a hostel dorm room in Bucharest, a visit to a windy cave town in Georgia, a Russian translator, nudity in Antarctica and a craft beer pub in Sofia. But it wasn't as simple as that. Jonny doesn't do simple. He also doesn't do lazy, dishonest or boring. He writes from an unwiltable heart and a boundless mind.

"You're a monsoon and a fire all in one" - Super Furry Animals.

Expect thrills and mishaps along the way. We read about Jonny's first ever trip to Poland, a Stalin inspired poem, a night on the rip in Poznań drinking grzane piwo and a chilling visit to the German Death Camps.

Expect football, friends and beer to feature heavily. Jonny likes a drink and isn't shy about it. He finds the comparisons between George Best and Kazik Deyna uncanny. Is it any wonder this Ulsterczyk ended up supporting the Polish green and white fifth tier club KP Starogard Gdański in 2016?

Working as a barman, a teacher, a PR rep, a travel writer and a broccoli farmer all add spice to this szalony journey. We end up in far flung places here. Tashkurgan in Afghanistan, Lam Tin in Hong Kong and Grödig in Austria all serve as geographical pins on this man's globetrotting odyssey to Poland.

When the sun comes up in your unknown Polish town, don't be surprised if Jonny Blair turns up cradling a dobra kawa and craving your Babcia's pierogi ruskie.

"Love remains the drug that's the high, not the pill" - Seal.

For A.M.

#ulsterczyk #nimip #northernirishmaninpoland
#północnyirlandczykwpolsce

Chapterski

Chapter 1 - Ulsterczyk *11*

Chapter 2 - Gerry Taggart Ruins Robert Warzycha's Night *14*

Chapter 3 - Best Break *18*

Chapter 4 - Polska Biało Czerwony / Poland White Red *22*

Chapter 5 - The Original Party Train Till Warszawa *25*

Chapter 6 - Coleslaw / Bolesław *28*

Chapter 7 - Big Bird *37*

Chapter 8 - Dog For A Girl *43*

Chapter 9 - Ferry Cross To Jersey *52*

Chapter 10 - Ulster's Number One *59*

Chapter 11 - La La Lafferty *65*

Chapter 12 - The Don't Stop Living Globe *68*

Chapter 13 - Living In A Land Down Under *70*

Chapter 14 - Tasmanian Devils *74*

Chapter 15 - We Will, We Will Broccoli *82*

Chapter 16 - One Small Step For Yer Man *89*

Chapter 17 - The South Pole *94*

Chapter 18 - Kong Phew *97*

Chapter 19 - Up Something *110*

Chapter 20 - Define The Gap *115*

Chapter 21 - A Hostel in Chișinău *120*

Chapter 22 - Whackpacking Centurion *124*

Chapter 23 - Basque In The Glory *127*

Chapter 24 - Gibraltar Ego *130*

Chapter 25 - Your Bacon The Pig *133*

Chapter 26 - Queue: Wait *137*

Chapter 27 - Magic Whip *140*

Chapter 28 - Last Plane Out of Hong Kong *143*

Chapter 29 - Chitty Chitty Gong Gong.............................. 146

Chapter 30 - Manama Na De De Du De Du 154

Chapter 31 - Freetown Christiania.............................. 157

Chapter 32 - Ladonia.............................. 159

Chapter 33 - Fare Auld World 161

Chapter 34 - Back To The Portman 165

Chapter 35 - Greece Lightning Strikes Twice.............................. 170

Chapter 36 - Stanislas Is Coming To Town.............................. 175

Chapter 37 - Grzaniec 178

Chapter 38 - A Bit of Krak.............................. 184

Chapter 39 - Don't Stop Lviving.............................. 187

Chapter 40 - Chernobyl's Witness.............................. 191

Chapter 41 - One Almaty Decision.............................. 202

Chapter 42 - Magnetic Kyrgyzstan.............................. 205

Chapter 43 - Nights Alive On Monday Town.............................. 209

Chapter 44 - Death Road.............................. 211

Chapter 45 - Ruud Bullet.............................. 223

Chapter 46 - The Wish Worked 240

Chapter 47 - Dashkent.............................. 248

Chapter 48 - Turkistan, not Turkmenistan.............................. 250

Chapter 49 - Get It India (Get It Intill Ye) 252

Chapter 50 - A Night In My Town.............................. 255

Chapter 51 - Holifest And The First Ever Pub Crawl In Bishkek 259

Chapter 69 - Left Out For A Reason, (I'm) All Nude.............................. 263

Chapter 53 - SV Grödig Baby.............................. 267

Chapter 54 - 7 Seconds Away 270

Chapter 55 - Crocodile Drumcree 274

Chapter 56 - Blarney Rumble 277

Chapter 57 - Zielone Ogórki (Green Gherkins).............................. 280

Chapter 58 - Kings of Lyon.............................. 284

Chapter 59 - Bruges That Won't Heal.............................. 289

Chapter 60 - Amsterdammed 294

Chapter 61 - I Went To Gdańsk With Somebody.............................. 296

Chapter 1
Ulsterczyk

Pub Tato, Bielany, Warszawa, POLAND (September 2020)

"Where it began, I can't begin to knowing" - Neil Diamond.

Zdrówko! Sláinte! I take another swig of my six złotych piwo here in Pub Tato and I ponder. I love it. I love my life in Poland. But I didn't plan it. I didn't mean it. I totally didn't expect to live here. Nevermind, love it. I didn't expect to be living in Poland. Ever. It's a big surprise, but a pleasant one. How on earth did that all happen?

Poland was never part of my plan. Life is a baffler. I am a Northern Irish nationalist. I love my wee country. I grew up on the streets of Marlo and Kilmaine in the Northern Irish seaside town of Bangor. It's a far cry from the streets of Poland. It's a really far cry. This book will try to make sense of how I ended up in Poland, and through it all, it may still not make sense. I'll be telling you stories along the way from my journey through over 150 countries.

My childhood was bliss. But looking back, as a kid, I knew virtually nothing about Poland. While reading books and studying European history, I was of course aware of the German invasion in 1939. I admit I did have a fascination for borders and countries from an early age. I was especially intrigued by the USSR, the whole Eastern Bloc, as well as Yugoslavia. I found it so fascinating how the Soviet Union broke up, communism ended in many countries and the 1990s brought a new world, a breath of fresh air. I remember the whole wallfall and how it was reported on the news from 1989 to 1991. In the middle of it all – there was a football World Cup. A football World Cup which would be the last one for four "countries" as they were – Czechoslovakia, The Soviet Union, Yugoslavia and West Germany. As the dust settled on a 1991

Northern Ireland, or upon a 1991 Poland, would life ever be the same again?

"Take me to the magic of the moment on a glory night" – Scorpions.

As a kid, I was a massive football fan, and of course I still am. You'll learn that in the duration of this book, if not from following my blogs. 1986 meant the World Cup. My Dad bought me a Northern Ireland scarf, a Northern Ireland shirt, Northern Ireland sweatbands, a green and white Northern Ireland caser and the Panini World Cup sticker album. In that album were stickers of footballers from the 24 qualified teams. In that book, Poland had two pages and Northern Ireland had two pages. So my first ever memory of anything Polish was getting a sticker of Zbigniew Boniek, a Polish footballer from the 1980s. I stuck his sticker in my book, mispronounced his name, but ultimately I knew who he was. He scored a hat-trick in a World Cup match in 1982 in a 3-0 win for Poland over Belgium, on route to Poland finishing third. 4 years later, I stuck his sticker in my 1986 book.

I owned a few football books as a child, one of which had stories, results and photos from every World Cup since 1930. Through reading those, at the time I was only ever aware of four Polish footballers (until Robert Warzycha in 1991). Those four Polish footballers would have spooky links to my life in Poland, later in life, they were -
1. Kazimierz Deyna (who was well known in the UK as he also played for Manchester City)
2. Jan Tomaszewski (who was even more well known in the UK as he basically stopped England qualifying for World Cup 1974)
3. Grzegorz Lato (who was top scorer in the 1974 World Cup as Poland reached 3rd place)
4. Zbigniew Boniek (who scored a hat-trick in the 1982 World Cup as Poland again reached 3rd place)

The irony would be that in 2017, I'd watch Tomaszewski play in a charity match in Starogard Gdański. Also in Starogard Gdański, I would end up dating a local lady. I also visited Deyna's childhood home, statue and pilgrimage in that same hometown. I'd also spend a night in the home cities of Boniek and Lato in my first 4 months living in Poland – Bydgoszcz and Malbork. It was all a spooky full circle.

While that was a mysterious start to my new life in Poland, the journey here was long and unpredictable. Hopefully by the final chapter, some of the Ulsterczyk jigsaw will start to make sense.

Wait - what or who is Ulsterczyk?

It's me, Jonny Blair, I am Ulsterczyk. "Ulsterczyk" is merely the translation of "Ulsterman" in Polish language. I am also Połnocny Irlandczyk w Polsce. That means Northern Irishman in Poland. I like the sound of Ulsterczyk more, though it craves more explaining, given that Northern Ireland in itself is only six ninths of Ulster. Ulster has 9 counties in it. Northern Ireland consists of 6 of those 9 counties – Antrim, Armagh, Down, Fermanagh, Londonderry/Derry and Tyrone. The actual moniker of "Ulsterczyk" was coined by Kamil Kowalczyk (brother of the famous Rafał Kowalczyk, who will feature in this book) in his flat while watching Mexico beat Germany 1-0 in the 2018 World Cup.

Nothing in Ulsterczyk's life has ever been simple…as you may begin to realise.

Chapter 2
Gerry Taggart Ruins Robert Warzycha's Night

Windsor Park, Belfast, NORTHERN IRELAND
(5th February 1991)

"Oh he can't believe it, can he?" – Mark Robson.

It was a cold February night at Windsor Park in Belfast and as usual, I had to be there. It was my third Northern Ireland match live in the stadium. Those first two matches were both in 1990.

The previous two matches were a 2-0 defeat by World Cup 1990 Quarter Finalists, Yugoslavia followed by a spirited fighting 1-1 draw with soon to be European Champions Denmark. I loved watching my country play live from an early age. In the 4 years before that, I had watched every Northern Ireland match or highlights that were shown on television. Sometimes, radio was all we had, especially for the away matches back in those days.

Next up was a winter friendly with Poland in February 1991. On my third ever match watching my country, could I finally get a Northern Ireland win to go with my draw and loss?

I headed to Windsor Park that February night with my Dad Joe, my friends Michael and Gavin McClelland and their Dad Brian. Neither Poland nor Northern Ireland had qualified for the 1990 World Cup, nor the 1988 Euros. Both countries were in an international lull having both been at the 1986 World Cup. We had home advantage which could count in our favour. But it was merely a friendly and a warm up for the qualifiers in March that year.

Before that match in Belfast, there was hype over two players. The first was Polish winger Robert Warzycha. It was rumoured that Everton wanted to sign him and they sent someone to the match in Belfast to watch him play that night. The second was Northern Irish midfielder Jim Magilton, who had left Liverpool to join Oxford United and was expected to make his international debut that night. Magilton had been unlucky at Liverpool, where he was an unused sub at Wembley in the previous year's Charity Shield final and officially he played for Liverpool only in a 5 a side tournament and for the reserve team.

We got into the stadium before kick-off and watched the teams warming up. I knew who all the Northern Ireland players were, but in the Poland team, it was only really Robert Warzycha we knew of and looked out for. In those days, there were no names on the backs of shirts, and players were of course numbered 1 – 11. It was fitting then that the two hyped players Robert and Jim, both played a big part in how the match unfolded. I'll never forget the match, nor would I have thought that 30 years later I'd include it in a chapter of a book.

Just 17 minutes into the match, we lost the ball in midfield. Down the wing in front of me (from the North Stand), Robert Warzycha ghosts his way through the Northern Ireland defence and blasts the ball home, past Paul Kee. Damn! Poland were winning 1-0 as we headed for half time. And of course it had to be Robert Warzycha.

But in the 44th minute, Northern Ireland get a free kick and the big boys go up. Colin Hill launches the ball into the box and there is centre half Gerry Taggart to head home. Going in 1-1 at half-time still gives me that chance of a first ever Northern Ireland victory.

Second half, on 51 minutes Stevie Morrow drifts into the box and is brought down for a penalty. Enter debut boy Jim Magilton. Surprisingly to all of us, World Cup hero Colin Clarke didn't take the penalty, but the confident 21 year old Magilton on his debut steps up and slots it home. 2-1 to Northern Ireland. Elation for a 10 year old!

We hang onto the lead and with 10 minutes left, we get a corner. The ball goes to the back post and big defender Gerry Taggart is there again, this time scoring with his right foot.

Final score from Windsor Park: Northern Ireland 3-1 Poland.

When we got home, we watched the highlights on TV. After Taggart's second goal, Northern Irish commentator Mark Robson memorably says *"He's done it again. Oh he can't believe it can he? Hahaha!."*

It was an unforgettable memory from my childhood. I often pondered over whether or not, one day I could visit Poland. But it was all a big dream to travel, back then.

After that match, Everton paid half a million pounds to Górnik Zabrze for Robert Warzycha. Robert was one of only thirteen players not from the British Isles to play on the opening set of fixtures of the newly branded FA Premier League a year later in September 1992. In a match that week, Robert scored for Everton in a 3-0 win at Old Trafford against Manchester United. By some crazy coincidence, this was the last goal scored by a Polish player in the English top flight until 2015, when Marcin Wasilewski scored. That fact often freaks me out a bit, as a football geek, as 2015 was also the year that sowed my seeds for moving to Poland. Robert Warzycha was also the first footballer from mainland Europe to score in the newly branded Premier League (English top flight / Division One).

Alas, I had now seen my country, Northern Ireland, win a match, at the expense of Poland. The 90s faded out of view and in the next century, I relocated to sunny sunny Bournemouth on England's south coast.

Poland, in its splendour, would still have to wait.

Chapter 3
Best Break

Mobile 2 Ice Cream Hut, Bournemouth Beach,
ENGLAND (May 2004)

"Everyone's changing. I stay the same" – The Corrs.

So while a scene was set back in 1991, with that first personal
Northern Ireland football victory, nothing of note even related to
Poland happened in my life for the next 13 years. Nothing. That
much is true. I never visited Poland in that time. I never met Polish
people in that time. There was no link at all in my life between
myself and Poland. Nothing. The journey, therefore, has been
somewhat remarkable and completely unpredictable.

The only real moments of note that reminded me of Poland in
those 13 years were also both football related. But we simply
cannot bore an entire book with footballic moments as if it's a
reason to move countries. Almost every country plays football, but
there were always some subliminal Polish football links in my
wacaday life.

Firstly, In February 2002, in Cyprus of all places, Poland beat
Northern Ireland 4-1 in a football match. It was a friendly match
and I didn't go. Though, of note, Steve Lomas's header in that
match was to be Northern Ireland's last goal for over two years. I'd
be at the match against Norway in 2004 when David Healy finally
scored our first goal in two years during a barren patch (which
involved 0-0 draws with Spain, Cyprus, Ukraine twice and
Liechtenstein). In the meantime, I also met Northern Ireland
captain Steve Lomas in The Northern Whig bar in Belfast, where
we had a whiskey together while watching the 2002 World
Cup Final.

Secondly, I did have a chance to visit Poland in August 2002. As a football fan, my team from Belfast, Glentoran FC were drawn to play Wisła Kraków in the UEFA Cup. I personally attended the first match in Belfast, where we lost 2-0 to Wisła Kraków. In the away match, a small selection of Glentoran fans went. We lost 4-0 away to Wisła Kraków, crashing out 6-0 on aggregate. Alas, I didn't go to the away match so even my debut visit to Poland would have to wait. Those two moments would be the only real times I thought about Poland at all in the intervening years.

Then, having moved to the English seaside town of Bournemouth, things were to change with regards my journey to Poland. I got a job in May 2004 working for Bournemouth Borough Council on their coastal retail units by the beach. It was an odd journey how on earth I even ended up in that actual job.

For a start, I had broken my arm on my birthday that year (a long story, and one I covered in my *"Backpacking Centurion"* book series – it's in Chapter 13's *"For Your Arms Only"* of Volume 1's *"Don't Look Back In Bangor"*). After that arm break, the next job I took on was one that involved using my arm to scoop up ice cream. I did that deliberately to get arm strength back and in the meantime, I had failed a year at university because of it. As an ice cream seller, I was working mostly in a unit called "Best Break" by Bournemouth seafront and harbour. One day, my manager Matt had placed me alone in a different unit known as "Mobile 2", it was here where I was selling ice cream on an incredibly busy day at Bournemouth beach.

It was a hot day and the queues for ice cream were relentless. Early afternoon, manager Matt came down to check out how things were going. I was low on ice cream, had run out of change and hadn't had a break since 9 a.m. Matt saw that I was being bombarded by customers and five minutes later, a new member of staff came in to help me.

His name was Piotr Oczkowski. He was from Warsaw in Poland. Piotr was the first ever Polish person I met in life. We would chat at length that day, in between busy times at work. Piotr was learning English. The following day, I was to work with Grzegorz and Aneta, two more Polish people. I met more Polish people that summer and the trend continued. Bournemouth is a popular international town and it changed my life. In that job at Best Break, I met people from England, New Zealand, Australia, Latvia, Poland, Germany, Spain, Colombia, Venezuela, Angola, Guinea, Wales, Scotland, France, China, Japan, South Korea, Ecuador… and many more countries. This was becoming an incredible journey already.

My world had certainly changed now. I had left Northern Ireland far behind and was meeting people from all over the world. 2003 – 2004 was an eye opener when I lived in Bournemouth. Bournemouth in England was one of the most up and coming cosmopolitan places in Europe at the time. One of the reasons for this was that it boasted some brilliant English language schools and foreigners often came here to learn English. On top of that, it had a rare sunny climate, often monikered with "sunny sunny Bournemouth." Indeed since I moved to Bournemouth, I developed a real passion for other cultures and I wanted to meet people from everywhere.

By the end of 2004, I had 3 different jobs in Bournemouth and had worked with and made friends with people from over 50 countries. As much as I had loved working in Northern Ireland, the culture there had been local and inward. I remember working with Chris from South Africa in Belfast, Henrik from Denmark in Springhill (Bangor) and Michelle from Australia in Ballyholme (Bangor). But except for some other British Isles workers, they were the only three foreigners I had known in my entire time of living in Northern Ireland.

The simple fact is that when I left Northern Ireland in 2003, I never moved back. The world was more exciting out there. All that said, I have still spent much more time in my home country than all the other countries put together. As of 2021, I have visited Northern Ireland 99 times and spent roughly 23 out of 41 years there. I am still an immensely proud Northern Irishman. My nationalism for my country won't ever wane. I love our little place, but from now on, Jonny Blair was out exploring the world.

From Bangor to Bobruisk, from Belfast to Bydgoszcz, from Strabane to Starogard. There was an oyster here to be mine.

Piotr for sure kickstarted the Polish oyster in this topsy turvy life. I have only met up with Piotr a few times in Warszawa since, but it's the history that counts. Every person and every instant can affect the rest of your life forever. And it's a beautiful thing. Fate and chance has controlled so much of my life, and it will probably control a lot of yours.

"We can't keep a hold on time; just receive what it will bring" – Tim Wheeler.

Chapter 4
Polska Biało Czerwony / Poland White Red

Hunter's Bar, Belfast, NORTHERN IRELAND (September 2004)

"Polska Biało Czerwony. Poland White (and) Red" – Polish football fans.

While working in Bournemouth that summer, I had by now met over 10 Polish people. By yet another crazy coincidence, the next international football match I would attend would be in Belfast between, you've guessed it – Northern Ireland and Poland.

I flew back to Belfast the day before the match having bantered the Polish contingent in England that Northern Ireland would win easily. Whoops.

I met up with the usual lads from back in the day – Brendan Burdoch, Michael McClelland, Ian "Skin" McKinney and Gavin McClelland plus a few others. We had pre match pints in the notorious Hunter's Bar on the Lisburn Road that day. It was a regular haunt at the time, being located near the stadium. I drank in there often before matches, or in the Four In Hand / Ryan's Bar and Grill.

In Hunter's, I took great delight in chatting to the Polish away supporters, saying *"Dzień dobry"* to them, now that I had learnt my second and third Polish words/phrases. The first, of course, was *"piwo."* The second, of course, was *"dziękuję."* We posed for some photos and had a good chat. Some of those Polish fans had travelled from England and Dublin for the game, having now lived outside of their home country. While chatting to the Northern Irish lads, we all agreed that in March 2005 we should go to the Poland away match. It was just a suggestion down the pub.

A lot of these notions don't come to fruition in real life. It's beer talk. We say them down the pub after a few beers but never go through with them. My mate Brendan swapped scarves with the Polish lot and myself and Michael headed to the corner shop outside the stadium to sell fanzines. In those days, I was a football fanzine editor and we had our 19th edition out that day. It was the end of an era for that fanzine, "Here We Go…Again" – it would be 12 more years until the 20th edition ever saw the light of day (in June 2016). Such was the busyness of life. The irony was that that 20th edition would also be sold at a Poland match (in Nice at the Euros in 2016, this time). Wow, another crazy coincidence on this wacaday journey.

Then on the football pitch that day, the horror show came. The contrast would be staggering. While in 1991 (see Chapter 2), we had swept Poland aside with a 3-1 home win, today was a total paradox. Poland easily beat us on the day. It was a 3-0 home defeat. We were toothless. We were a shadow of the 1991 match. We were well beaten and we drowned our sorrows post-match in Lavery's Bar, I met up with a few of the South of England based Northern Irish lads and some other Polish fans. We simply congratulated the Polish lads and lasses – the better team had won. They were ordering the vodkas. We were drowning our Steve Morrows.

I flew back to England. Over the next 6 months, I met a load more Polish people working there, plus I dated a Polish girl briefly in Bournemouth, Ania. We met twice, but there was no spark. Then with my Northern Irish mates, we finally made concrete plans to go to Warszawa for the Poland away match. It wasn't just beer talk anymore, it was really happening. We were going to Poland!

This was to be special. By no mean coincidence, that match was on my 25th birthday and to be held at Legia Warszawa's stadium, Marshall Józef Piłsudski's Municipal Stadium (Stadion Miejski

Legii Warszawa im. Marszałka J. Piłsudskiego) on Łazienkowska 3. We simply had to go there.

And so, around 300 Northern Ireland fans got booked for Poland away. Flights were cheaper now and this match was to be part of a double header. My mate Michael McClelland would have his birthday celebration on the Saturday before, while we watched England v. Northern Ireland at Old Trafford in Manchester. That match was a World Cup qualifier, as was the Poland match.

After that, we had booked a flight from Manchester to Berlin. We would spend two days in Berlin sightseeing before taking what was dubbed as "the party train" from Berlin to Warszawa Centralna. It was also to be my first time in Germany, as well as my debut in Poland, aged 24.

Everything was booked and life carried on, I was busy working and studying in Bournemouth, where again I was working with Polish and English people. We partied in Manchester in March 2005, then suddenly we were in Berlin with a big group of around 30 Northern Ireland football fans on route to Poland. The other 270 would be arriving in Poland in different ways. It was a magical time. I was young and vibrant.

Chapter 5
The Original Party Train Till Warszawa

Ost Bahnhof, Berlin, GERMANY (March 2005)

**"When the day is dawning, on a misty Belfast morning"
– GAWA.**

My first time in Germany had been short, yet action packed. By the time this book was released, I had amassed over ten trips to Germany, visiting more than 10 different German cities. On this first trip however, it was merely a brace of days in Berlin. It was a lads football trip.

The journey to Poland began from Berlin East Bahnhof. It was such a crazy day, and one that I have documented on my blogs numerous times and in my travel book series, *"Backpacking Centurion."* So I won't go into all the details. When the morning came to leave Germany behind, I was first up and out of our hotel, Aldea in the former East Berlin part. This hotel was like a textbook grey communist block. I had breakfast at 7 a.m. after being out with Dean Nutt until 4 a.m. the night before (yes, 3 hours sleep – we were hardcore in those days). Our group of about 10 of us all hopped on the U-Bahn. In that group, I think it was Skin, Mike, Gav, Dave, Dean, Andrew, Colin, Tim, Charley, Roan and Wendy, but I'm not 100% sure. At the Ost Bahnhof, we met up with other Northern Ireland fans who had already boarded the party train at Berlin central. They flew green and white scarves and Northern Ireland flags out the train window to signal where the party was at. That group was the North of England based Northern Ireland Supporters Club. Just before that, I grabbed a 4 pack of Becks, Dean munched an ice cream after #barfgate (it's a river of vomit story which features grotesquely in *Chapter 16 – Barfgate* in the pages of *"Backpacking Centurion"*) and we found the correct platform for the trip to Poland.

Also at the train station in Berlin, Mike and I hurriedly tried to get our train tickets changed as we had booked the wrong day! We had the wrong tickets but thankfully, we got them sorted and boarded on time. After all the commotion, we all left Berlin on time and in one piece and we were on the party train till that there Warszawa! I cracked open a beer as we waved goodbye to Germany…

"Auf wiedersehen Deutschland" – me, in 2005.

The "party train" certainly lived up to its name. I joined the North of England lads – Toddy, Nolers, Rob Gray, John Hart, Owen Millar and a few others. They had a booth further from ours so I just stayed in the corridor/aisle and drank my carryout there. Neither the German guards (in Germany it was legal to drink on trains) nor the Polish guards (where carryouts were not permitted) told me to put my carryout away. We got stamped out of Frankfurt an der Oder in Germany and arrived into Słubice in Poland. For the bizarre record, I've never actually been to Słubice! I have passed through it on trains only.

On that there party train, Garreth Todd (Toddy) from North of England NISC had his trademark GAWS (green and white snake) which caused some amusement amongst shy Polish girls dandering past us to the bogs on the end of the corridor.

I had my ghetto blaster (no iPods or smart phones back then) with me and I had physical CDs of Oasis, Ash and Snow Patrol pumping as well as spare batteries. These days, all that material fits into a smart phone. The train journey was madness. I chatted to a Polish lady called Anastasia, who revealed she was a student violinist. She then whipped it out and played us a tune!

Apart from Słubice (unknown but borderic), the first Polish city I saw out the window was Pozzie – Poznań. I checked my old passport out of curiosity, and it appears that I got my passport stamped out of Germany, but not into Poland that day, even though both were now in the EU. We continued with the music, beer and banter and were joined by a Polish "chav" to whom we lent a beer. We arrived into Warszawa Centralna station late afternoon but it was still bright. In the madness of all of that, I was in Poland for the first time ever…it was the fourteenth country I visited in my life.

This is where and when my physical journey to Poland all began. Warszawa Centralna train station. Tuesday 29th March 2005. Jurassic Park.

Chapter 6
Coleslaw / Bolesław

Warszawa, POLSKA (March 29th, 2005)

"Is this the way to Amarillo? Every night I've been hugging my pillow" – Tony Christie.

As documented in Chapter 5, we had now arrived in Poland. When I look back at the order of the countries I have visited in life, Poland was the fourteenth country on my list. It was one of the early ones. At the time, despite having met people from all over the world, I had no idea that I would visit over 150 countries in the next 15 years. This was just a small step along that dream. I was still living in Bournemouth in England – we were only here for a football match.

I wasn't really budget backpacking on my first trip to Poland either. We had decided to book a swanky hotel – the Hotel Intercontinental. There was a large group of us booked here and the Northern Ireland football team were also staying here. We got to meet and chat to the whole team, we spoke to journalists and were interviewed for Northern Irish television.

After checking into our hotel room and admiring the superb views (the Palace of Culture and Science was out my window), it was time to eat, drink and explore. But this also wasn't really a backpacking or sightseeing trip. We were here for the football match, to have some beers and to enjoy a few nights out.

Memorably on day one, Dave Watson in our group said he was extra hungry and opted for the "big burger" on the menu. The Polish waiter told him "be aware, this burger is huge." We all had a laugh about this as nobody else ordered this gigantic burger. When it arrived, it was certainly huge, Dave had no mission of finishing that burger. Already I had some really crazy memories from Poland. The massive burger that Dave could never finish, getting a lift in the hotel with Northern Ireland international Warren Feeney who recognised me from AFC Bournemouth matches, the chav drinking our carryout on the train, to Anastasia's violin playing. We hadn't even seen any of Warszawa yet. Now it was time.

The first night in Warszawa, I met up with the Northern Ireland team to get their autographs on a Tony Christie CD cover I brought with me *("Is this the way to Amarillo?")*. Most of them signed it in the hotel lounge. On the party train the day before, we had been singing along to that Tony Christie song on my CD player, changing the words to *"Is this the way to Northern Ireland?."* Now the team had kindly signed that CD cover for me. It was the song of the trip, and that song will always remind me of that first Poland adventure, those crazy days.

We had a beer in the hotel before going out to the local sports bar, "Champions" on Aleje Jerozolimskie (Jerusalem Avenue). After a few beers on the first night in there, we headed to the Old Town. That night, as well as Michael, Gavin, Skin, Dave, Colin and the boys, I was drinking with some new Northern Irish friends – Marc Vannucci, Rodney Ferris, Stuarty Mellon and Silver. My old school friend Gareth Walker was also there. We got into inventing new football songs in the bar and one ridiculous song came up, stuck in the memory briefly, yet would be forgotten again, never to be sung on the terraces.

We had been singing the Amarillo song again but changing it to *"Is this the way to Legia Warsaw?"* after one of our group had checked our match tickets and realised that the next night's match would be played at Legia Warszawa's stadium. As we sang, the question arose *"what rhymes with Warsaw"?* And somebody came up with "coleslaw"! Coleslaw rhymes with Warsaw and of course, the song was born after a few beers. Legia Warsaw had played against Glenavon in Europe and indeed, Glenavon fan Skin from our group had been impressed that the city's Irish Pub (Pub Irlandzki) still had a Glenavon shirt hanging up in it.

As well as Glenavon, Legia Warszawa had also played Blackburn Rovers and Manchester United in the 1990s in European tournaments. In 2020, they also played Belfast Linfield in a Champions League qualifier. However, a song was now born, and it was pretty dire but it summed up the boisterous drunken mood of our group and of that trip, and it was locked in that Warsaw moment. We sang, shyly…

"Is this the way to Legia Warsaw?
Every night I've been eating my coleslaw.
Dreaming dreams of Legia Warsaw.
Carrots, cabbage and mayonnaise.

Sha la la la la la la la Warsaw!
Sha la la la la la la la Coleslaw!"

There was another irony here for the history buffs amongst us, that Bolesław (pronounced differently than "Coleslaw") was the name of a former Polish king, as well as a town in Poland.

The next morning, it was my birthday. I was now 25, having been born at 2:43 a.m. Oddly, no hangovers existed, we must have been hardcore back then, because before 10 a.m. we had munched our breakfast and filmed a video for Ulster Television (UTV) of us doing the Conga with pink and green shirted "GAWA girls". The GAWA girls who joined us for the video, oddly I never saw them again – not on that trip, nor on any other future trip watching Northern Ireland football matches. I often wonder what on earth happened to those sexy pink and green GAWA girls from that trip. That video for UTV was made in front of the Palace of Culture and Science and was presented by Claire McCollum. This is an iconic

Warsaw building, which was built by Stalin's Soviet empire back in the 1950s.

In fact, this building was completed in 1955, so we were there on the fiftieth anniversary of its dominance in Warsaw's skyline. The building splits opinion in Warsaw. Some love it for its beauty. Some hate it because it contains reminders of Stalin's reign. My first glimpses of this building were memorable. I was impressed by its beauty. I didn't see the ugly here, but I researched it. As you'll learn in later chapters, this building would play a bigger part in my Polish adventures in days to come. By the time of this book's release, the building would no longer be the highest building in the city.

After doing the Conga, we did our bit of sightseeing in Warszawa. This was really basic tourism – we admired the streets and didn't go to museums or anything. We walked down Nowy Świat and Krakowskie Przedmieście. These two streets are part of the main thoroughfare through Central Warsaw. For me, I love the walk down it. I still walk down this street brace very often. It always reminds me of that day in Warsaw in March 2005, on my birthday. The first day I ever walked down it. Also to this day I have never seen that Conga video we filmed for UTV, though my parents saw it on TV back home at the time.

That morning was cold and there were not many tourists out but the memories are still very vivid. I have always hated DickMonalds but for some reason, some of the Northern Ireland fans had gone to the fast food joint on the corner of Świętokrzyska for lunch. We met them outside, and then walked down towards the Old Town together in a group.

On the way, we stopped to admire three churches, one of which was the prominent Holy Cross Church on Krakowskie Przedmieście – when we went inside, there was a mass on. It feels sad now. The day we arrived in Poland, Pope Jan Paweł II (Karol Józef Wojtyła) was still alive, but rumoured to be unwell. He was to die within a week. The man is very widely respected in Poland and all over the world for his part in Catholicism over multiple decades. A football geek fact is that the Pope once attracted a bigger crowd to Barcelona's Nou Camp than Lionel Messi or Ronaldinho!

As well as the church, we passed the Polish parliament building, with Józef Poniatowski on a horse statue outside it. I always draw parallels with this statue to the statue of Edward Carson in Belfast, Northern Ireland. The reason is that both statues are in front of the parliament – with Edward standing high above Stormont in Belfast. Both men were from countries other than where their statue sits – Poniatowski being born in Vienna, Austria. Carson being born in Dublin, Republic of Ireland. Of course, at the time of their births, those countries had different names and regimes. Another Polish hero on a statue nearby, Józef Piłsudski was born in Zułow, which is currently in Lithuania.

We arrive in Warszawa Old Town for the first time ever. We pass the Royal Palace and Zygmunt's column. This is a memorable and remarkable entrance. I won't forget it. We all arrived here together. It was my first time to see any eastern European old town. Before that, I had only really seen old towns in Spain and England. And yes, Poland is in eastern Europe. Spain is in western Europe. Northern Ireland is in northern Europe. Italy is in southern Europe. Many people argue that Poland is not in eastern Europe, but for me, I cannot count all of Russia as Europe just to satisfy them. When people argue that Poland is in central Europe, I disagree with them. Besides, I never wanted to live in central Europe. Places like Austria, Czechia, southern Germany, Liechtenstein and Cheatzerland are the only real central European countries to me.

And I don't want to live in any of them. There is no charm for me there. The charm for me has always been further east.

We mingled in the Old Town square (Stary Rynek) where the bars were all open, all lively and a good crowd had gathered. There were over 100 Northern Ireland fans drinking beers here. It was great fun. I could see that I liked the bar culture here – there was no issue with what we were wearing. Drinks were cheap, bar staff were fun. In Belfast, at that time, we couldn't have got into most bars wearing Northern Ireland football shirts and brandishing flags. I loved this part of Polish bar culture already. The customer matters, not the venue buck eejits. In the Old Town square, we were joined by some Polish fans and a Legia Warsaw photographer took a snap of Michael and I.

From somewhere, Michael had been given a pink flower. Little memories like that stick in the head. The flower is in the photo, I don't remember where the flower came from. When we were back in the UK, we noticed that that photo had been posted on the Legia Warsaw website. Back in those days, social media didn't properly exist. I had joined Friends Reunited and Bebo only. Instagram, Facebook and Twitter however - none of us were on those platforms in 2005. I was offline for the entire trip. None of us had mobile phones or laptops on that trip. My wind on disposable camera (24+3 exposures) did however capture some great photos from that first trip to Poland. Nobody had a mobile phone and the only photos were on disposable cameras or cheap cameras with films. Glory days loyal.

We spent quite a bit of time drinking, mingling and chatting in the Old Town square before returning to the hotel to freshen up for the big night out and the main event – the World Cup qualifier between Northern Ireland and Poland. The match was a 20.45 kick off. Before the match, we were drinking with the GAWA (Green and White Army) and some more Polish fans in the Champions Bar again. The Polish police had agreed we could march from that bar to the stadium, so we walked it, with carryouts.

The whole day was really good banter, there weren't any major problems at all. The walk to the stadium was cold. Once inside the stadium, we were placed on the right hand side (looking at the pitch) of a covered stand in the corner by the corner flag. There were about 300 Northern Ireland fans here, up in the warm top part of a home end. There were 14,000 Polish fans, some were in front of us shaking hands before kick-off. The stadium was old and worn. It was a textbook football stadium, I liked it. At the time, Poland were in the process of upgrading their national stadium (Stadion Narodowy). A new one would eventually be built and opened in time for Euro 2012. For the time being however, Poland played their home internationals in a few different stadiums.

Poland were hot favourites to win. They had beaten Azerbaijan 8-0 in this very same stadium a few days earlier. Poland had beaten us 3-0 in Belfast the previous year. England were top of the group and had beaten us 4-0 just a few days ago. Poland were second in the group. The top 2 teams would qualify for the 2006 World Cup, to be held in Germany. For Northern Ireland to stay in with a chance, we'd need to win tonight and then produce a few more wins in home matches against Azerbaijan, Wales and England plus an away match in Austria. It was a tall order.

In the first 20 minutes though, we almost scored. We were strong tonight. Keith Gillespie took the defender on many times, firing crosses in. From one of these it eventually fell to James Quinn who fired a fierce shot, which the Polish goalkeeper, Jerzy Dudek (then of Liverpool FC) smothered. Minutes after that, Quinn went off injured and Warren Feeney came into the fray.

We weathered the storm for the first half and most of the second. Maik Taylor was strong for us in nets. We brought on ex-Glentoran players Andy Smith and Stuart Elliott – both attacking changes. But we couldn't get a winning goal. Instead, Poland scored an 85th minute header from a corner and won it. Maciej Żurawski scored the winner. It was a harsh defeat to take and we were basically now out of the World Cup. Poland would go on to secure second spot in the group and qualify for World Cup 2006. We lost 1-0, but on the final whistle, Polish fans had stopped to applaud us for our singing throughout the game. It was certainly one of the friendliest atmospheres at a football match that I had experienced.

The rest of that evening was interesting to say the least. In the hotel bar, we grabbed beers, a chat and a photo with Northern Ireland players Keith Gillespie and Andy Smith before heading out on the town again. A few other players popped in and out of the bars. The entire team were very chatty. There was never much distance between the Northern Ireland team and the fans. Some of the players knew fans by name and face.

The fact that it was my birthday had still kind of passed me by, but I reminded the guys of this as we decided to head out into a few bars. We were in Warszawa after all, we were on holiday and although we had lost the match, beers were cheaper here than in Bournemouth. At some point, and for whatever reason, the idea of going to a strip club came up. This idea didn't sit too well with me for a few reasons. Firstly, exactly a year before, I had broken my arm on my birthday, in a strip club in Bournemouth! (A story which appears in *"Backpacking Centurion's"* Volume 1 *"Don't Look Back In Bangor"* in Chapter 13's *"For Your Arms Only"*). Secondly, strip clubs are dear. Thirdly, I had a girlfriend, Lauren, who was back at home in England. I spoke to Lauren on the phone that day from the landline phone in my hotel room (it was an expensive 3 minute call in those days!) because it was my birthday and she actually said it was okay to head to a strip club! Somehow, we were convinced of it and about 15 of us headed to a basement club with red lights. We didn't spend the whole night in there, but most of it.

At one point, a few Polish guys offered me some vodka shots. I usually hate vodka but this was polite to take them and for sure in those days, it was easier to get drunk and survive a hangover the next day. Overall I had a great birthday night out in Warszawa on what was my first delve into Poland.

Back then, I had no idea I'd ever move here to Poland, nor want to. Despite having a great time, it didn't seem like a place I would later live in. Life has a funny way of surprising you.

After the Poland trip, I attended the National Student Television Awards in Loughborough in England before returning to Bournemouth for a busy summer.

I would be working hard in Bournemouth again, making many more new Polish and international friends.

Chapter 7
Big Bird

Sesame Street, U.S and A (1969)
Best Break Cheeseburger Stall, Bournemouth, ENGLAND
(Summer 2005)

"Alan. Alan Connell Alan" - AFC Bournemouth fans.

If the summer of 2004 working in Bournemouth was fun, the summer of 2005 was funner. This one eclipsed it for sure. I worked with even more foreign people, I made even more new friends. I got a job promotion to seasonal supervisor (so I was on slightly more money) and it was a busy life.

Just before I started back in that job, my English girlfriend Lauren and I decided to split up. We had only been together a few months but that romance had filtered out. This isn't a book about love stories. I'm an epitome of the failed romance in many ways.

When summer started, the ice cream huts got busy and work was fast, furious and relentless. It was often a 7 day week. As well as selling ice cream, hot dogs and cheeseburgers, I also worked a few times per week in Tesco in Branksome, Poole.

At the end of July, myself and my flatmate Jody organised a huge house party in our flat. The end of our lease was up and we wanted to host a big party to say goodbye to many friends as well as that flat. We invited everyone from work. In those days, parties were always happening in Bournemouth. You'd be invited to new ones every week. At this house party in our flat, it was dominated by English and Polish people. It was the first time I'd try Żubrówka. Żubrówka is basically a Polish flavoured vodka, which contains a bison grass blade in every bottle. The name itself, comes from the Polish word żubr, for bison.

I had even more new friends to meet now. After that party, Jody and I moved into a shared room together in Cranborne House and we basically worked every day, partied as many nights as we could and got ready to finish another year of university in Bournemouth. After the Poland trip, I had started to travel a lot more.

One of my first jobs as supervisor of the Best Break and ice cream units was to organise the staff into positions in the morning for the shift. Basically, you'd spend the first hour of work getting all the food and drink ready for the day. The boss Matt wanted me to be in charge of the main Best Break unit and I was allowed Saturday afternoons off work when the Cherries (AFC Bournemouth) had a home match.

One morning, there were two new Polish lads in work and I had to organise them to pack hot dog and burger boxes into freezers etc. They'd have to take a roll cage down the seafront to a hut with stock on it with ice creams and drinks. It was such basic work but we all loved that job and I got to meet new people and have fun. These two new Polish lads were called Artur and Rafał. Just another dot on my globe and just another two people to meet eh?

Not so. This is mad.

As I prepare to write and release this book about my journey to life in Poland, I've now met Artur and Rafał in three different decades. Thriced it. Hat-tricked it.

Rafał and I became best friends. We are best friends. **There ain't no better man outside my family than Rafał.**

You wouldn't expect that back then – sometimes summer jobs are just party times to meet people that you will never see again. But basically – Rafał, Artur and I were a mini team here. I later went to Artur's wedding and have met his kids. I still meet Rafał almost every week. There is no doubt, this was a catalyst and a turning point in my long road to Poland. I just didn't know it then.

Back then, in the summer of 2005, I would take the orders from the customers and try to keep the unit tidy and clean. Rafał would prepare the hot dogs for the customers. Artur would prepare the chips (French fries to the non-Northern Irish) for the customers. It was boring work and mundane at times, but these were my friends now. After a few days working with Rafał, I realised that he had been at the very same Poland v. Northern Ireland match I was at. It was a ridiculous coincidence. We were both in the stadium that night. He was in the home end. I was in the away end. But we never met each other or knew each other until 4 months later. Rafał hails from Warszawa and is a big Legia Warszawa supporter. The match that night had been in the Legia stadium. We had an immediate connection. I liked my workmates. The girls would usually work on the other side of the hut, selling ice cream and drinks. The guys would be on the hot food side. Sometimes we'd work a 12 hour shift on a "firework Friday" and I used to love those shifts the most. You'd work 9 a.m. to 9 p.m., watch the fireworks on Bournemouth pier and go down the pub straight from work.

In work to relieve the boredom, we'd have the radio on, we'd do football quizzes, we'd chat, we'd organise nights out on the beer. It was basically a Polish and English contingent at work now, plus me the token Northern Irishman, Julio the Colombian, Massi the Algerian, a mini "Spanish contingent" and a few others.

But the title of this chapter is "Big Bird" and this chapter isn't about me. It's about the new Polish friend I made in Bournemouth in 2005. It's about Rafał Kowalczyk. I'll move over and he will be the star of this show. Forevermore.

You see, Rafał took a chance on a long bus journey from Warszawa to Bournemouth to try and get some work in England and earn some money. Similarly to many adventures in my life – it was a risk and a chance he was taking. He didn't speak English, he had never been to the UK, he had no UK tax details or bank accounts or anything remotely English. He just wanted an adventure. So he boarded that long overland bus to Bournemouth. Artur Gorecki was on the same bus and was the connection that made Rafał take that risk.

At the time, it was widely known that there were many summer jobs in Bournemouth. I'd hazard a guess that Rafał Kowalczyk in his 2005 world had never heard of Bournemouth. At least he'd heard of Irlandia Północna. However, when Pan Kowalczyk arrived in Bournemouth Town, he didn't get employed immediately. There is a twist in the tale.

"Now you'll understand that this is not the promised land they spoke of" – Noel Gallagher.

Basically Bournemouth had become increasingly popular that summer. Tourists were everywhere, Polish people were everywhere now too. Poland had joined the European Union in 2004, so now there were many Polish people moving away from their beautiful native land. It was a crazy time.

When Rafał arrived in Bournemouth, before he worked in Best Break, he couldn't find a job at the start.

Rafał is over 7 feet tall. How can such a tall gentleman not find a job?

"Could you tell me how to get? How to get to Sesame Street?" – Joe Raposo.

Him and his mates came up with an idea to raise some cash in this English coastal town. Rafał would dress up as Big Bird. The yellow character Big Bird from Sesame Street. They'd walk around the street and encourage kids and their parents to pay for a photo next to Big Bird! And that, was what Rafał Kowalczyk did. Rafał Kowalczyk was Big Bird!!

Rafał and I still laugh about that. If he'd have been a more successful Big Bird, I'd never have met Rafał and who knows if I'd have not visited Warszawa again in 2007, would I have wanted to move here? Life is all about fate and moments changing your destiny.

One thing is for sure is that I had made a friend for life here. My Polish brother. Rafał Kowalczyk. He is my best friend, my lifelong friend. He is honest to me. We don't argue because we understand each other. Fate directed us to meet.

In my later journeys, as you'll read, it was my encounters with Polish ladies which would have further influence on me. There's something so romantically charming about their beauty, intelligence and conservatism that can be hard to resist. Caught in the here and now, nobody was to know.

In September 2005, I took Rafał (as well as another Polish friend Robert and three Spanish friends – Nacho, Elena and Rodrigo) to the AFC Bournemouth v. Swansea City AFC match in the English Third Division (then called "League One"). At the end of the summer of 2005, Rafał and Artur both headed back to Warszawa. Even though I had made new friends in Rafał and Artur, ultimately they returned home to Poland. Who knew if I'd ever see them again.

I had new Polish friends, but I also had friends from all over the world and for the rest of this book, and this journey, I began to travel more and more.

Chapter 8
Dog For A Girl

Nowy Świat (New World Street),
Warszawa, POLSKA (August 2007)

"This; a present from Stalin's reign" – Artur Gorecki.

By now, and by Chapter 8, it is clear to see that my journey to living in Poland was an extremely long process and a slow burner. It was gradual. In fact, 2007 was only my second visit to Poland. By now, I had already been around the world a fair bit. Moving to Poland certainly wasn't on my mind.

I had now started a travel blog (called "Don't Stop Living," https://dontstopliving.net/). I got the name for that travel blog from a High School wall in Toronto, Canada. I stole it from a wall I noticed on a walk somewhere near Wellesley Street and Yonge Street. I did that on my first visit to Canada in 2001. On my second visit to Canada in 2007, I started my travel blog in Toronto. I started uploading the posts onto a Blogspot page. I was a novice to blogging, but as ever, I had been writing for most of my life. I had always been a writer. The release of this book is no surprise to anyone; the surprise is that I moved to Poland.

My entire journeys had been documented with pen and paper. Long before the internet or laptops existed.

But what was the incentive for my trip around the world in 2007? It was because from 2006 – 2007 I had left Bournemouth and moved to London. I was now working in a high profile job in PR, Public Relations. I worked at Ravenscourt Park for Bite Communications. Days were long and office based. Yes, it could be seen as fun work and one to bring rewards. But part of me always despised such office work. I felt like I'd enjoy life more selling ice cream by the beach, or pouring pints in bars. I was right of course – I did prefer those jobs.

"The days are long and the nights will throw you away because the sun don't shine" – Noel Gallagher.

But that year in London made me eager to escape. I had to get out of the rat race, I had to escape the generic 9 – 6 job that I found myself in. The way I chose to do this was to go backpacking solo around the world.

On that trip, as well as starting my travel blog, I would go skydiving in New Zealand, visit the Great Wall of China, tour Red Square in Moscow and visit a bar once owned by George Best in Los Angeles. It was a really crazy world tour, all booked quite spontaneously on a budget. I even surprised myself as a backpacker, how cheap I could be.

After that trip, the decision was made to return to Bournemouth and finish my degree in Public Relations. Before I did that, Poland was ready for another visit – this time I wasn't with my Northern Irish friends at all. I wasn't here for a football match. I was here to meet my Polish friends, to see their culture for what it really was. This was the real thing.

I was the tourist in Poland and this was an incredibly inspirational visit to Poland. Just before that, I found myself in Bobruisk in Belarus. Again, as lunatical as it might sound, I was in Bobruisk for a Northern Ireland football match. However, this time it was Northern Ireland women's team away to Belarus and I was the only supporter for Northern Ireland. This was a crazy enough trip as it is. Belarus had about 1000 supporters that day. Northern Ireland had one – me. I won't write about that trip in this book though. Not because it was uneventful, quite the opposite. The reason I won't be writing about that trip in this book is because that trip has already featured on my travel blog, as well as as a separate chapter in THREE different books –

(1) Chapter 16 – Five Nil and You Still Don't Sing in Albania to America (With Belfast in Between) by Shaun Schofield. 2010.

(2) Chapter 26 – Multiple B: Beaten By Belarus In Belshina Bobruisk By The Berezina River in Backpacking Centurion – A Northern Irishman's Journey Through 100 Countries – Volume 1 – Don't Look Back In Bangor by Jonny Blair. 2020.

(3) Chapter 29 – We're In The Army Now in Champian Stewartnova by Jonny Blair. Due out 2022.

After the madness of Belarus faded out of view, I had the simple matter of a flight from Minsk to Warszawa. It was to be my second time to visit the Polish capital but I had no idea that it would be a sign of things to come. Nor that 10 years later I would actually live here.

What brought me to Poland this time? Well it was a concoction of many things really. Firstly, I felt that in March 2005 on my trip to Warszawa, that I had neglected the usual tourist things. I didn't really see the city. That was basically a lads holiday and party to watch the football match (which Northern Ireland lost 1-0), but it felt that there was something more to it. The fact that I didn't really delve into Polish culture properly, yet came away loving the country, had lingered in my mind. Even more so given the sheer number of Polish people I had met between 2004 – 2007, including Piotr Oczkowski, the first ever Polish person I met in life.

Secondly, I saw Poland as a cheap and easy stop-over after Minsk and Moscow. Thirdly, I would be spending time together with two good friends, Rafał Kowalczyk and Artur Gorecki and making many new friends in a short timeframe.

The memories of this second visit to Warszawa are quite distant and faded now. I can tell you what we did in the day time and night time but there was something stronger here. A magnetism that would later influence my entire life. For now, Artur and Rafał turned up at Warszawa Chopina Lotnisko (airport) bearing an "Alan Connell" sign. It was, of course, an in-joke aimed at making me laugh and welcoming me to their country again. Alan Connell, or "Alan Connell Alan" was one of my favourite AFC Bournemouth strikers during my first few seasons watching the Cherries. Connell even left the Cherries for a few years and came back, and despite injuries, he remains some kind of cult hero to me. I hope other AFC Bournemouth fans agree that Connell played a big part in many happy moments down at Dean Court, scoring some important goals and generally running around the pitch always looking for a half chance to put away. For now, with blonde hair and a slim figure, I was Alan Connell on arrival in Warszawa.

A nice joke from Rafał and Artur and a great introduction to Polish life, again.

From day 1, the guys had planned my trip well. I remember they had mostly taken days off work just to see me and hang out. I had dinner and drinks with Rafał's family in the Bielany district, north Warszawa. That felt good, as it gave me a chance to see the raw and local Polish lifestyle, the real Polish hospitality and escape the tourist floods of Warszawa's city centre and old town (Stare Miasto). Of course, being an obvious tourist was also on the agenda and one by one, I ticked off a phenomenal amount of sights in the city, including one sentimental one.

We visited the Old Town, we went out drinking nightly in the bars in and around Nowy Swiat. I was trying Polish food and drink, falling completely for the dream hangover cure, Kefir. A product simply non-existent in my Ulsteric hometown of Bangor. Kefir is a dairy based milky, yoghurty, salty concoction, which is totally perfect for the morning after a night on the rip. Sightseeing wise, we toured Wilanow Palace and Łazienki Park, but it was the trip to "Stalin's building" that brought about the most significant part of that journey to Poland's stolica.

Warszawa just didn't seem as busy in those days. Gorecki parked his car on a hungover Thursday morning at the city's Plac Defilad. We alight and stare peakingly at the sky. A well-designed grey building pierces it. This was a building opposite the posh hotel (Intercontinental) me and the Northern Ireland fans had stayed at, back in 2005. This grey structure is known as Pałac Kultury I Nauki (The Palace of Culture and Science) and was ordered to be built by Jozef Stalin during the Soviet era. In fact, Stalin's Soviet regime had built similar looking buildings in a lot of the former Eastern Bloc / Soviet / Communist countries. I have seen similar buildings in Riga, Minsk, Kiev, Moscow and of course, here in Warszawa.

As he inhales a well-deserved draw from his cigarette, Artur Gorecki's words to me are simple, true, pure, slowly spoken and memorable. Unforgettable, I'd say. Harshly, with deep feeling and without remorse, Gorecki professed:

"Jonny, this, is our present from Stalin's reign."

Artur Gorecki is almost angry as he says it. He's a tough lad, Artur. He mixes his anger with his happiness here. The building looks down on Artur, itself guilty.

Staring up at this monstrosity in a city that is changing gave me some kind of goosebumps. I don't know why, but this was deeper than visits to other cities, and to other buildings. I didn't know much about Warszawa, or Poland. I had read Stalin's book while at Newtownards Tech and I had studied the Soviet Union regime during the same history course. Suddenly a mixture of sadness and happiness came together all at once. It was quite sensational and indescribable. The Russians and the Polish were not good friends.

The wars hadn't been kind to this town, or to Poland. Poland was sandwiched in between Hitler's German Nazis and Stalin's Soviets. It was a country that needed to be strong and stand up for itself. And the thing is, it did.

Having worked with Artur and Rafał in England, I knew these guys. I knew their sense of humour, their way of communicating. There was a sense of hate, of love, of life, of honesty. There wasn't much bullshit with such guys. I could feel the fear in the three of us as we walked over to Stalin's "Palace," oxymoron that shit if you must. We were going inside to take the lift to the top floor to get a vantage point over the whole of the city.

I had my backpack with me and as the Polish security staff called to me on the way in, it was something they said like *"Skąd jestes?" ("Where are you from?")*. I had been taught about 20 words of Polish on this trip, and proudly could reply, when prompted by Kowalczyk *"Jestem z irlandii polnocnej" ("I am from Northern Ireland")*. A quick welcome and we are whisked in a Stalinic elevator to the viewing terrace to overlook the city.

I had a permanent marker in my backpack in those days. I often carried multiple pens of assorted sizes, shapes and colours. The pen is mightier than the sword and always one of my favourite inventions. This was a black permanent marker and at the top of Stalin's building, we had the chance to sign the wall. I signed it

twice. Once with Jonny Scott Blair and the date. The second time, simply with "Alan Connell," my pseudonym for the trip, kind of.

We stopped for a beer at the top of this magnificent building and I liked that. Here we were at the top of a building given as a "gift" from a country that didn't exist anymore (USSR) to a country that took the gift, and still had it. Here I was with two friends I had made while selling cheeseburgers in England. You can't make this sort of shit up. We were happy. I think we were the winners here, the lucky ones. Stalin had been and gone, with a good riddance to his Soviet Regime. Poland had entered the European Union in 2004 and was revelling in a new sense of freedom, second wave if you like, after the post-1991 progression to a democratic republic.

Soon, we were back down on the terracotta. Artur parked his car and we headed to a bar which had cherry vodka shots. This felt like another telling point. Telling, not turning. From Bournemouth to Stalin, from Alan Connell to Cherries, from beer to vodka, it was a magical time. As we sat in that bar, I pulled out my paper and pen and started to write a poem, more a song really. It was clear what the poem and song would be all about. It would be about Polish people, my friends here and my experiences in Warszawa. The main line of the song was to be: "This; a present from Stalin's reign."

Almost as if, I was envisaging Artur pointing to that building, while acting as a real life tour guide. After a few cherry vodka shots, I added the line "but you have your life again," and there it began. Within a few hours, the poem / song had been written, no doubt over more Polish beers and maybe a meaty kebab. Here, I share that poem's lyrics for the first time in print. It has been on my blog before, and on YouTube but never in a printed book.

You Have Your Life (Warszawa Skies)
Yesterday I was a dog for a girl,
Waking up in a different world,
Showing them the best of you, showing them the worst of you.
Warsaw skies they won't rain on you.
Warsaw skies they won't rain on me.

Yesterday's African party,
Up on stage false celebrity,
And you bow to the friends you made, you'll bow down to the
friends you made.
Warszawa skies they won't rain on you.
Warszawa skies they won't rain on me.

This; a present from Stalin's reign,
And you have your life again,
And this passion speaks a world to me, Polish passion speaks a lot
of you.
Warszawa skies they won't rain on you.
Warszawa skies they won't rain on me.

Looking out for the Lolek bar,
A foreign dream can it stretch this far?
She plays violin for me, most of them won't remember me.
Warsaw skies they won't rain on you.
Warsaw skies they won't rain on me.

On my final day in Poland, on this trip we visited a pond
somewhere in Warszawa (I still don't know where that pond is) and
Rafał asked if I was going to throw a Polish coin into the pond,
along with the rest of coins

already in there. I wondered why.

Rafał said to me, *"Jonny, if you throw a coin in, it means you will
be back here again in Warszawa, one day."*

It was a no brainer. I pulled out the nearest Polish złotówka coin I
had in my pocket and flicked it high into the air above the pond. It
landed, predictably in the pond. I didn't linger on the fact this
meant I'd be back here. Life doesn't give us what we want, need or
expect. We might not even get a tomorrow. Nobody is promised a

tomorrow. But my coin was in the pond, and perhaps, maybe, one day I'd be back here. Who knew? I probably thought I'd never be back. Rafał, like many Polish people I met in life, was correct.

"See you tomorrow, if God spares us"
– Mary Blair (my Granny).

My grandmother Mary Blair always always professed to me on leaving her flat, "See you next time, but only if God spares us." It was always "if God spares us." I loved it. The quote changed my world. Every single time, I left Granny's flat, she'd muse "if God spares us." In the circle of life, I knew that Granny said that because she knew, that one day God wouldn't spare us. One of us would die and the next meeting wouldn't exist. I thought Granny's quote would linger in the same way as Rafi's coin statement.

I was emotional at the airport too when I was leaving. We were joined by new friend Piotr Pawelski, who I met on this trip and we shared many a story about football and beer on some magic nights in the Polish capital. I boarded my flight from Warszawa to Prague in Czechia and the Polish adventure was over, for now.

The coin told me that I'd be back in Warszawa one day, but really, nobody could tell...

Chapter 9
Ferry Cross To Jersey

Weymouth Harbour, ENGLAND and Jersey, CHANNEL ISLANDS (May 2009)

**"Hat-trick of crescents and an unstoppable please Knoxville"
– Chris Bilsland.**

You can tell that I had to skip loads of what really happened in my life in order to cram and fit all of this into this book. Of course, after I left Warszawa in 2007, Poland wasn't exactly forgotten. But it wasn't exactly at the forefront of my mind either. Just a dot on my globe, well now a double dot on my globe.

When I returned to England, my first shift in my new job working at Bournemouth Pavilion Theatre was with a Polish girl. This was Kasia from Kraków. But it wasn't Kasia from that job that was to change my life. It was someone else.

I started that job in October 2007 and for the next two years my topsy turvy life would mean moving flats three times, passing my degree, having four different jobs, falling in love and quitting my chairmanship of the SOENISC (South of England Northern Ireland Supporters Club). I bunged all that into one paragraph, I won't have time to go into too much more detail.

Of those things that happened in my life between leaving Warszawa (August 2007) and the start of this chapter (May 2009), at Weymouth harbour, it was falling in love that had the biggest impact on my life.

I met a girl.

Again.

Same old story. Except this time it was real love. In 2008, whilst working on the bar in Bournemouth Pavilion Theatre, I went to the coffee shop (Piacetto) and in there, I met Hungarian dancer, Noemi Linzenbold. I was in love immediately, though I didn't know it then. I enjoyed every minute with Noemi. I couldn't be without her. I wanted her by my side, always and forever.

"So ferry cross the Mersey cos this land's the place I love"
– Gerry and The Pacemakers.

Noemi and I toured a few parts of England together in my car in the cold winter – we went to London a few times, to Southampton, to Portsmouth, to Poole. We also spent a lot of time together in work and outside work. By coincidence when I met Noemi, she lived round the corner from me. She lived on Southbourne Grove while I was living on Arnewood Road.

Again, life had become really busy for me. I was working in the bars at Bournemouth Pavilion Theatre and Bournemouth International Centre. I also started working back on the seafront services in March 2009. I then got a job working on Condor Ferries. At one point, it felt like all I did was work. Yet when I wasn't working, I'd only want to be with Noemi.

I had never met a girl like her before, nor have I since, nor will I again. She changed my world. She turned my world inside. Out. I've tried but I can't talk her down. By February 2009, I had quit my role as chairman of the South of England Northern Ireland Supporters Club and I had given up alcohol and football. I just gave them up completely for Noemi. I still held a season ticket for AFC Bournemouth, but I only went to one more home match in the next 6 months. I still held a block booking for the Northern Ireland home matches and while I still went to the final 3 home matches on that ticket, I gave up away matches and decided not to renew that block booking in late 2009.

The beautiful blonde haired, blue eyed Noemi seemed to like my taste for adventure. I thought of taking us to Peru and Bolivia together. I was aiming to make plans for all of that. Our first trip abroad came in April 2009 to her native Hungary, just after we celebrated Noemi's birthday together. I would be staying with Noemi's Mum Ilona, and also Noemi's cousins, Beata and Maria. On another side, was her other cousin, Karola Moszik. We flew Bristol to Budapest and back the same way on a one week trip. It was my first ever trip to Hungary. Hungary was my 34th country on my journey and I truly loved it.

It was blissful being with Noemi, I was learning some Hungarian words, loving the food and I especially loved Noemi's home city, Debrecen. Debrecen was like an unknown gem. It is a beautiful city, where a shining bright yellow church dominates the main square. This yellow church is the Nagytemplom. When we were in Hungary, we already knew that in May – June 2009, Noemi and I would also travel to Venice together. I had booked that trip for Noemi as her birthday present.

Noemi was a year younger than me, but I could tell that she had never been with a boyfriend who was taking her on crazy trips before. I could see the magic in her eyes. She admitted she loved the fact that I had already backpacked in China. It was like another world for her.

After the Hungary trip, we were both busy working and then our Venice trip crept up. I had told Noemi all about my backpacking lifestyle and the places I could go, backpack on a budget and make every day an adventure.

"Every day is all there is; in my some kind of bliss"
– Kylie Minogue.

As a treat, I had booked us into a swanky double room in the Hotel Noemi in Venice! Yes the hotel of her name. Days were brilliant. We toured the city together, we loved the canals and using the hop on and hop off boats. We went to Lido beach and had great fun there.

I was now totally in love and knew I had the girl of my dreams. Noemi was my girl for life. She was, and always would be, "my Wonderwall." I didn't need anyone else. I had Noemi and I would have done everything for her. But a bombshell from "golden locks" was just around the chimney corner.

After Venice, Noemi told me she didn't want to see me anymore. I don't remember exactly where she told me that, but it was on the Sunday. Maybe she told me in Venice town, maybe in the hotel, maybe on the bus to the airport, maybe at the airport, maybe on the flight, maybe in my car when we arrived back in England, at Stansted Airport. The next morning, I had to be in Weymouth to start a new job. There was no time to linger.

"Maybe maybe it's the clothes we wear" – Suede.

I would be working for Condor Ferries on the Weymouth and Poole, England to St. Malo and Cherbourg, France routes as well as serving on the Jersey and Guernsey routes.

I had no time to mourn the death of my love affair with the beautiful Noemi. We were finished and I cried my eyes out, physically for days, weeks and months. I worked 8 days a week. Yes, 8 days a week, not 7. 4 days in one job. 4 days in another job. 2 days overlapped.

At work I pretended to be all cool and normal. It was all a pretence. I came home every night and cried my eyes out. EVERY night for the whole of June, July and August 2009. One night, I drove to a notorious suicide spot and was close to killing myself. I went to Hengistbury Head. But I had survived.

That year, Welsh rock band Manic Street Preachers released an album called "Journal for Plague Lovers" and it was written by Richey James Edwards. The guitarist and lyricist who disappeared back in 1995 - a suspected suicide. I listened incessantly to that album and it helped keep me sane. Yes, that album kept me level headed, and it kept me alive. Without it, who knows what might have happened. I stick on "Journal for Plague Lovers" onto my MP3 player regularly and I feel good about it now. I love that album, it's fucking class.

"Only a God can bruise, only a God can soothe"
- Manic Street Preachers.

To prove to myself that I had turned the corner, I booked a one way ticket to Taiwan. Even if I'd never use it, I knew I was getting back on the road again. I had spent almost 6 years (give or take the odd backpacking stint) in Bournemouth by this point. With Noemi living round the corner and reminders of her every night I drove home, I had to leave the town of Bournemouth behind. Going to work and back, I'd drive past her flat twice a day. I vowed never to return. I just had to kill the ghost of her and of Hengistbury Head. The memories will linger forever and I can't forget her, but 2009 was a dark, dark year.

I wasn't well. I had deep depression. If you're suffering from mental health or depression, make sure you tell someone. Don't keep it all in – go let it out.

"You'll never change what's been and gone" - Noel Gallagher.

Because I had given up alcohol for Noemi, I knew I had saved money by doing this so I decided to continue with my abstention from it. It worked a treat, it helped me save a load of cash and afford that one way flight ticket to Taiwan. I didn't dwell on it, I just kept working. Working non-stop helped me actually, I had changed and was not boozing anymore. This was the big positive in fact, looking back. My fast relationship with Noemi had helped me kill any desire to drink alcohol.

But it came to the point where I was on a countdown. I'd be saying goodbye to Bournemouth town and it would be a forever. Even then, I sensed my clock had ticked on this town and like a rat out of heaven, I was gone in the morning sun. But ridiculously, it was at this very point in my journey that I met some of the funniest and coolest people in life to date. People that could have kept me in Bournemouth, people that just made me laugh so much. My job at Best Break had introduced me to a load of new people, most notably "Frog" – Maxime Froger from France. He helped me through some of the bad times and I wore a frog suit on his farewell from England. Even better, I went to France with him in the summer on a rare day off from work. I got him and his mate Martin a discount on the ferries that I worked on. While Frog and I backpacked our way through the streets of St. Malo, I was haunted by the ghost of Noemi. We ordered a coffee. It comes with a receipt. "You were served by Noemie (the French spelling)" it says on it. "Was I fuck?" This girl couldn't leave my life. I'm ordering a pizza and I'm asked if I want Italian or Hungarian salami on it? "Get over it," said many. I couldn't. Frog and I said our goodbyes in St. Malo and I headed back to Poole in England to finish my non-stop summer of work.

I worked on the self-dubbed "Café Cherbourg" onboard the Condor Ferries between England, France and the Channel Islands. It was there that I met more Polish people, including a hat-trick who I car shared with – Dorota, Maria and Marta. I owned a car, a Hyundai Accent (from the year 2001) and I was their driver for the whole summer of work.

My best mate at work was Doncaster lad Chris Bilsland, who ran the west wing of "Café Cherbourg" with me. We'd take it in turns to serve food, do the till and generally crack jokes with customers. It was a fun job and a fun time, post-Noemi. As soon as that job ended, it was time to leave England behind for Taiwan.

Although this girl hurt me, I dedicate this chapter of my story to the Hungarian dancer and coffee shop assistant, Noemi Linzenbold. I hope you sleep in peace tonight, Noemi. By the way, it took me over 5 years to get over you, but I've stopped crying my heart out…

I'm really over you now, Noemi. But also, I really did love you.

And Noemi, thanks for everything you did. Especially your honesty, passion and love. I wish you all the best in life. You really deserve it.

"And after all, you're my Wonderwall" – Noel Gallagher.

Chapter 10
Ulster's Number One

Windsor Park, Belfast, NORTHERN IRELAND (March 2009)

"Artur Boruc. Artur Boruc. Artur Boruc, Ulster's number one" - GAWA.

While madly in love with Noemi, the Hungarian dancer, there was a two week period of pure sadness and madness. My life; it's a roller-coaster.

On Saturday 21st March 2009, I worked in Best Break by Bournemouth seafront. After work, I had dinner at Noemi's. Then I went home and the next morning, I'd come to Noemi's for breakfast before giving both of us a lift to work. We were both working from 12 noon until close the next day, which was Mother's Day. I haven't told this story to anyone before but now is the time.

I arrived at Noemi's flat, probably around 9 am. I told her I'd call my Mum and wish her Happy Mother's Day. I did that for Mum, never for myself or anyone else. I personally don't agree with Mother's Day, Father's Day, Saint Valentine's Day etc. We can show our love anytime we want, never when we are forced, not least by commercial excrementors. But down the years, I did those days as others wanted me to.

On this day, I phoned Mum.

"Good morning Mum. Happy Mother's Day" - I said, joyfully, Noemi by my side.

But it wasn't a happy mother's day. I won't forget Mum's words, *"it's not a happy mother's day, Granny has just died."* And that was it. I was basically grandparent less.

Officially the grandmother I never met (on Mum's side) was still alive in Australia, but time and consequence prevented us ever from meeting.

The memories of all my grandparents gushed back. All were tinged with an emotional sadness or swansong. Granda Charlie who I never met. He died before my Mum was even married. Great Granda Whinney (John Mawhinney) whose flat we watched the 1992 FA Cup Final in, as a family, before he died a month later.

Granny Scott, Mum's Mum. Mattie Scott. After witnessing the birth of my brother Daniel in 1994, the week before Christmas 1995 was a sad one when Granny passed away. I was 15.

Four years later, it was a poignant farewell to Granda Sam. He chose to bow out before the millennium came round. He died on 9.9.99. The 9th of September 1999. My parents had just moved into a new house, it was a sad end to the 1990s, a decade that I had loved, but lost many relatives, with Auntie Anne also dying in 1997.

In 2005, my great grandmother Annie died, three years short of her becoming 100 years old. Now, it was Granny Blair, Mary.

Mary Blair, was an inspiration, she always told me "if God spares us," every time I left her flat. Those were her words, "See you next time Jonny, if God spares us." This time, as I cried my eyes out, it hit me deep. God hadn't spared her, and I would never be able to hear her say "if God spares us" to me again.

Granny was gone. I hung up the phone and cried.

"If God spares us" – Mary Blair (My Granny).

I called my manager Matt (at work) and told him I couldn't go to work. Mum booked me a flight back to Belfast, whilst Noemi swapped shifts to spend the day with me. I'd fly back the next day, but I was in no position to work, for once.

I drove Noemi and I to the New Forest. We stroked and fed horses, we had a day in nature. We went to a local pub somewhere in Bransgore. That night, in the pure sadness I was in, Noemi slipped her clothes off as I lay in bed. She pulled my pants down and pleasured my desire. It couldn't hide any sadness, but there was no better girl in the world that I could have been with that day, but Noemi Linzenbold.

In the circle of life, I'd later meet Noemi's Mum and grandmother, in Debrecen. She was destined never to meet either of mine.

For now, I was back in Belfast. I toured many places with Dad on this trip back. The funeral passed by and Dad and I went to Belfast Castle, to the Titanic Dock, to Longs for a fish and chip.

The day after the funeral, through no mean coincidence in life, Northern Ireland played Poland in Belfast. Granny died on the Sunday, her funeral was on the Friday and Northern Ireland were playing at home on the Saturday.

Before Granny died, I already had a flight booked back to Belfast, ironically that flight was supposed to be on the day of her funeral. As a block booker for Northern Ireland matches, I had already planned my trip for the upcoming brace of Northern Ireland home matches, Poland then Slovenia.

Saturday morning came and I was back on Tates Avenue, meeting the boys and going to the match at Windsor Park. Only this time, I wasn't drinking alcohol. I had given it all up for Noemi.

I met the lads as normal in the absence of the usual Harp and we headed into the stadium. This was to be an unforgettable match and one that, later in life would supply me with an odd decade hattrick, all because of Artur Boruc. Artur was soon to become "Ulster's number one."

The place was buzzing. At this point, the group was wide open. 5 teams were trying to get two slots for the World Cup, the second of which would be a play off. I had been to every match in that group so far. I went to Slovakia, Slovenia and San Marino away. I was at Czechia and San Marino at home. Now, we had 7 points and we had two home matches. To get 13 points, with two wins would be a phenomenal dream. Surely we couldn't do it.

At Northern Ireland matches in those days, we were always in the Kop end. I've watched Northern Ireland from all 4 sides down the years. We usually wanted our captain to win the toss so that we could play down towards the vociferous Kop in the second half. This worked wonders in our victories over England in 2005, Spain in 2006 and Sweden and Denmark in 2007.

We won the toss against Poland and would be playing down to the Kop in the second half. God help any goalkeeper defending that net in front of the Kop. Today, that slice of bad luck fell on Poland's Glasgow Celtic based goalkeeper, Artur Boruc.

We went 1-0 up through Warren Feeney after 10 minutes but Poland soon equalised.

Then, just after half time, Jonny Evans put us 2-1 up from a corner.

A moment of madness was to come. We wanted to rock DJ. Damien Johnson had the ball in midfield and pressured his marker, Michał Zewłakow. Zewłakow tried to avert the danger of us going

3-1 up, by passing the ball back firmly to Polish goalkeeper Artur Boruc.

The ball was rolling towards the net and as Artur Boruc made a swipe for the ball to blast it upfield, the ball hit a divot and rolled over his boot and into the net!!

The ball was in the net. We went wild. Totally crazy. We were in disbelief. This was a professional footballer making a schoolboy mistake! It was hilarious!

Boruc had previously kicked up a divot on the gracious Windsor Park turf whilst taking a by ball. As Boruc attempted to clear the ball, it sailed delightfully over the divot and into the net!! We were 3-1 up. It was a comical moment and led to a chant of Artur Boruc, Ulster's number one.

Artur Boruc is still deemed a hero to Northern Ireland fans and we often sing his praises for his part in our victory. No doubt the Glasgow Rangers fans enjoyed it even more since he was at Celtic.

That story doesn't even end there, as I'd later watch Artur Boruc multiple times live in the flesh in the Championship and Premier League after he joined AFC Bournemouth. I saw him save a pelanty at Birmingham City away (in an 8-0 win) and give away another calamity goal at home to Watford (in a 1-1 draw). From 2020 onwards, having relocated to Poland, I'd watch Artur Boruc live more than 20 times, when he re-joined his beloved Legia Warszawa. In short, I've seen Artur play live in 3 different decades, for 3 different teams, in 3 different stadiums in 3 different countries.

But here now in 2009 in Belfast city, it was 3-1. Northern Ireland were destined to do something ridiculous in my life cannon. In the first year of the 90s (February 1991), we beat Poland 3-1 at home.

The last two goals came at the Kop end. I covered my attendance of that match in *Chapter 2's "Gerry Taggart Ruins Robert Warzycha's Night."* In the last year of the next decade, the 00s (March 2009), we were 3-1 up on Poland at home. The last two goals came at the Kop end. Was this history repeats?

While 3-1 up, Poland started to attack and we sat back on a 3-1 lead. And they were loud now. I feared the worst. I had already seen Germany, Turkey and Austria score thrice here.

I had even seen Spain smash 5, Norway smash 4 (twice) and a fake Ireland team also managed 4 past us at Windsor Park.

But here, with Jonny Evans, Gareth McAuley, Stephen Craigan and Aaron Hughes commanding the defence, no chance were Poland getting 3. They did manage to fluke it back till a 3-2 but we hung on. Parties ensued in Belfast city.

I went home, called Noemi on Skype the next day and then on the Wednesday night, Dad and I headed back to Windsor Park again for Slovenia at home. This was another World Cup qualifier. The winning goal was textbook.

The ball came in and Warren Feeney headed it home at the Kop end right in front of us. Maybe, just maybe we were heading to the World Cup in South Africa. We had three matches left to play - Slovakia at home, and away to Poland and Czechia. Three wins would guarantee at least a play-off.

My summer was action packed with work. I cried every night over Noemi and in my final month living in England, there was the Poland v. Northern Ireland match to watch down the pub, before I headed off on my journeys again. Taiwan, Singapore and Malaysia were to follow, not before Kyle Lafferty almost had us dreaming of the World Cup.

Chapter 11
La La Lafferty

Walkabout Pub, Bournemouth, ENGLAND (September 2009)

"Fermanagh's Ulster Goal Machine" – Jonny Blair and Davy Hunter.

Before I left England behind in 2009, there was one final twist. Northern Ireland had to play Poland away again. This fixture just kept coming up in my life on my journey to Poland, and I remember all of them. This time, if Northern Ireland won, we could be four to six points away from qualifying for World Cup 2010.

In order for that to happen, we'd have needed to beat Poland away, then beat Slovakia at home and then win or draw away to Czechia. The group was very tight and I really thought we would come second and make the play-off. It was a group of six, with five teams that were all on quite an even par, at least in my opinion, yet two had to nab the automatic World Cup spot and the play-off spot. Slovenia, Slovakia, Poland, Czechia, Northern Ireland – we were all around the same level. The other team in the group, was San Marino, who everybody beat twice.

But unlike my 2005 adventure, this time, I wasn't going to the match in Poland. This was known in advance to me. I had messaged Rafał about it and he also skipped that match. Plus – Poland were getting their stadiums ready for Euro 2012 and therefore that match had changed venue a few times and the location was unclear. It was rumoured to be in Warszawa, then Szczecin and finally they said it would be in Katowice. It wasn't though – it ended up being in Stadion Śląski in Chorzów. I gave up Northern Ireland away matches in early 2009 due to Noemi and so

I always knew I wasn't going to this match. However, Noemi-less, I decided to watch the match on television in a bar in England.

I arranged to meet a mixture of Northern Irish, English and Polish mates in the Walkabout Pub in Bournemouth. I booked us a table and we aimed to watch the match in there. It was a great atmosphere in the pub. I was with Chris Bilsland, my aforementioned English mate from work, Simon McCully and Matthew Rutherford, two Northern Ireland fans plus the standard Polish contingent from work, including Maria, Marta and Dorota. There were a few others there but I don't remember too much about the whole evening as the beer was flowing and this was the end of my time living in England. I was on a countdown.

On the pitch, Northern Ireland broke through and we went 1-0 up just before half-time. It was the fans hero Kyle Lafferty who opened the scoring. As I write this book, Kyle Lafferty is still playing for Northern Ireland. His international career has spanned three decades. At this point, it looked like Northern Ireland would hang on to win 1-0. Martin Paterson burst through and had a chance to put us 2-0 up. This was where our World Cup hopes faded out of view.

Paterson missed. Then Poland equalised through Mariusz Lewandowski and the match finished 1-1. In the end, neither Poland nor Northern Ireland would qualify for that World Cup in 2010. It would be Slovenia and Slovakia to make it through our group. Of note though, while Mariusz Lewandowski scored that night, his surnamesake Robert Lewandowski came on as a substitute.

At that time, none of us had heard of Robert Lewandowski, but there he was playing against Northern Ireland in 2009. As I edit this in 2021, Robert has just broken Gerd Mueller's scoring record at Bayern Munich with 41 goals in one season (2020/2021) and is a global superstar, one of the best footballers in the world.

After that evening watching the Poland v. Northern Ireland match, I was counting down my days before leaving England. After splitting up with Noemi, I had been in touch with an Estonian friend called Natalja. Natalja was at a low ebb in life too and we both sook a change in our lives. Natalja agreed to backpack through Taiwan with me, then we'd dive into a couple more countries in South Asia before heading on an adventure to Australia, assuming we could both get our working holiday visas.

I had known Natalja for 4 years. The first time I met her was whilst selling cheeseburgers by Bournemouth beach. She worked in the bucket and spade shop opposite and we became friends. I didn't expect that Natalja would be keen to go to Taiwan with me. She fell asleep in my bed one night and I realised she would come with me and trust me and that I had to be strong and keep her happy. I did fancy Natalja sometimes, but nothing romantic ever occurred. It was friendship only. Though, she looked really good. I always loved looking at girls like Natalja. She held the same beauty as Noemi. And later in this book, I'll mention another Slavic girl. Natalja, Noemi and that Slavic girl all held the same beauty. They were blonde, slim, blue eyed and they came from countries that were once in the former Eastern Bloc. It was a trend in my life to fall for that history and beauty all in one. I'm weak to it, but strong within it.

As Bournemouth faded out of view and I left the United Kingdom behind, Natalja and I were off on an adventure. And when I look back on it now, it's now two decades since I lived in the UK.

Chapter 12
The Don't Stop Living Globe

Xinying, TAIWAN (October 2009)

"It's a small world after all" – The Sherman Brothers.

Natalja and I had never met outside England before and yet now we were suddenly backpacking it together in lands afar. In a four-trick of countries neither of us had been to before. We would backpack through Taiwan to start with – and we certainly did that hardcore back in those halcyon days. While in Taiwan, we visited the stunning Lotus Lake in Zuoying, we went dipping in hot springs at Kwan Tzu Ling and we backpacked cities like Tainan, Xinying and Chiayi to a hilt, with nonchalant aplomb. I blogged about all of that and those were the most popular blog articles my blog had ever seen. People other than my Mum and mates were reading "Don't Stop Living" now. Another memorable road trip for Natalja and I was the trip to Eluanbi, the beacon of South East Asia.

England, Northern Ireland and even Europe had been left selfishly behind. They were a distant memory. I had a moment to ponder here as I sat on the rocks at Eluanbi. At that exact moment, I was further south east in Asia than any other person. It was there I decided I would travel the world hardcore. It was a stark moment of realisation.

Slowly but surely, I would do it, I would backpack the world.

First though, we met up with a Taiwanese friend Eva, who helped us backpack up the east coast through cities like Taidong and Hualien to wind up in the tranquility of Tiansiang, in the heart of the rainforests in the dreamlike Tailuga National Park. We knew Eva Chung through Millwall Neil, my former (and future) flatmate who I had travelled with before and who was the catalyst for the visit to Taiwan. Millwall Neil lived in Taiwan. He is a London lad and has been my friend since 2004 when we met at Bournemouth University. Neil's barmy life in Taiwan was the intrigue. He said Natalja and I were welcome to visit and he was kind to allow us to sleep in his flat for our time in Taiwan. Ultimately, Taiwan was a gamechanger in my backpacking life.

It was also the place where I posed by a huge globe, at a Primary School in Xinying (Shinying). This globe became notorious as the globe that headed my "Don't Stop Living" blog and profile photo for years. It is forever known as the "Don't Stop Living" globe.

After Taiwan, Natalja, Neil and I had secured 1 year Working Holiday Visas for Australia. On route to Australia however, Natalja and I toured Malaysia and Singapore and had some more truly great backpacking moments together. For the time being at least, Millwall Neil stayed in Taiwan as he had a job contract there as a Native English Teacher.

Without further ado and like two kids on their first playground visit, after a night of karaoke in The Beatles Bar in Kuala Lumpur, Natalja and I got the train to Kuala Lumpur international airport and boarded a one-way direct flight to Australia. This was the crazy stuff.

Chapter 13
Living In A Land Down Under

Parramatta, AUSTRALIA (2009 – 2011)

"On a hippy trailhead full of zombie" – Men At Work.

Without flinching an eyelid, and for the first time ever for the pair of us, Natalja and I landed in Kingsford Smith Airport, Sydney and we were suddenly in the land down under. I never ever dreamed of living in Australia as a kid. But here we were. This was life now.

After what had happened with Noemi, I just had to leave Europe behind. Plus, I was still in my 20s and I wasn't getting any younger – I needed to see the world now. Before I arrived in Australia, I had already been to just over 30 countries. However from the day I arrived until exactly one year later, I didn't leave Australia so I didn't add to my country count but I certainly smuggled endless memories into my backpack brace.

This was a crazy year, and a busy one. That day, we arrived in Australia at 9 a.m. but with the time difference and the last few crazy weeks in Asia, it felt like 9 p.m. at night. In a quick moment of Google searching in Singapore, I had done two things –
1. I booked a random hostel in Sydney with a name I liked the sound of – "Chili Blue Backpackers."
2. I emailed a random Irish Pub somewhere near Sydney in a place I'd never heard of, asking if they had any jobs – this was "PJ Gallagher's Irish Pub in Parramatta."

The significance of that brace was to hit me and was to be the most positive impact on my life in that month. That year. That decade perhaps. And forevermore. For, on the first night at Chili Blue Backpackers, I met Daniel Evans. This is all about fate. Daniel was travelling with two female friends. I was travelling with one female friend. On the first night, Natalja and I were sharing a dorm with Martha, from Colombia. While chilling in the lounge, I don't remember how it happened, but a group had gathered to head down to the Opera House at night and then go for a beer. Of course, immediately Natalja and I were up for that. We were jet lagged but after arriving at the airport at 9 a.m., the hostel allowed us to check into our dorm room at 12 noon. We grabbed a short nap and were up for the night out. It felt so magical. We were free. But their 9 p.m. felt like our 9 a.m. and for once in my life, I realised we both had jet lag and a lack of time knowledge. None of that would matter, anymore.

That night, we all walked down to Sydney Harbour together. It was a big group. We had people from Finland, Sweden, Germany, Denmark, France, England, Estonia and Northern Ireland. Weirdly, I hardly met any Polish people in my entire time in the land down under. You were maybe expecting another Polish catalyst in Australia, but no – it wasn't to be.

Daniel and I got talking about football soon and we organised a few five a side matches with the hostel crew. One of these was a hangover match on the Sunday after Halloween. Daniel is a Derby County fan and we went to watch Sydney FC together in the stadium and watched a fair few matches down the pub – we'd head to the Sports Bar at King's Cross. Daniel and I became best friends. Natalja had met other friends too and was having fun. It just felt wild and free but nights on the booze as a backpacker in Sydney took their toll, on the liver. We were drinking a lot, in fairness.

Daniel, Natalja and I ticked off all the main sights in the first few days. Museums, Cathedral, Sydney Harbour Bridge, Bondi Beach, Sydney Opera House. It felt like the best time to be a backpacker. Every night there was an offer for a cheap meal somewhere, and bars lured you in with a free drink to start off. Nights out were wild. I was single but never found love there. There was a huge Halloween party with 30 of us all in fancy dress and as November 2009 homed into view, Daniel and I headed to the Blue Mountains to escape the big city life. We felt so mainstream and back then we were. We packed our backpacks and headed on the train up to Katoomba, where we stayed in the Katoomba Backpacker Hostel. We needed a break from city life and wanted to trek and hike in the Blue Mountains. Just before that, came a sad and tearful sentimental goodbye.

I had to bid farewell to Natalja.

I wished her good luck, we hugged at King's Cross metro station in Sydney and off Dan and I went. I didn't actually see Natalja again until 2015 when I met up with her in Bournemouth, England again. Natalja is a Mum now. Life changed for us all.

The next significant dot on my globe was that email I had sent to that random Irish Pub before I landed in Sydney. Just before I headed to the Blue Mountains, I attended a job interview at PJ Gallagher's Irish Pub in Parramatta. Parramatta is a CBD of its own and whilst officially in Sydney, it felt like a separate place. That interview was with Angela Gallagher, the wife of Pat Gallagher the owner of the PJ Gallagher's Irish Pub chain. I had never properly worked outside Europe in my life – blogging then was only a hobby for me. I had no Australian bank account, no Australian Tax File Number, no Australian mobile phone but I did have my Australian Working Holiday Visa and I did have my enthusiasm and passion. I wanted that job a lot but I wasn't sure they would employ me. However, I needed that job. Failure wasn't an option.

I didn't dwell on it though, because Daniel and I were backpacking through the Blue Mountains every day. There was one day we got back to the hostel totally drenched from torrential rain. I dried up and checked my email and there it was – a Godsend. I had been given the job in PJ Gallagher's Irish Pub and was due to start work in a few days' time! I was so delighted, since I was down to my last hundred or so dollars. Backpacking had taken its toll on the wallet this time, rather than the liver.

On the Sunday, Daniel and I viewed a flat in Westmead (by Parramatta) and convinced them to let us share a room at discount price. On the Tuesday we moved in. On the Wednesday I had my job training. On the Thursday I had my RCG (Gambling certificate) course and on the Friday I started work in the land down under! It had been a crazy month in my life. Leaving Noemi behind, backpacking through Taiwan, Malaysia and Singapore with Natalja and now I had a job and a flat in the land down under. The journey got more and more wild from hereon in.

Poland, was still not anywhere near my radar.

Chapter 14
Tasmanian Devils

Tasmania, AUSTRALIA (February to June 2010)

"Where women glow and men plunder" – Men At Work.

The one year working holiday visa for Australia can be extended for a further year if you have done 3 months (or 88 days) of "rural work". There are certain criteria that you must meet in order to get this visa. I wanted that extra year of visa, but I also wanted to explore parts of Australia and ensure that when I left the country in October 2010 (on the 1 year anniversary of my arrival) that I would have a trip to remember planned.

After 3 months working in PJ Gallagher's Irish Pub in Parramatta, I had a chat to my boss, Ian Corke. I told him that I loved the pub and my job there and that I didn't want to lose my job but that I wanted to do my farming work to ensure I could extend my working holiday visa for another year. He agreed and we organised a mini party for my "going away drinks." I promised I'd be back in the pub again, but nobody really knew. I had only 8 months left on my first working holiday visa. To secure the second year extension, you had to work in a rural job for 88 days. Working in a pub in the city of Parramatta wasn't acceptable to pass for that. And while I did well over 88 days working in the Irish Pub, I also felt like I wanted to do some farming work. I just wanted the experience of it and my choice was suitably inspired.

I've skipped some parts of the story here of course. But basically Daniel Evans and I shared a room in Parramatta in a flat with Ruben, Rebecca and Peter. However, in December 2009, Millwall Neil had also moved into the room with us. Neil had left Taiwan and got work in Australia now. We were saving money by having three of us living in the same room. It was never any issue – Neil worked days teaching and I usually worked nights in the bar. Even though Neil and I had decent jobs here in Parramatta, we all decided we should leave them behind and live the dream. Neil however did expect and intend to return to his job in Sydney.

We planned an adventure down to Tasmania. To this day, I will never know the exact catalyst for going to Tasmania, but for sure as hell it changed my life for the better. I have a feeling that the only reason we decided to road trip it to Tasmania was that Dan and I had been in a bar in Sydney one night (Scruffy Murphy's) and noticed an advert for apple picking in Tasmania if you stay at the Pickled Frog hostel (in Hobart). At that time in my life, I didn't expect we'd actually do either of those things. It was a notion on the rip we concocted.

But now that Millwall Neil was on board, we had a good hat-trick of lads here. The plan was hatched. We'd leave Parramatta on the last day of our rent, head into Sydney to the main bus station and get a bus to Canberra. After a few days there, we'd head to Melbourne, then tour the Great Ocean Road and then we'd actually go to Tasmania by ferry, on the Spirit of Tasmania.

There were some mishaps along the way but that was the plan. I finished work at PJ Gallagher's Irish pub at 4 p.m. My leaving drinks party was at 7 p.m. in The Albion Bar in Parramatta. The next morning we were up rise and shine and on route to the capital city, Canberra.

Canberra, is a hugely under-rated city. We loved it. We had our first afternoon chilling and meeting black swans at Lake Burley Griffin. At night we headed to King O'Malley's Irish Pub, where we had an encounter with a lunatical local dancer who we nicknamed "Wolverine." We toured the War Memorial Museum, the Australian Parliament, Mount Ainslie, Black Mountain and we even had a dip in the soothing lakes at Casuarina Sands. Canberra was blissful and relaxing.

From Canberra, we headed on a nightbus to Melbourne. This became a wild period of life in a crazy week in Victoria. We met one of the characters from TV show Neighbours while doing a tour of Errinsborough to Ramsay Street (which is a genuine real street called Pin Oak Court!). We had a bit of a gang together by now.

As well as Daniel and Neil, we were joined by Paul from York and a few girls – Lynsey, Gemma and Ali. We were walking down by Melbourne's Yarra River the day after the Australian Open tennis tournament. I dandered over and saw some camera crew and journalists, before saying to my friends *"That's Roger Federer!"* and it was him! So by chance we also met the man often considered to be the world's best ever tennis player!

We joined a pub crawl of Melbourne, where I famously won a karaoke competition by belting out a fired-up rendition of Pulp's "Common People" in a bar full of self-declared "ex-pats."

After touring the Great Ocean Road, Neil, Daniel, Paul and I boarded "The Spirit of Tasmania" ferry and headed south to Tasmania. This was where the dreams all began.

As I wrote before, I had only been to around 30 countries when I landed in Australia. However, I wanted to work hard, earn as much money as I could and bump up my backpacking experience and country count.

We arrived at Melbourne Harbour at dawn and there she was. The massive, impressive vessel, the Spirit of Tasmania. This was our ship to take us from Melbourne in Victoria across the sea, south to the city of Devonport on the magical island of Tasmania. It was another dreamy adventure to twist all of our fates again and take me to a land far away from Northern Irish Bangor.

There were four of us now in the backpacking gang, it was Neil, Paul, Daniel and I. We had met Paul in the Urban Central hostel in Melbourne and he had also attended what I had classed as *"The Defining Backpacker Victory Night,"* which was the aforementioned karaoke story that appeared in Chapter 45 of my *"Backpacking Centurion"* series. It's in Volume 2 of that series, *"Lands Down Under"*.

As we got off the ferry around sunset in Tasmania, I had no idea what the future held for me or for any of us. Nothing was planned or booked ahead. Nothing! We had nothing booked except one night, we had a bed sorted for the first night and that was it.

Little did I also know that we arrived as four friends yet when I'd get round to leaving Tasmania, I would be travelling back to the mainland alone. All three of my friends having already left not just Tasmania, but all would have also left Australia by that point. It's a spooky thought, pondering back on it now.

They'd also all leave Tasmania by flight, yet I'd be back on this same ferry again, alone, almost five months later. It would be an odd full circle again for me. Hindsight tells me that. For now, we buzzed as four good mates and all was good. We had booked one night in a hostel but I knew there was room for lots of madness here. On arrival at the Gingerbread House Hostel – a last minute hostel we (Neil or I – don't remember) had booked, there was a friendly welcome in store. I recognised an accent and there was a Belfast lad called Chaz Fitzsimmons working here and soon enough I had a new mate! Radaboutye big lad! Not only was Chaz a Belfast lad, but also a Glentoran and Northern Ireland fan!

The next night we moved hostels to stay in Molly Malone's Irish Pub, which had cheap dorm rooms on the opposite side of the lough, but I kept touch with Chaz. I had picked up a flier for a free beer for everyone in town as well. After a day exploring Devonport, Neil cooked us all a tasty pasta and sausage meal and the four of us were having a great time. That was a Saturday night and as Daniel and I went to an internet café to get the Derby and Bournemouth scores, something bad was around the corner. Perhaps it was good news to follow the bad, who knew. But I didn't see it coming. I expected the next day we would check into our third different hostel, Tasman Backpackers and first thing on Monday morning, Daniel and I would go into town and look for every conceivable possible job available – probably picking apples, and to start as soon as possible.

Life, is simply not like that…

On the Sunday morning around 11 a.m., when we had been only around 40 hours on the island of Tasmania, the bad news arrived from my new best mate. Daniel had made up his mind and dropped a bombshell.

Daniel had decided to leave Devonport already, yes within 40 hours of being there, he was leaving.

Neil, Paul and Daniel hired a car between them and they were off to explore the island for a few days before jetting out. The lads had made up their mind. They also knew I had made up my mind. I was staying here in Devonport.

I had landed in Australia with Natalja in October 2009. I met Daniel Evans on the first night in the country and he quickly became my new best mate. I said goodbye to Natalja in November 2009. I worked hard for three months in Parramatta and lived with Daniel in our flat. In the last five months, Daniel and I had backpacked together all over Sydney, Parramatta, Blue Mountains, Canberra, Melbourne, Great Ocean Road and so on…now it was February 2010 and I was destined to be alone again. I basically knew nobody here.

I had never ever felt this lonely before in life. I was so far away from home now. There was no chance of me ever catching a flight back "home," wherever "home" even was, so now I had to make this my "home." I was still in my twenties of course…

"Oh my God I can't believe it. I've never been this far away from home" – Kaiser Chiefs.

I decided I was staying here in Devonport and that was it. I wasn't going anywhere so I booked an extra night in the hostel above the Irish Pub, the Molly Malone's. I would sleep in the same bed, in the same room that four of us had slept in the night before. By 1 p.m., I had waved goodbye to Neil, Daniel and Paul. They got in their hired car and off they went. Daniel and I had bought a football and we kicked the ball about in the car park just before they left. It felt like the end of something. I was really emotional kicking that ball around the car park.

Once the car drove out of the car park, I went into my bedroom in that hostel dorm above Molly Malone's and cried my eyes out. I was so sad. There were three empty beds of my best mates.

Three Korean backpackers came in to take their places shortly after and I couldn't bring myself to say anything other than hello. I was really sad.

I slept the whole day and night. I didn't even have dinner but I took the complimentary pint of Boag's offered by the Irish Pub. The next morning, I checked out of Molly Malone's Irish Pub alone and I prepared to move into Tasman Backpackers. It was a lonely 20 minute walk there. Suddenly, backpacking didn't seem like such a golden dream anymore.

Then there was a weird thing that intervened, to give me one last bit of time with the lads and a future inspiration to head to Antarctica. So, this is what happened. On the Monday morning, Daniel, Paul and Neil had travelled far south towards Hobart. I Facebooked Daniel and he confirmed they would spend the night in the Pickled Frog Hostel. Him, Paul and Neil were all heading back to the mainland on the Wednesday morning and that would be that – it was booked. No way was I leaving. This was my dream here in Tasmania and I wiped away my tears and checked into Tasman Backpackers, but there was a problem. The hostel was full. The God damn hostel was full. Yes I could have blagged my way onto the sofa, but for some reason, I felt this was a turn of fate…

"Oh, we're overbooked" said Guillaume on reception at Tasman Backpackers. So, there was now no room for me here for the night. It was a stroke of fate though. Upset and downbeat, I said "when is there a spare bed in a dorm?," "in two days' time!" said Guillaume, "Okay, book it for me and I'll be back."

Then, I saw on the wall that they hire cars so I decided to hire a car immediately for those two days and sleep in it. I could drive all the way south to Hobart to have a final farewell and drink with the lads before they board their plane on Wednesday, then I could head north again. It might scatter my sadness, my loneliness and tears over a few days and we could backpack some places hardcore, for one last time.

I did just that! I covered the story a few times before in blogs down the years. But those last two days with the lads were brilliant. We saw Tasmanian Devils, fed Kangaroos and toured the harbour at Hobart, plus a few more pints together. On the final night, we drove past the Tasmanian Antarctic Research Centre (by chance) and I pulled over to grab a photo. We stopped on route to the south of the island at a remote place called Gordon, near the Huon Valley.

As Daniel and I leaned on planks over the river for sunset, I told the lads I was going to work hard here in Tasmania and then book a trip to Antarctica. I'm not sure any of them believed me. We returned to Hobart late evening and after a quick drink in a bar near the Pickled Frog Hostel, we bid our farewells this time.

This time, it was for good. This time, I didn't cry.

As I write this now, I can also reveal that I haven't seen Paul since that day. I didn't see Daniel Evans until **exactly** five years to the day (5th February 2015) and of course I was reunited with Millwall Neil again by 2011 in Seoul, South Korea and many more places since. But it was the end of the four of us backpacking together and it was definitely an emotional moment. When I think back on it now, it was so sad to hug them and say goodbye at the Pickled Frog Hostel.

Chapter 15
We Will, We Will Broccoli

A Lonely Broccoli Farm, Poatina, Tasmania, AUSTRALIA
(February – June 2010)

"Don't know what I'm doing here, I'll carry on regardless"
- The Beautiful South.

I was now alone and I was also jobless. So, I returned north in the hired car and moved into Dorm 40 in Tasman Backpackers. I had a top floor bunk bed in a dirty 8 bed dorm. My room was full of guys from Hong Kong who were noisy and into video games, staying awake and chatting Cantonese until 4 a.m. I hated it. But there was one Australian guy in the room, Damo and he was a cool lad. But I was work focused. It was my first few hours in this hostel so I stormed out of the room and walked down the street on my own and found a job centre. In here, I applied for a position working on farms with a company called Work Direct. They invited me to their office to fill in an application form. Diane, the boss, asked me the following questions to which I gave the following answers.

Diane - *"What kind of work are you looking for?"*
Me - *"Any."*
Diane - *"When can you start?"*
Me - *"Now."*
Diane - *"How long can you work for?"*
Me - *"As long as you want."*

As I walked out of the office that day, I didn't hold my breath. I didn't expect a job. Diane had looked at my application form and asked, *"don't you have a phone?"* *"No"* I said, *"I'm an old school backpacker – I don't want one!"* She immediately told me to get a phone, an Australian phone or I wouldn't get a job. I hadn't used a phone properly since September the previous year and enjoyed not having a phone, but if I wanted a job, they'd need to phone me. I popped quickly to the K-Mart and bought the cheapest phone they had for $30 AUD and gave Diane my number. An hour later I headed to a local pub for Happy Hour, they included free food with any beer purchase which was $5 AUD. I am not kidding, as I took my first sip, the phone rings…

"Hey Jonny, it's Hayley from Work Direct, can you cut broccoli tomorrow?"
"Hey Hayley, definitely! What time?"
"We'll pick you up at the hostel at 7 a.m.!"
"Brilliant" I said, *"I can't wait!"*

And that was that. I was absolutely ecstatic. I had gone from utter sadness yet within 24 hours, I had a job!! From that point on, I was living a golden dream and I grasped it with both hands. Nobody was taking this away from me now.

Ask me when I was a teenager at Tech in Belfast if I thought I'd be working as a broccoli harvester when I'm 29, and I would simply have laughed at you! But there I was, aged 29, working on farms in Northern Tasmania as a broccoli harvester. Loving it.

I got into it totally by chance and fate, aided by my unfussy insistence and "get up and go" attitude, which has paid off a number of times in life. I won't go hungry and I don't do lazy. The world doesn't stop turning.

As somebody I can't remember once said "you don't just sit in a rocking chair and build a revolution" (maybe they didn't even say that, but it fits). Manual labour and harvest work are common jobs for travellers and new Australian immigrants to do. For those like myself initially here on a one year visa (my first "Working Holiday Visa"), by doing this type of work, you can extend your visa. For most "Working Holiday Visa" owners, this gives you an extra 12 months on your initial 12 months, meaning you can stay in Australia working for 24 months or 2 years in a row (or in two separate spells each of 12 months).

After this, you have to get a sponsored visa or become a resident or a student to work (or do it illegally cash in hand). I really didn't think I'd like Australia that much to stay longer, never mind wanting to spend my days working on remote farms and fields. But life takes you where it does, and it took me here...to the wilderness of places such as Squeaking Point, Longford, Poatina, East Sassafras, Kindred, Moriarty and Wesley Vale. I mean where the fuck is Wesley Vale?

Basically, Wesley Vale is a farming area 12 kilometres or so west of Devonport. It has a local shop and that's about it. It's barely a village or a hamlet – it's simply just a farming area. And it was there on a spanking hot day in February 2010 that I started my new job as a broccoli harvester. I guess you could call it broccoli picking, broccoli farming, broccoli cutting, but I reckon the best way to describe it is broccoli harvesting.

I met a lot of new friends on the broccoli job, mainly the (Tasmanian) Australians, French and Taiwanese. I also worked with people from England, Italy, Germany, Hong Kong and Canada. It was some experience and I cherished every minute. My days on broccoli have been covered further on the blog many times, including being lucky enough to work on the world's first broccoli harvester. And yes, it was luck, but also a fair amount of arduous work on the way. I was earning about $18 AUD per hour (which was £10 Sterling at the time) and this rose to about $19 AUD when I was upgraded to a level 2 broccoli harvester. I normally worked from 7:30 a.m. to 5 p.m. with 2 fifteen minute breaks and a thirty minute lunch break. I will never work out the exact number of broccoli boxes I filled **personally** but it must be somewhere in the region of 1000 boxes, maybe around 500,000 bits of broccoli. Yes, half a million. It was a dream life and when I look back now it seems like I was a happier man back then. Life was damn good and the money I earned came in very useful on my upcoming adventures. The whole thing had worked like a golden dream.

I ended up working on farms all over Tasmania for the next five months. I hardly had a day off work. I worked from 7 a.m. to 7 p.m. often, trying to earn as much money as I could. I worked weeding cabbage paddocks, planting pyrethrum, weeding bean paddocks, purifying echinacea, picking fruit, harvesting broccoli and cauliflower. Any job that was offered, I took it. The more obscure the better and I travelled all over Tasmania for jobs – no place was off limits for me. I was also offered a job on Bruny Island at one point, but that was an unpaid role so I turned it down. However, it was the broccoli harvesting that was the overarching triumph. This was my victory.

After a month of working on broccoli, I bought a car for around 1,000 Australian Dollars and I slept in it for weeks as well as camping out sometimes. By doing that, I saved a lot of money on accommodation and was given more and more work in remote parts of Tasmania. If I worked from 7 a.m. to 3 p.m. one day, I'd spend the rest of the day exploring, touring and sightseeing. I smuggled so much tourism from Tasmania into my backpack. I was taking photos and making videos of towns, villages and farms that I knew I would never ever be back in. In this life, I was right. Alcohol had also been and gone, again.

I had my last alcoholic drink for 5 weeks on my 30th birthday, we had a decent group of hostel friends and broccoli workmates to celebrate with me in the Molly Malone's Irish Pub in Devonport that night. I worked on the day after my birthday and I slept in my tent or in my car (I bought a Toyota Hilux) after checking out of Tasman Backpackers in late March 2010. I was also offline most of those 5 months that I spent in Tasmania. Once every few weeks, I would go to the internet room in the library in Longford, email Mum and Dad and type up my blog stories from the farms of Tasmania.

In total, I spent 5 months in Tasmania, working almost every day in some capacity but I also got to explore a lot of the island. Due to the fact that I had been working long days concurrently with no breaks and had no internet or no contact with anyone outside the farms, I didn't know how much money I had. I wasn't drinking, I was basically eating cheese, ham and bread every day and drinking only water, tea and coffee. I was hardly spending any money as I slept in my car or my tent now.

Then came the shock.

I really had no idea how much money I had earned. I had just been working on farms every single day for months and wasn't spending much money at all. In mid-May 2010, I finally went to an ATM (in the city of Launceston) to check my bank balance and there the shock arrived. I had thousands of Australian Dollars in my bank account!! Some of the weeks on the broccoli farms I had worked 12 hours a day for 7 days a week, earning $1,300 AUD a week. When I cast my mind back 4 years earlier to my time at Bite Communications in London, I had earned more money in a WEEK here than I did in a month there. It was unbelievable.

Money doesn't usually drive me or inspire me, but this particular time, it did – the fact I had so much money for once, it made me feel so amazing. My hard work had totally paid off and I also had now completed more than the minimum 88 days needed to extend my visa. I had amassed well over 100 days working in farms! One night while heading to sleep in my tent in lonely Poatina, I decided that the next day I would drive to the internet room in Longford and book the entire Antarctica trip. That was it. I had earned it.

There was a special offer trip with GAP Adventures for $ 5,000 AUD if you booked it now, you would get the 13 day cruise for the price of an 11 day cruise.

From that internet room in that library in Longford, I booked myself on a November 2010 trip to Antarctica. A trip, which, you've guessed it would turn my life on its head, again!

I have covered the farming story of how I booked Antarctica before on my blogs, but this is it in short really. I had earned the money now, so I paid it in full and I knew that in 6 months' time, that was it – I was heading to Argentina, Chile, Uruguay and Antarctica! From the amount of money I earned in remote lonely farms in places like Wesley Vale, and later while living in Poatina (camping out or sleeping in my car), I was able to book my trip to Antarctica and still have a few thousand dollars to spare. I had turned the corner in life, I was happy. I had forgotten about Noemi and I was on a mission to travel the world again. Suddenly, I had money in life.

I continued to work in Tasmania though – the work was ongoing and regular there and I wasn't just a broccoli specialist now. I also worked in weeding, sorting, pyrethrum planting, echinacea purifying and cauliflower harvesting. I also briefly met up with Chaz Fitsimmons and Andrew Power (a Rangers fan from Bangor in Northern Ireland – now living in Hobart) where we formed a temporary Northern Ireland Supporters Club in TasmaNIa. We called it the Green Devils – the TasmaNIan WilderNISC. I watched a few 2010 World Cup games on TV with Andrew including England v. USA.

But now that I had earned all that money, completed my farming work and was isolated in Tasmania, I decided it was time to return to the Australian mainland. Believe it or not, I visited about 40 different settlements in Tasmania, all during that work time – I'd often sleep in my car in random villages just to check out another village! After touring some truly remote parts of Tasmania – Stanley, Strahan, Rinadeena, Bruny Island, Kettering (and a longer list), I left Tasmania the same way I had arrived on it – onboard the ship The Spirit of Tasmania.

Leaving Tasmania that night also felt like a full circle for me and it felt like a sentimental end. I loved Tasmania, I really did – I loved the people there, the hard work ethic on the farms and the fact that this beautiful island had allowed me to work hard and live my dream.

I treated myself to a final night of luxury - I spent my last night in Tasmania in a bed for the first time in months by staying at the Molly Malone's hostel in the same dorm as the one with the lads five months earlier. I bid my emotional farewell to my work bosses Hayley and Diane and I thanked them immensely – they had been brilliant to give me that job and stand by me the whole time. I was heading back to Melbourne for a few days, then a road trip up to Queensland with a few stop overs on the way to meet up with a few friends, notably George Sutton (my Australian mate in Coolangatta) and Owen Millar, my Northern Irish friend who was on the original Warszawa Party Train (see Chapter 5) who now lived in Brisbane.

After that, I returned to Parramatta and PJ Gallagher's Irish Pub where I worked as many shifts as I could until the day my visa expired (October 2010). After that, it was time for my first ever visit to South America, and of course – that crazy dream. I'd be visiting Antarctica and had visited all 7 continents by the age of 30.

(to Tasmania, the night I left) "We may never meet again, so shed your skin and let's get started" - Hunters & Collectors.

Chapter 16
One Small Step For Yer Man

Barrientos, ANTARCTICA (November 2010)

"It just don't matter anymore" – Buddy Holly (though I'm actually thinking of a different song which even Google couldn't find for me).

After long hours on the broccoli fields in Tasmania, I was finally in Ushuaia and I boarded my boat bound for Antarctica. Everything seemed to happen in a hasty daze. I had a few days in Buenos Aires, did the Maradona, Tango, steak and red wine, then I flew to Ushuaia in Tierra Del Fuego. It all happened very quickly. Soon, I would be on-board the MS Expedition boat, southbound for Antarctica. Yes, I was going to live that dream.

Due to the fact that my journey was long and varied, it is simply impossible to document it all in here. There is not even enough room for just a snippet from each country that I dipped into on my adventures. A lot of my crazy backpacking days were already covered on my travel blogs down the years but then again when I moved to Poland, not a lot of people knew my history. I started freshly in Poland in 2016. It was like a new life, I turned over a new leaf. However, for the basis of this book, I will still be including a few morsels from those crazy backpacking adventures down the years in those years that led up to my move to Poland. While I was in Argentina, Chile and Uruguay around the same time, this chapter is where I fell in love in Antarctica.

Yes I fell in love **IN Antarctica**. Not with Antarctica!

There it was. The magical. The dream really happened, and it happened at a place that most of you reading will NEVER have heard of - Barrientos. I stepped foot in Antarctica. Be honest, if you haven't been to Antarctica, would you ever have heard of "Barrientos"?

So what is Barrientos exactly? Barrientos is a very small island in a group of cold Antarctic islands known as The Aitcho Islands. The Aitcho Islands themselves are part of the even larger group of islands called The South Shetland Islands. It would be here in remote pure wilderness where myself and my boat buddies would officially land on Antarctic soil or snow for the first time ever.

The term "glory days loyal" is all about this. Backpacking in Antarctica. Barrientos away.

"Live the dream" – Cast.

The night before our arrival in the continent of Antarctica was a memorable one - we had passed the worst parts of the dreaded Drake Passage and were called into the main lounge bar room for a summing up and preparation for the next day. We were ahead of schedule and Julio, the Gap Adventures leader announced that we were going to have our first Antarctica landing the next day in the early afternoon. Everyone was so perked up and hyped by this stage.

The announcement revealed we would land on little known "Barrientos" in The Aitcho Islands. It's likely that nobody except the crew had heard of The Aitcho Islands. For sure none of us tourists had heard of Barrientos.

Within a day, I'd never forget either. This was a life changing day. A truly life changing day.

I fell to sleep in my cabin room onboard the MS Expedition. My roommate was Mark, from Australia. We had a red wine each and fell to sleep now that the Drake Passage was behind us. The following day, the 8th of November 2010, after looking out on deck and seeing the land of white magic, I saw with my own eyes....Antarctica. It is that breath taking, it is that awe inspiring. Once you've been to Antarctica, it's hard to beat it. Surely the only thing that will surpass this is landing on the moon. Seriously.

"If you believe they put a man on the moon, man on the moon" – Michael Stipe.

So we landed on Barrientos, we danced and dived in the snow. We met hundreds of penguins – the locals here in Antarctica. We saw some seals too. I had done it – I had visited the world's southernmost continent and I was buzzing. I was ecstatic!

But that wasn't even the highlight of the 8th of November 2010. No, landing in Antarctica wasn't even the highlight. The meal onboard the boat **after Barrientos** was the event that would truly change my life. Everyone on the ship was buoyant from our first landing. It was magnificent! That night, for dinner I sat at a six person table. I was the last to join that table – we always sat at different tables and with different people every night. At the table already was John, one of the leaders and beside him was Paul Gray who I had already got to know well on the trip. To my left was a French couple and then the other person, diagonally left to where I sat was a Hong Kong girl, a budget backpacker like myself. This lady, was Panny Yu.

We dined together that night. This was the first time Panny Yu and I spoke. 8th November 2010, off the coast of Barrientos island in The Aitcho Islands in Antarctica. Panny Yu, in her calm splendour and Jonny Blair, in his wacaday enthusiasm were destined to meet. It was fate that we were to meet that night.

"You've changed my life completely. I'm touched by your love" – Wet Wet Wet.

Although Panny and I had now met in life, and liked each other in life – we were too busy for all that just yet. We had the rest of our Antarctica adventure to enjoy! It was wild! Antarctica gave me the chance to swim in the coldest waters I had ever known. This event occurred at the magic of Whaler's Bay in Deception Island. Deception Island itself is just sensational. Our Bulgarian captain, Asparuh Chorbadzhiev invited us all up to the deck as he veered our ship, the MS Expedition through the narrow "Neptune's Bellows" and into the nucleus of this oddly shaped island.

The entrance into Deception Island was full of marvel and wonder. It really was like a James Bond film scene. Even standing on deck waiting to pass through "Neptune's Bellows" you could sense the mist of intrigue in the air. It was cold and chilly on deck and a wee bit windy. A brave crowd had gathered on deck to view our narrow entrance through this slim channel into Deception Island.

To the right of our ship as the captain sailed her gallantly through the tight gap. Why a tight gap? you may ask and why make a big deal of it? The reason is...Deception Island, by its very shape is like a small "c" letter from a bird's eye view. And the entrance is like going into the letter "c" so this was a special slow motion part of the Antarctica adventure, another exciting time to be up on deck as our Bulgarian legend sailed us calmly through this narrow entrance at Neptune's Bellows.

It was one of a few times I visited the bridge of the ship during the trip and it was quite busy - everyone wanted to hear and watch the captain at work in what is a tricky job. Deception Island forms the entrance to Port Foster, in the South Shetland Islands. Of course it is named "Neptune's Bellows" after the Roman sea god Neptune, apparently coined by American sealers prior to 1822 because of the strong gusts experienced in this narrow channel. We made it in safely.

The same Neptune would feature in the journey later on, significant six years down the line when this weary backpacker wound up in Gdańsk in Poland, whose Ulica Długa houses a Neptune statue in the fountain in the pretty market square.

Aside from all of that, there were too many highlights on my special "13 days for the price of 11" Antarctica tour to mention. I've written about them many times since 2010. We hiked to the top of Cuverville Island. We got jiggy with it at Jougla point with dancing penguins. We landed on mainland Antarctica on the Danco Peninsula at a place called Neko Harbour. We passed the Argentinian and Chilean bases but didn't visit. We got stranded on pack ice somewhere near Peterman Island and Pleneau. We had Happy Hour drinks onboard the boat, once opting for Port to celebrate our "any port in a snowstorm" adventure. We built a snowman on deck. We had snowball fights. We had live music onboard in the bar. We chatted to penguin enthusiast Frank S.Todd. We cruised around Foyn Harbour, where a bronze shipwreck, The Governor was instantly Instagrammable before most people even used Instagram.

Also during the Antarctica trip, we visited the British Base at Port Lockroy. And another base that feels appropriate and significant now given that I was on route to Gdańsk with somebody. Ahem.

Chapter 17
The South Pole

Henryk Arctowski Station, King George Island,
POLISH ANTARCTICA (Listopad 2010)

"Boom shake shake shake the room" – DJ Jazzy Jeff.

It wasn't all a dream. It was a magical fairytale. I did something on a British passport that the Queen of England didn't do. Boom shake shake shake the room. I got my passport stamped at the British Base of Port Lockroy in Antarctica! I also posted postcards from the post office there. Life was wild and free. I had worked hard for such moments. And then, our final stop in Antarctica would have repercussions years later, which I wasn't to dwell on in 2010's Listopad. Yes, it was about Polska.

Poland was to come back into play. We didn't actually go to the "South Pole" itself of course, it's just a pun for the chapter title – you know I love doing puns for chapter titles and blog posts. Anyway to visit the actual South Pole – well, that would be either extreme or expensive for such a budget backpacker as I. But there was a "South Pole" to come – that was by surprise, by chance, by fate. We weren't supposed to have this "South Pole" experience yet here's how it all happened that day.

On a windy day, we had planned to land on Penguin Island around 2 p.m. But adverse weather conditions worked against us. The captain and crew were forced to abandon that idea and anchored instead off the coast of King George Island. However, this was a welcome change of fate. Thanks to bad weather, we would instead be visiting Polish Antarctica!! The Polish Antarctica base was here at Admiralty Bay off the coast of King George Island. When we anchored, two of our crew went to check how windy it was and how treacherous the waters would be. Unfortunately, it was dangerous here too. Those two crew members, John and Scobie boarded a zodiac and headed away from our ship. They headed on a Zodiac towards King George Island.

As we watched from the deck of the ship, the unthinkable horror happened. Their Zodiac overturned in the rough seas. It was turned upside down and John and Scobie were in the ice cold waters. This was an act of survival. Thankfully, by the grace of God, they were saved and back on the boat to recover from hypothermia. At that point, we felt that no landings would be made that day.

Just after eating, our luck was to turn. An announcement was made that the Polish base would welcome us here at Admiralty Bay by King George Island and that the waters to cross to it, were calm enough. As mentioned before, we had previously visited the British Base at Port Lockroy, which has a post office and a museum. Now it was to be Poland's turn. I should also mention that on my Antarctica tour, two other countries bases refused our visits. The Ukrainian Base (which has a bar in it, apparently) and the Argentinian Base.

We hopped onto these Zodiacs from the boat, the MS Expedition, and we arrived at the Henryk Arctowski Polish Base in Antarctica. We saw penguins nesting and had a quick circle tour of parts of the island. If you had wanted to speak Polish here, you could as a few of my shipmates did. There were some Polish staff working here and even more incredible were two things.

Firstly, the shop was open and sold some extraordinary Polish Antarctica gifts! This was unique. I bought a t-shirt and a badge at the Polish base. I was a cheapskate, tight budget backpacker still so couldn't afford much more from the gift shop, even though I wanted it. They accept złotych, US dollars and Euros here in Polish Antarctica. I didn't have any złotych on me though so I paid in US dollars.

Secondly, two of my shipmates – Russell (from Sydney, Australia) and Rodrigo (from Sao Paolo, Brazil) and I had brought a beer each and decided we would have our one and only beer on Antarctic land here. It felt so fitting that we would do that "in Poland." A country that I had drank many piwos with down the years and knew I would do so again. I *"Na zdrowied"* and *"Slainted"* in Antarctica! It was always my Polish friends who liked a sneaky drink. We toasted to our trip and our final night on Antarctic land. This was a really ice cold beer and a superb celebration for the memory. Life doesn't have quite so many unique defining moments as this. That was a high.

"We're an all-time high" – Rita Coolidge.

The next day, we circled Elephant Island without landing. The day after that, it was time to head back to Ushuaia in Argentina.

When the Antarctic dream came to an end, I was back in the southern Argentine port of Ushuaia. From here, I would backpack my way through a good chunk of South American countries. In fact, I'd visit almost all of them, leaving only Guyana and French Guyana unbackpacked. Not bad for a farmer and barman who plied his trade in Australia.

Fate and fortune had reared its head now though. My travel blogs were becoming more popular and I had met Panny Yu.

I had met Panny Yu in Antarctica.

Chapter 18
Kong Phew

Lam Tin and Lan Kwai Fong, HONG KONG (June 2011)

"Warm sun feed me up cos I'm leery, loaded up"
– Gavin Rossdale.

This certainly isn't a book about love stories but it would be impossible not to write about love on my journeys since they played a major part in influencing the travel decisions in my life. In 2009, I had only gone to Hungary because of Noemi. I also only booked Venice because I wanted to take her there. At that point in my life, I wouldn't have backpacked Venice on my own. I was madly in love with Noemi from 2008 until 2009. I can proudly say that I am no longer in love with her (as of 2021) and even by 2010 most of my love for her was gone. She was a super girl but God had my destiny elsewhere, and her's too. So what came next in Jonny Blair's love life cannon?

After Antarctica, I had 3 months of extreme travel ahead. I stayed with a local family in Montevideo, Uruguay to brush up on my Spanish. After that, I backpacked hardcore through Uruguay, Argentina, Paraguay, Brazil, Chile, Bolivia, Suriname, Peru, Ecuador, Colombia and Venezuela. All of those stories were shared on my blogs and social media at the time and many of them feature in my book series *"Backpacking Centurion – Volume 2 – Lands Down Under"*. That South America trip still feels like my finest hour of backpacking. Everything was new and exciting. I was young. Every day was an unpredictable adventure. I felt like I was the only tourist in Paramaribo, Suriname. I did the 4 day Inca Trail hike in the rainy season, culminating with the descent down to watch the mist clear over the lost city of the Incas, the awe-inspiring Machu Picchu, on Christmas Day 2010. I toured the mines of lofty Potosi, where we let off dynamite in the wild. I slept in a salt hotel and got naked at Incahuasi, the Atacama desert area that straddles the Bolivia to Chile border. I crossed the equator on foot at Ciudad Mitad del Mundo in Ecuador. I partied in Colombia on New Year's Eve. I got mugged in Venezuela the week of the black market crash. I went white water rafting in Juquitiba in Brazil. It was an intense few months.

However, as mentioned earlier, it was on the Antarctica trip that I had already met Panny Yu. Panny was a Hong Kong budget backpacker, she shared my passion for cheap and random backpacking travel. Panny and I became friends on the boat to Antarctica, we officially met and spoke for the first time after docking in Barrientos on November 8th 2010. Panny and I met up again in Argentina and Uruguay. We then decided that we could meet up further afield soon – either in Hong Kong (where Panny lived and would return to) or in Australia (where I had planned to return to, having secured my second Working Holiday Visa). It was love. I was in love again. It all happened very fast.

Panny came to Australia to visit me in April 2011. Just before that, I had applied for a Working Holiday Visa for Hong Kong. At the time, Hong Kong granted 100 Irish passport holders a Working Holiday Visa every year. Only 100 lucky people would get that visa. I was convinced it wouldn't be me. I was convinced they were looking for IT, office and banking professionals to work there for a year. I was a glorified barman and a hobby blogger. In those days, my blogs were not bringing in any money. Nevertheless, I applied for that Working Holiday Visa. I filled in all the paperwork in Australia, where I lived and worked in Parramatta. I then posted it all to Panny in Hong Kong and she made sure I had all the correct documents before submitting the visa application.

At the time, that visa option was available for Irish passport holders, but not for British passport holders. I don't recognise myself as Irish or British though. I will only ever be Northern Irish

– that's my nationality. I'm Northern Irish. I'm a Northern Irishman. I'm a Northern Irish nationalist. I love our six county country. However, as Northern Ireland doesn't officially have a separate passport, residents and Northern Irish people can apply for both a British and an Irish passport. Naturally, I have both and luckily this gave me a chance to be able to work legally in Hong Kong, on a "holiday."

It was actually the exact same type of visa I already held for Australia.

As the clock struck midnight on 30th March 2011, I now oddly held the unique honour of simultaneously holding three Working Holiday Visas for three different countries. I was currently living in Australia, using my Australian Working Holiday Visa, which would run from February 2011 to February 2012. I had also got myself a New Zealand Working Holiday Visa, as a back-up and while I was still young enough to get it. That was actually a two year Working Holiday Visa and would run from October 2010 until October 2012. Now, I had secured my Hong Kong Working Holiday Visa, which would begin and be activated from the day I'd land in Hong Kong to use it, and for 12 months after that.

It was an interesting situation I found myself in. I could literally have chosen any of those three countries. But Panny was in Hong Kong. It was also the most exotic out of the three options. I had already been to New Zealand twice. It was cool but I knew if I went there, I'd end up working in bars, hotels, restaurants or boats again.

I already lived in Australia at the time and though I had worked on many farms and in two bars there, it felt like I needed to move to Hong Kong. So I did it. However, it was a move that involved a crazy twist of fate and luck.

Initially I had saved enough money for a one week trip to Hong Kong from Australia. That trip also involved two stopovers in Singapore, on one of those I could meet my cousin Chris Scott who had now moved to Singapore. It was the first time I had seen him since meeting in London in 2006.

How I ended up in Hong Kong was crazy. On my first day there, I was tired but still did the sightseeing. On my second day there, I plucked up the courage to use my Hong Kong Working Holiday Visa to secure my Hong Kong ID card. I spent the morning unfazed by a visit to the immigration office at Ngau Tau Kok. I was the only *"Gweilo"* (a Cantonese expression, slightly derogatory for a white ghost/foreigner) in there. On my third day in Hong Kong, Panny and I were walking through Tsim Sha Tsui when by chance we passed an Irish Pub there. That Irish Pub, also by chance, that day happened to have a sign outside saying they were looking for staff. This was a Godsend. That Irish Pub was Delaney's. So we went in, Panny and I.

I met the boss, Colin Williams and the staff and filled in the application form. However, it felt like they were giving me the job already. I just felt it.

That felt weird though, because I was only here on holiday for a week. I already had a job. In Australia. On a Working Holiday Visa. In an Irish Pub. I was now trying to get a job. In Hong Kong. On a Working Holiday Visa. In an Irish Pub. I now had a Hong Kong phone and SIM card too. On the fourth day, the pub phoned me and asked me to start work the next day. It was day 5. I started work in Hong Kong while I was on holiday in Hong Kong! But I hadn't told them that I was only here on holiday for a week. I was due back in work in Australia on the Sunday evening, yet here in Hong Kong I was working on the Friday and Saturday evenings, my first two shifts in Hong Kong. It was actually the first "work" I ever did in Asia, at the ripe old age of 31.

In the end, Panny and I couldn't work out what to do. It was a no-win situation. It was a lose-lose situation. And even though 22 is my lucky number in life, this was a Catch 22, the escape from which we didn't have a clue.

Catch 22 - If I stayed in Hong Kong and didn't get my flight back to Australia, I'd lose my job in Australia, lose the money on the flight, have to pay rent for a place I wasn't sleeping in and all my belongings were in Australia. I'd have to fly back there anyway and get them.

Catch 22 - If I left Hong Kong and went back to Australia, I'd lose my new job in Hong Kong, almost certainly. And I'd not be with Panny and I'd have failed in my first week in Hong Kong.

I abhor failure though, it don't become me. Losing was never an option for me, so I worked really really hard those two nights in Hong Kong, to ensure the staff would notice that. They would see my value and hopefully allow me to head back to Australia and pack my bags and come back.

However, I worked just two shifts in Delaney's Irish Pub in Hong Kong and went to the airport 3 hours after my last shift. For one day, in a 24 hour period, I'd work in an Irish Pub in two different bars, in two different cities, in two different countries, in two different continents, in two different time zones, on two different visas. This was lunacy. In between, I'd have a double flight from Hong Kong to Singapore and from Singapore to Sydney. I clearly wasn't Superman, but for one day it was crazy. I worked from 0.00 – 03.00 a.m. in Hong Kong (having also just worked the Saturday 6 p.m. to 0.00 a.m. – i.e. it was a 9 hour shift), flew to Singapore at 6 a.m. Spent a few hours in Singapore, then flew to Sydney. I went straight back to my flat in Sydney to change clothes and by 7 p.m. I was in the Irish Pub in Sydney working.

A day later, the pub in Hong Kong confirmed that they didn't want me to work there, as I had let them down on my first week by starting and then leaving. Colin, the manager at Delaney's Irish Pub in Hong Kong didn't want me there as I had worked for 2 days then left. I was gutted as I knew my heart belonged in Hong Kong now, and with Panny. The next 7 days were tough on my mind. I was sad that I wasn't with Panny, that I wasn't in Hong Kong.

For whatever reason that God dealt me, Colin, had a change of heart. He liked me there even after two quick days. I was depressed and working in the pub in Australia and I came home from work one night to check my email at 2 a.m. Colin had emailed to offer me the job. Within a few hours, I had spoken to Panny, booked my flight (one way this time) back to Hong Kong and told the pub in Australia I was leaving. That was it.

It all happened so fast but I was now where I wanted to be in life. As opposed to nowhere I wanted to be in life. I was living in Hong Kong, with Panny. We were together, we both had good jobs and were working and saving hard. Another catalyst and twist was to bring even further surprise and for this reason, I felt blessed in Hong Kong. I had touched down in "lucky land." For once in my life, everything had seemingly worked out the way I had wanted it.

"She was lined, and I was home to the lucky land…
the legal pads were yellow. Hours long, pay packets lean. The
telex writers clattered where the gunships once had been"
– Donald Walker.

An old Bournemouth University friend, Chris Anderson now lived in Hong Kong and though I had hardly seen him in years, he knew I was now working in the pub in Hong Kong. He invited me to a house party one night, at the end of August 2011. The house party at his flat would run from 3 p.m. to 3 a.m. That night, I had to work from 6 p.m. to 3 a.m. in the pub so I really didn't think I could attend that party. But Panny and I decided to arrive at 3 p.m. to at least say "Hi" and then we would leave at 5 p.m. so that I could start work at 6 p.m.

On arrival at the house party, at 3 p.m., there was a guy from Portsmouth in England there – Simon Skinner and an Irish guy called Ronan. I told them about my job in the Irish Pub and the guys all found it a huge surprise that I was a Northern Irish guy living there for a few months and working in the Irish Pub. That day, Simon had an opportunity arise for an English teacher job. Simon was already a qualified teacher. He asked if I wanted to apply for that job. I laughed and said, "I'm not a teacher, I have never taught any English."

I told Simon I was working in the Irish Pub and had to dash off to serve pints soon. But he insisted that his contact was looking for a Native English teacher to start teaching right away and he kind of offered me an interview. It was another twist of fate. If I hadn't gone to Chris's House Party, I'd never have even met Simon and Ronan and I'd certainly never have been offered a job interview a few days later. I might never have become a teacher.

You have to believe me that I said, "no way," "I couldn't do that" and basically brushed aside the idea completely. But Simon gave me his contact on e-mail so I jotted down the e-mail address anyway. Panny and I had to leave the house party early, at 5 p.m. and I was in work by 6 p.m.. I headed to work in Delaney's Irish Pub and Panny went home. Then I thought how confident a guy I always am, so I decided I would at least apply for the job Simon had mentioned, what harm could it do to apply for it. I texted Panny on my tea break. "When I get home, I'll send my CV to that e-mail address and see what happens" I texted Panny. I was home at 4 a.m. and I sent the e-mail. Over a cup of the Earl Grey.

By the Sunday evening I had an e-mail back inviting me for an interview in North Point on the Tuesday morning. Wow! I had an interview at 9 a.m.. For a teaching job?! I had never done any teaching in my life and obviously had no chance. A complete underdog but weirdly they had given me an interview. I was so busy though. I was working in the pub everyday 6 p.m. to 3 a.m. and getting home to Panny's at 5 a.m. most days. I said yes to the interview but realised I would be too tired to get up for it, or most probably wouldn't get the job. I had zero experience of teaching English, I had zero qualifications and I was a barman working in Tsim Sha Tsui. Like the ultimate backpacker victory night in Melbourne or the night Northern Ireland beat England 1-0, underdog loyal, surely there was no chance I would get this job?

Tuesday morning came and I had no sleep. I went from work in the pub to Panny's flat for about 4 a.m.. Panny and I had a quick chat and she told me to buy some fruit to take into the interview and explain to the interviewer how I could teach children different fruits and colours. I was knackered but I went to the job interview anyway, which was at 9 a.m..

I got the MTR from Lam Tin in rush hour, changing at Yau Tong and onwards to North Point. I didn't have a Smart Phone or any of the like, of course I didn't have Wi-Fi. Panny used to laugh at my choice of a 2001 phone, here in 2011. I only had an address and a map of Hong Kong Island on me. It was 8.55 a.m. now, and I couldn't find the interview venue! It was just such a hot day and I was sweating. I had bought the fruit and I was lost. I had failed the interview before it started by not even finding the venue. I felt like giving in. Why was I doing this? I wasn't going to get the job anyway, like I said I was a barman! The interview was in five minutes time and I was hot, lost, tired and smelly. All alone on Hong Kong Island.

But something in me spurred me on and I managed to find the interview venue by asking and begging locals to tell me. I was early in the end as the interview team weren't going to start until 9.30 a.m.! There were two others being interviewed for the job. Again, I knew I had no chance. They looked sharp. I looked knackered. Bags under my eyes, sweat everywhere, dirty shoes. I looked like a backpacker who had got out of bed and rolled up to an interview. The others being interviewed also probably had teaching qualifications. Should I lie? Should I pretend I have the teaching qualifications? I thought about all this and then just went into the interview, confident and natural. I decided to be totally honest if they asked about my teaching experience and qualifications. In the end, such questions went unasked. In fact, I would say I went in and used the gift of the gab to blag it.

There were four ladies and one guy at the interview. The four ladies were all school principals. I wasn't one bit nervous. I was very talkative, very sincere and I meant business. *"Why do you want the job teaching in a kindergarten?"* one of the principals asked.

"I'm buzzing about Hong Kong. I love it here. I see all the happy people. I see the smiling children. I'd love to be a part of it. I'd love to help out. I'm so new to this country but I sense I belong here." Well that was something like what I said. I was so enthusiastic, positive, happy, and smiling.

Still, I left the interview room and back into the hot smoggy Hong Kong Air. I had to go for a coffee, get changed (in a public toilet) and go straight back into work at the pub for 3 p.m. that day. There was no time to go home and change and back out. Or sleep.

I decided to get the boat across from North Point to Hung Hom. The weirdest thing I just realised now when I type this is that this is the **only** time I have ever done that route. I have been in and out of Hong Kong Island, Kowloon dozens of times, yet this day I took that unusual ferry. But I'll never forget it.

As the ferry docked into Hung Hom, my phone rings. It's Simon Chan from the Education Agency, *"Jonny you've got the job"!*

"What?" I couldn't believe it. Speechless, in disbelief. This felt like a true underdog victory. *"Excellent Simon. That's amazing! When do I start?"*

I sat down on a bench on my own in Hung Hom, stared at the sky and sipped some water before phoning Panny. *"I got the job."* Panny too was in disbelief. She couldn't believe it. I'm not exaggerating here to put this shock into practice. I had no right to get that job. But somehow the principals interviewing me preferred me with my zero experience and zero qualifications to the others who had all taught English before. It must have been my Northern Irish charm and passion. They could see the happiness running through my veins! I couldn't believe it. This was like Greece winning Euro 2004! This was like Goran Ivanišević winning Wimbledon in 2001! I was today's Toto Schillaci – the man with Sicilian eyes who scored 6 goals and became top scorer at Italia 90 having been previously unknown and ranked the 4th or 5th best striker in Italy. The wildcard had won it.

When I got into work in Delaney's Irish Pub, I told my manager Colin the bad news (for him) and good news (for me). I said I'd love to go part-time in the pub, working weekends especially during the Rugby World Cup as the pub would be busy. But ultimately, I was now ridiculously a school teacher in Hong Kong. Without any real qualifications, experience or any reasoning. A true victory for passion and belief over useless certificates.

In the course of three days, I had doubled my wages, cut my working hours by a day per week and was guaranteed holiday pay and a visa extension. All from a crazy passion and desire to succeed. I really, really believed it now – if you want something in life and put your all into it – you get it. I really wanted that job you know. I became over excited at the interview and they gave me the job. It was ridiculous, truly ridiculous!

So, on the Tuesday I told Colin I had a new job. On the Wednesday before work I had to go and sign the contract for the teaching job. On the Thursday before work I had to go and buy my clothes – shirt, trousers, shoes. On the Friday it was my only day off that week and I had to go into both the schools I'd be teaching at to introduce myself, meet the teachers, and get my timetables. It was a crazy busy week. On the Saturday and Sunday I was back in the pub working 9 hour shifts each day.

On the Sunday night, my shift rolled into 3 a.m. on Monday morning as usual. My first ever day at the Kindergarten in Tsuen Wan began at 8 a.m. that day. I got home to Panny's at 5 a.m.. I left at 6.30 a.m. for my new job.

I had 1.5 hours sleep before teaching English professionally for the first time ever. Until now, nobody except Panny and I knew that. I was knackered to say the least.

When I look back on all that, especially that week, I wonder how on earth I did it all and didn't fall asleep or pass out. I guess I was 31 feeling like 21. From that Monday morning on, I could now call myself a Native English Teacher. I don't even remember being nervous. I don't think I had time to be nervous. Life moved pretty fast.

From my job in the kindergartens, I got offered extra work as a private teacher and as a teacher in Primary Schools and Secondary Schools. It all happened quickly. Life dealt me another ridiculous full circle when I was told I could earn 900 Hong Kong Dollars for

3 hours work every Saturday as a bonus in a Primary School. This was 300 Dollars more than I earned for a 9 hour shift in the pub (before tips). When I accepted this extra job, the Primary School was in…Yuen Long.

Yes, Yuen Long - the place where I had met Simon Skinner at Chris's House Party and a twist of fate, total chance had changed my career and life on its head. I'm not reading too much into this but:

1. If I hadn't known Chris Anderson from my time in Bournemouth (I met him through my PR coursemate Emma Broomhall, "Australian Emma")
2. If I hadn't known Chris was in Hong Kong (We were friends on Facebook)
3. If Chris hadn't invited me to his party (He didn't need to invite me)
4. If I hadn't gone to Chris's party (Panny thought I'd be too tired)
5. If Simon Skinner hadn't gone to Chris's party… (Simon was there).

Indeed, if any of those scenarios (or many more) hadn't happened, I truly believe I would never have got into teaching English. This was total chance. It was a complete twist of fate.

I just feel blessed when I look back on it. It was my reward for being passionate and hardworking and wanting it.

"Always want it" – Liam Gallagher.

I have now taught English in 10 different calendar years and in over 10 different schools and 50 different businesses along the way. I taught English in Hong Kong from 2011 to 2015. I have since taught English in Poland to Polish people, Ukrainians and Belarusians since 2016. In life now, I have over 10 years of experience as an English teacher, including teaching English in kindergartens, primary schools, secondary schools, high schools, businesses, offices and individuals. I can teach English face to face or online. I have my experience in it, I have my qualifications and I believe I could step into any English teaching job tomorrow around the world if I wanted to. And in that job, I could be an excellent teacher, or as good as I can be. It's a crazy world sometimes.

So that is the story of how I became an English teacher, told for the first time in this book, not even my mates down the pub heard this full story before.

Thanks Chris Anderson. Thanks Simon Skinner. Thanks Simon Chan. Thanks to the school principals for believing in me. I hope I did a good job as an English teacher for you all. It's a truly charmed life. I was blessed.

While based in Hong Kong from 2011 to 2015, many more adventures happened including visiting almost every country in Asia, working for Internations and becoming a professional travel blogger. In the middle of all that, some other things happened too. This book couldn't possibly have enough space to tell you all of that.

Also although I believe I am a decent teacher and barman, my heart has always been in writing – which of course links in to teaching in classrooms. I'm a natural and passionate writer and I want people to remember me as a man who loves writing. I write poems, songs, travel blogs, books, I write anything. I just love writing.

Chapter 19
Up Something

Uplistsikhe, GEORGIA (October 2013)

"Up something" – Rafał Kowalczyk.

After relocating to Hong Kong in 2011, Panny and I travelled a lot together. We backpacked all over China, a load of South East Asia, I headed to Africa again on a sponsored trip and we also toured the Middle East and Europe. Any time we had off work – we went on an adventure, even if it was just a weekend. By September 2013, we had both saved enough money for a 4 month trip. However, I was now working for myself as a professional travel blogger and was getting sponsored trips, tours, accommodation and food. My main website, "Don't Stop Living" had started to earn advertising revenue in late 2012. This meant that during those 4 months, I would continue to work online, as some kind of modern-era "digital nomad". We toured Israel, Palestine, Druze and Jordan before deciding to visit Georgia and backpack through the Caucauses. Georgia brought a huge catalyst that changed my journey to Poland.

When I talk about full circles and backpacking blues, our time in Georgia encapsulated this theory to the maximum. For my first four days in the country I was wearing the same clothes. Turkish Airlines had lost my bag. I seem to have had more bags lost by airlines down the years than anyone else I've ever met. Nine; and counting. It was a bad start to life in Georgia.

As soon as we arrived in Tbilisi airport though, we headed on a double marshrutky journey to the seaside town of Batumi. Batumi begins with a "B," a fact which gave me a smile and a reason to believe it would be lucky and we would get our visas okay here.

I'm coastal "B" towns on the brain remember. I grew up in the "B" of Bangor, Northern Ireland. I studied in the "B" of Belfast, Northern Ireland. I worked in a butchery in the "B" neighbourhood of Ballyholme, Northern Ireland. I later moved to the "B" of Bournemouth, England. I later had season tickets for the Cherries in the "B" of Boscombe, England. I broke the trend a little bit in Australia by living in the non-coastal "Ps" of Parramatta and Poatina, and my coastal residences in Australia were an "S" of Sydney and a "D" of Devonport. Perhaps that was why I had to spend a week in the "B" of Brisbane and a few days in both "Bs" at Byron Bay and Botany Bay. Hong Kong saw me live in Lam Tin, Lai Chi Kok, Ma Wan and Yau Tong so "B" seaside towns escaped me until I rented a flat in Poland in 2016. Where was it? You guessed it – in a "B" seaside town just by the beach. I lived in Brzeźno, a coastal part of Gdańsk. For now, back to Batumi...

We got soaked to the bone on the walk from Batumi bus station to the city centre in search of a hostel. We were a week too late for summer season and many hostels were closed completely. This was one of the rare nights on our travels where we think we may have been forced to stay up to explore, not sleeping to rest; all night without a bed. The place was soaking in torrential rain, and was a ghost town. That night we arrived in Batumi was one of my worst introductions to a country ever. But things would change.

We finally found the D'Vine Hostel, which was reluctant to take us in! They were about to close for the winter and the owners wanted to head back to Tbilisi to help out in the other hostel, the Why Not Hostel? In the end perhaps the wet rain and howling wind helped us, aided by my production of the "Don't Stop Living" travel blogger business card. Finally, we struck a good deal with them and during a three week stint in Georgia, we stayed a couple of nights in Batumi in the D'Vine Hostel and then headed to the "Why Not Hostel?" in the stolica Tbilisi which became our base for touring the Caucauses.

Why Batumi? Batumi was the easiest and cheapest place to secure an Azerbaijan visa. The first morning we headed straight to the Azerbaijan Embassy to get the visa. Panny and I were both told we could get the visa the next day. Northern Ireland were due to play Azerbaijan in Baku in three days' time so I was cutting it tight. In the end we got the visa, not without drama of course.

After touring Tbilisi, we headed on a night train from Tbilisi to Baku and spent 12 days backpacking in Azerbaijan including a few nights in the gorgeous mountain village of Xinaliq. Northern Ireland lost 2-0 in the World Cup qualifier with Azerbaijan, but we enjoyed a good few nights on the rip in un-nocturnal Baku. Then we returned to Georgia and it was time for a thrilling reunion and full circle again as we headed to Gori.

Before I tell my story of the trip to Gori, a bit of background is needed here. In 2005 I visited Poland for the first time, I was in Warszawa / Warsaw (see *Chapter 5 "The Original Party Train Till Warszawa" and Chapter 6 "Coleslaw / Boleslaw"*). Warszawa is the city where Stalin built the Palace of Culture and Science. A few months later I was working in Bournemouth selling hot dogs with Rafał and Artur - two top Polish lads who became good friends. I kept my promise to Warszawa and revisited in 2007. This time we went up to the top of the Palace of Culture and Science - Stalin's Building. It was here that I wrote a poem which became a song. That story makes up *Chapter 8's "Dog For A Girl"*.

Then 6 years passed. 6 years! And finally, Rafał and I would be in the same country again. How completely ridiculously fitting that the country was Georgia! Georgia being the home of Jozef Stalin, linking us spookily back to the Palace of Culture and Science, again mentioned in *Chapters 5, 6 and 8*. The reunion night with Rafał was in Tbilisi; Georgia's proud and reserved capital. We met in Liberty Square and toured the bars that night along with new friends Kamil, Wojciech and Ania. We probably hit the liquor a bit hard that night, many shots were consumed...and we hatched a plan. We were only 81 kilometres from Gori, Stalin's town. So we all agreed we would head there in the morning, hungover or not!

We were staying centrally in the "Why Not Hostel?" and that morning we walked to the metro. We got the metro from Liberty Square to Didube. From Didube we took a bus, slightly bigger than a Marshrutka. The bus took us all the way to Gori main bus station. We were hungover and slept the entire way!

On arrival in Gori, we made the journey straight to the Stalin Museum. Gori is a small enough town and everything is walkable. However, this is no paradise – remember that. Stalin is from here. Since my trip to Gori, I have also endured solo trips to Amna Suraka (Saddam Hussein's "House of Horrors" in Iraq) and Braunau Am Inn (Adolf Hitler's hometown in Austria). Bring your heart, but pray it won't wilt.

You probably know a bit about Stalin. I studied Politics for Media in Belfast and European History at Newtownards Tech. On both courses, there was a large chunk of it on the 1917 Revolutions and the Bolsheviks rise. Quite simply, Jozef Stalin, from Gori in Georgia was a ruthless communist ruler of the former USSR. The man that Lenin insisted should not take over the country. However he did, and he lasted a while...and the rest is history. The museum has 2 floors and also contains Stalin's train and mock house. Entrance fee was a modest 10 Lari. The Stalin Museum is massive and full of many items from Stalin's history. You should try to spend a couple of hours in here. This is probably the most extensive Stalin "tribute" on the planet. Stalin's schoolbooks, Stalin's early notes, photos of Stalin through the years, things that belonged to Stalin. Stalin's copy of Mein Kampf is here, along with war medals, guns, Communist symbols. I read my Stalin books while studying in Belfast and Newtownards many moons ago. For now, I was simply here to ponder on the errors of the past.

As well as all the information and memorabilia, as I wrote, there is a mock of Stalin's house and Stalin's train. There is also a shop. I didn't fancy backpacking the globe with a Stalin T Shirt...or drinking from a Stalin mug. The Stalin statue itself was removed from the town in 2010, though a smaller statue of Stalin still sat outside the museum. There are less than 20 surviving Stalin statues in the world and the Gori one is the only one I have seen to date. There is a smaller museum on Stalin Avenue which is dedicated to the war heroes from Gori and is unrelated to Stalin. Yes, that's right – there is still a "Stalin Avenue" in his hometown. It was a poignant and sombre day trip to Gori and we also took time late afternoon to tour the nearby cave town of Uplistsikhe, which Rafał and I called *"Up something"* as we found the name of the place unforgettable and unpronounceable. We still laugh about that to this day.

I felt a return to my history studying days here, to back when I studied the whole Russian Revolutions of 1917, the demise of Lenin, the rise to power of Stalin and the horrific regime where millions were killed under his reign. For the record, Jozef Stalin was born in Gori, Georgia in 1878, he ruled the USSR from 1945 - 1953. He died in 1953 in Kuntsevo Datsha, Soviet Union. He was an atheist and had 3 children.

We had some more drinks with Rafał and his Polish friends Kamil, Ania and Wojciech in Tbilisi. I would later meet all of them again, in Poland. In fact, I would later live with Kamil and travel to Belarus with Kamil, Rafał and Wojciech. For now, stuck in 2013, post-Georgia it was time for Panny and I to travel through Armenia, Nagorno Karabakh, Iran, Turkey, Qatar, UAE and Iraq.

But the fact that I had met up with Rafał again here and had another few crazy days with him was another point on the map which would eventually lead me to Poland again. But just not yet.

Chapter 20
Define The Gap

A far cry from home, PLANET EARTH (Yearically 2007 till 2015)

**"Never go back you tell me it's the worst thing you can do.
But I must go there till I find out where it is I'm going to"
– Highly Likely.**

Some of you reading might be curious as to why there are so many huge gaps in my journey to Poland story. Why not just include every year? Why not just include every country? Well this chapter isn't meant to simply give reasons for or "define" that entire gap, but I do want to explain that my journey around the world was long, tiring, weary and relentless. And also – it certainly wasn't about Poland or Northern Ireland. They are simply two countries on my globe that happen to be very significant.

My Northern Irish nationalism has always been there, but it wasn't until I had visited 100 countries or more that I realised how strong a nationalist I was. It was the reason I loved travel. I just love borders, real countries, national traits, separate things in each country and the joys of entering a new country, getting my passport stamped, seeing their flag, using their money, drinking their beer, meeting their people and feeling like I am *really* in a new country. I don't dream of the world ever becoming one big borderless country, I detest the EU and the Euro. Bring back the Greek Drachma, the Deutsch Mark and getting my passport stamped on entering Belgium, please! I love the visa thrills, the currency exchanges, the passport stamps, the immigration chats, the border crossings! It's boring when places are the same and they don't feel like separate countries. I love each place to be different, and separate. That's the charm for me.

So when I travelled, I always found that my best friends in life were those proud nationalists from every country. Panny for example, flew a Hong Kong flag in Bolivia. She wasn't from China, or Tibet, or Taiwan, or Asia or the UN – she was from Hong Kong. I loved it.

I'd meet people who called me British, or from the UK or Irish, and while in their worlds, they might think they are correct. While in my world, they were wrong. I'm Northern Irish.

Of course, 2013 had meant meeting up with Rafał again, but that was a brief encounter and my journey sauntered on. In 2014, I spent 5 months working flat out teaching English in Hong Kong as well as working online for myself as a professional blogger. I was working non-stop yet I still managed to visit Hong Kong, China, Indonesia, Thailand and East Timor in that time. Then, it was World Cup time.

The 2014 World Cup was to be held in Brazil. Panny and I decided to go. We had secured tickets for two matches – the Brazil v. Mexico group match in Fortaleza and the World Cup Final – Germany v. Argentina. How prestigious that would be. It was a childhood dream. Northern Ireland had been at three World Cups – 1958, 1982 and 1986 but only two after I was born and as I was getting older, I felt I just wanted to be at a World Cup even if Northern Ireland weren't there. Of course, the fact that it was in Brazil was also amazing. It was the first time Brazil had hosted the World Cup since 1950. Yet in that time period, they'd won the thing 5 times!

For each of the two matches Panny and I had 4 tickets. For the final, I wanted Mum and Dad to be there and also wanted to show them some of South America as neither of them had been before. It was also some kind of dream of my Dad to visit Brazil and to play football on a beach. We were living these dreams. For the other match, I invited my brothers and sister first but they declined. My close friends all declined as well, so in the end Panny and I would have two spare tickets for the Brazil v. Mexico match. Even my Brazilian friends didn't want to attend. In the end, my Norwegian friend Lief took one of the tickets as he was nearby in Natal and would overland for a night for the match. The other ticket, we'd sell to our hostel dorm room mate, Dorian from Canada, who by coincidence lived in Winnipeg, where I had been years before for my cousin Alison's wedding.

On this adventure, to the World Cup in Brazil, Panny and I decided to close our doors on South American countries. I had two countries there that I hadn't been to – Guyana and French Guyana. So we swallowed the brace as well as my return to Brazil and Suriname. I still have plans to return to South America though – as I neglected to visit Easter Island in Chile and the famous Galapagos Islands, owned by Ecuador. But countrywise, we'd have nailed them all after this trip.

We met my parents in Sao Paulo and toured Iguazu with them before we spent 5 days in Rio De Janeiro encompassing the FIFA World Cup Final. I'm racing quickly through that marvellous time but I'm really proud that I took Mum and Dad to the World Cup Final. Part of me knew, that my Mum wouldn't travel very far again after that trip. Indeed, 7 years on, that is Mum's last time outside Europe and for the love of life, and our family, my Mum doesn't need to leave Europe again.

My Dad, equally is not a huge traveller, so sometimes it's a mystery to me where I get my wanderlust from. I love the adventure of travel yet nobody in my family, save cousin Paul, shares this love.

"Been around the world. Been around the world and there's no place like home" - East 17.

It has been clear that my journey to Poland was far from obvious. In fact, after the 2007 trip to Warszawa, I didn't visit Poland again for a whopping 8 years. It was 2015 when I wound up in Poznań. Can you believe that? I should have written this at the start of the chapter, but basically in this chapter, I will aim to define that 8 year gap and give some reasons for it. My Polish friends were as surprised as me by that gap. On arrival back in Poland in 2015, one wrote to me that she was completely surprised by the gap and that she hoped it wouldn't be another eight years until the next one. She was invariably correct, but in fact for the next concurrent eight calendar years, I'd be primarily in Poland!

The main reasons for the 8 year gap from Poland are simple though - I was focusing on global travel for those 8 years and Europe wasn't included in much of that. In fact from 2009 to 2015 I didn't actually even live in Europe! I lived in Australia and Hong Kong.

Despite all that, I still worked with Polish people just before my move to Australia in 2009. We worked together on England to France ferries and I made new Polish friends on my travels too. This included Paweł from Wrocław who I met in Paraguay, Agnieszka and Cez who I met in China, Ewa and Milada who I met in Azerbaijan and another lady who I met in Moldova. Polish people were always in and out of my life. For whatever reason God threw at me.

It's also true that outside of England and Northern Ireland, my best friends have consistently been Polish. I can't explain it any other way than I like Polish people, I usually have a great connection with them and I find them very welcoming, friendly and similar to me.

"Although we view the world through different eyes. We share the same ideals of paradise" - Pet Shop Boys.

However, perhaps the biggest catalysts on my move to Poland during this "Define the Gap era" are now clear to me. A few of those will be mentioned in the next few chapters. One was backpacking in Georgia and visiting Stalin's Town, Gori, with Rafał Kowalczyk in 2013. Another came in a hostel in Moldova in 2014, another came in a bar in Kraków in 2015. How intriguing. Nobody could tell what was around the chimney corner. Not even a sultry lady, who had now entered my life in Chisinau.

Chapter 21
A Hostel in Chișinău

Dorm 2a, Tapok Hostel, Chișinău, MOLDOVA (November 2014)

"You became the light on the dark side of me" – Seal.

While it might seem from some of the early chapters that I was destined to live in Poland, the actual clincher probably happened in Kishinev, now known as Chișinău. I know that now. It was a night in Chișinău in Moldova, and a chance meeting with someone there, that influenced my life ever since. I thought a lot about this chapter and to be honest, this chapter was edited so many times and deleted at one point. But I'm putting it back in but calming it down a notch. It's to protect myself and others. Especially the person I was to meet in Moldova.

"I've got your number, but so does every kiss and tell who dares to cross your threshold" - Rapid Eye Movement.

On that fateful night in Moldova's capital city in November 2014, so many things happened. It wasn't clear to me that I was influenced by this lady, but looking back, I was. One of my biggest faults in life is that I don't realise how important or relevant things are, at the time when they happen.

This chapter was actually supposed to be a big influence on the book as a whole. But now, it's just a boring extra catalyst in the journey. It doesn't fit well now. It became a blackened nightmare. It wasn't even Chișinău or Moldova's fault. I liked Moldova and Chișinău. This Chapter definitely belongs in the book, but for reasons of legality and from God, it cannot be written here. Hence, it doesn't actually belong in the book now, perhaps in a future book. Perhaps in a fantasy book. I don't know anymore. There are too many ifs and buts. There are too many "what ifs?." The fact is that fate led me to somehow meet a person in Chişinău, Moldova. For better or worse? Again, I don't know anymore. I left Moldova and headed back to Romania and then onwards to Bulgaria - in early December 2014 I arrived in Gorna Oryahovitsa in Bulgaria. By 27th March 2015, I had visited 100 countries and completed writing my book series *"Backpacking Centurion"*.

The chances of the event in this chapter happening are slim. This was all down to fate.

A professional travel blogger, a broken laptop, a Northern Ireland match, a border crossing to Moldova, a locally based lady with charm. All of those led to one crucial event.

For whatever reason, in life, Jonny Blair was destined to meet this lady in that hostel.

Likewise, for whatever reason, in life, that lady was destined to meet Jonny Blair.

It happened here, in the unlikely city of Chişinău in Moldova. It happened by total chance. A series of occurrences led this to happen.

Firstly, there was the coincidence of the timing. Northern Ireland were playing Romania in Bucharest just before that and I had decided next to head straight to Moldova. I was here in eastern Europe for the football first and foremost. I had decided that about a month earlier. It was standard for me really. So that decision played the first part into the hands of fate. I would definitely be in Romania, Moldova and Transnistria that November.

Secondly, there was the fact that as a professional travel blogger, I was now getting free hotel and hostel stays in exchange for reviews. How did I choose those hostels? I'd usually email about

10 in each place I was visiting next. I'd pick the first one to reply or the most attractive one to me from the first few replies. On this particular fire of life's cannon, it was the Tapok Hostel. They offered me accommodation in exchange for reviews and some promotion.

Thirdly, there was the laptop failure. Again. My laptop broke. It came as no surprise. It was a horrendous Apple MacBook. It had broken about 6 times before that. But that happened across the border in Bucharest - I needed to go to a shop in Bucharest on the Saturday and buy a brand new laptop at short notice as I couldn't get any work done. It meant that I had to leave my Apple laptop in to get fixed and it would take days. I had already seen Bucharest so I decided now was the time to head to Moldova. If my laptop hadn't broken, the timings would have been different and that exact night, I would not have slept in the Tapok Hostel.

Fourthly, and finally, for whatever reason in life, that lady had decided to book a night in a dorm room in Chişinău. That lady smiled a lot and she reminded me of my onetime teenage sweetheart Vicky Everitt. Both ladies had a smiling charm, blonde hair, blue eyes and both, to me, were drop dead gorgeous. They also fitted into the same bracket as Noemi and Natalja – two eastern European girls mentioned on my journeys so far. This lady was about to walk into my life.

In short, those were just a few little decisions which meant that fate had dictated us to meet.
- If Northern Ireland had not been playing Romania on Friday 14th November 2014, I would never have crossed into Moldova and met her, or even been in eastern Europe that time.
- If I hadn't been a professional travel blogger, I wouldn't have stayed in the Tapok Hostel in Chişinău, therefore I would never have met her.

- If my laptop hadn't broken, I would never have met her as I wouldn't have been in Chişinău, Moldova that time.
- If that lady hadn't been in Chişinău, I would also never have met her.
- Plus there was the fact that every night when I stay in hostels, I'll probably only ever meet about 10% of my fellow guests. We are too busy to meet everyone. The chances of me meeting this lady were slim. Really slim. But we met.

Even when we share a hostel, or a dorm room, we may not actually meet that person. One of us could have been on the rip that night and got home late, straight to bed.

That's all water under the bridge now though. The fact that I met that lady, or that she met me it sure as hell influenced the rest of my life.

She started to follow my story and she left Moldova after that to ply her trade in another country. She had me curious about her and her *dla mnie*.

Again, I don't know why and I cannot dwell on all of this, but please remember that in November 2014 I was four years into a relationship with Panny Yu. We were engaged and I was not interested in other girls. This was a travel friend only.

The rest of this chapter was deleted and might never ever be told in writing – only down the pub when you meet me. I won't apologise for that. I've spent my life apologising for things.

Time for that 100 country celebration me thinks!

"That's entertainment" – The Jam.

Chapter 22
Whackpacking Centurion

Tunis, TUNISIA (March 27th 2015)
Barcelona, CATALONIA (April 2015)

"Sometimes I feel like I'm in Barcelona" - D.Kay & Epsilon.

So the trilogy series of "Backpacking Centurion" closed its doors and I now had the rather selfish and proud title of being a "Backpacking Centurion." I had visited 100 countries just before my 35th birthday. A few years before that, I had already thought of the title for my book series – it was to be called "Backpacking Centurion." It was a phrase I coined myself for many reasons. I love both words – backpacking and centurion. At university (in Bournemouth, England) we used to play a game called "Centurion" where you'd get a lot of alcohol together and mates and go round in a circle drinking a shot of beer each counting to 100, once you all had 100 shots of beer, you were a centurion and you'd head out to the bar lit. It was a natural title for my book series once country 100 was hit with my passport.

But I did it all too crazily – my journey wasn't normal. It wasn't without taints and honours either. Despite labelling myself a "Backpacking Centurion," I was a "Whackpacking Centurion" in reality. I monikered it "Whackpacking Centurion" as "backpacking" still felt too mainstream. The book title was already decided though, so at least the word "whackpacking" survives itself into a chapter title: whackpacking means backpacking in a crazy way and I invented the term myself. I love to invent new words. There are quite a few in this book that I invented and I have listed them all at the back in the "Wactionary" as well as on my websites. So yes, I was whackpacking. I'm a whackpacker. I whackpack. The term "whackpacking" was one I coined when I realised I was going backpacking in a crazy way – visiting remote villages like Ta Pa Tsune (China), touring remote islands like Sloth Island (Guyana) and backpacking countries that most people have never heard of (Austenasia and Podjistan for example). And now, in the city of Tunis, Tunisia I was to become that "Backpacking Centurion," and would celebrate with my wife to be, Panny Yu.

Panny and I were together for 5 years from 2010 to 2015. In March 2015, to celebrate my 100th country, we visited Tunisia together and backpacked it hardcore. Tunisia was my 100th country. Looking back now, that was our last trip together, it was our 44th country together and in our 7th continent. We split up shortly after that. I had visited 100 countries, I had books to release and I was working only for myself at that point. I was a professional travel blogger. I earned all my money through the "Don't Stop Living" platform and a few spin off sites and projects.

I finished writing my "Backpacking Centurion" book series in April 2015 on a bus from La Linea de La Concepcion to Malaga in southern Spain. Just over a year later, July 2016, from a bar in Poland's Starogard Gdański, I made the final edits which I then closed the door on in the quirky back room bar at Jozef K in Gdańsk, in late 2016.

From 2020, I finally released that series one by one. "Backpacking Centurion" had been done and dusted. That was it all over. I had now been to 100 countries. I had a hat-trick of books written (but not yet released) and life was to calm down. Perhaps I'd return to teaching in schools? Or even go back into the world of Public Relations? Or just work in a bar next to a football stadium? Well yes, I should have done. But by April 2015, I had now been working only as an online travel blogger, writer and marketer for 10 months without any other jobs. When I looked back even further, at the time, in the previous 22 months, I had only really had one job that wasn't freelance. That only job where I wasn't working for myself was from February to June in 2014 working at a kindergarten in Tsuen Wan in Hong Kong and a Primary School in Yau Tong. If I could survive and backpack the world earning money from my laptop for basically 18 months of my life, I could do it forever. But there were reality checks, moments of high stress and deep depression.

All of these things together meant that to be working only as an online blogger was soul destroying and certainly not the promised land they'd spoke of. Depression was always a black dog sitting eagerly on my shoulder.

"Now you'll understand that this is not the promised land they spoke of" - Noel Gallagher.

However, I had cash in the bank and after country 100, I was suddenly in Algeria, Catalonia, Basque Country and Gibraltar. My backpacking odyssey certainly didn't stop when I hit 100. It was only the start of the next chapter of my journeys…

Chapter 23
Basque In The Glory

Donostia / San Sebastian, BASQUE COUNTRY / EUSKADI (April 2015)

"There was a time when time didn't matter, only the time of day" – Highly Likely.

After catching up with cousin Paul in Barcelona, in Catalonia, it was high time I realised that there were two other countries or disputed regions nearby that I hadn't yet been to – one was the Basque Country, Euskadi and the other one was Gibraltar. It was time to do both and to fire Madrid in the middle. 100 countries and 800 settlements deep and I still hadn't been to Madrid…

After bidding farewell to Nuria and Paul in Barcelona, I decided it was time for me to tour a few more of the world's smaller countries, disputed territories and mini states. In the years prior to that I had visited The Vatican City, Frestonia, Artsakh / Nagorno Karabakh, Druze, Israel, Palestine, Transnistria, Kosovo and Austenasia (amongst others). Over the next 9 months, I'd visit Catalonia, Basque Country, Gibraltar, Lovely, Ladonia, Podjistan, Christiania, Kuwait and Bahrain. These were wacaday adventures to the core. I dreamt big and lived fast.

"The sink is full of fishes; she's got dirty dishes on the brain" - Noel Gallagher.

At the time I was working daily for myself as a professional travel blogger and was documenting all of these journeys while working for new clients online in travel blogging, online reviewing and marketing. It was truly an inspirational time.

I was getting a bus from Catalonia to Euskadi / The Basque Country blogging along the way. That journey itself conjured up magic over my 7 a. m. Maxwell from Barcelona's Sants Bus Station. I was backpacking from Catalonia to Euskadi while the European Union tried to convince me that the whole thing happened in Spain.

"Another paper tells it the way it isn't. How wrong they were" - Jonny Blair.

In Euskadi, I would tour two cities Donostia (San Sebastian) and Bilbao. I had shocked myself by leaving that brace and this country so long until its jigsaw entrance.

100 countries deep and travel never ceased to surprise me. I was amazed by Donostia. It is a stunning city. Make no bones about it. I could live here and the thought crossed my mind during an aimless late afternoon beer crawl in a downtown bar sampling tapas and txakoli (a sparkling dry white wine, popular in Donostia).

I was backpacking it alone. Panny was back in the Kong for now. Beaches, mountains, old town, bars, cafés all aplenty and an identity. Nationalistic charm. Basque nationalism of course.

As I toured the sights of Donostia, I sensed a little bit of freedom lost on days in the Kong. I didn't know why Panny wasn't here with me. We could have hiked together, lazed on the beaches and she would have loved it. Panny hadn't been to the Basque Country before either. I didn't know why she wasn't here with me. I couldn't fathom it. We had split ways but not split up. I didn't know why we weren't still travelling everywhere together. Maybe I was too busy blogging about my life every day. Maybe it was my fault.

Donostia old town is a charmigator. That's for sure. I missed not having clothes or a charger for my camera. I was still wearing the same clothes every day no thanks to Tunis Air, who lost my baggage. Yes, again luggage loss – this happened a lot to me on my journeys and so now I am hand luggage loyal only, on every single flight.

In Donostia, I also visited the football stadium before three Valencia girls let me share a ride with them to Bilbao. This hospitality was welcomed.

On arrival in Bilbao, I checked into my hostel before realising that the local team, Athletic Club de Bilbao were playing at home to Valencia that night.

I toured part of the old town then headed to the football stadium. I arranged to meet my Spanish girl hattrick in a bar later that evening, these were fine young ladies. All my clothes were the same, for sure they giggled or questioned my style. I never had one, and now, no thanks to Tunis Air, I was even less stylish than before.

Wearing the same clothes, and having been inspired by the Basque Country, I boarded a bus for Madrid. Believe it or not, but 100 countries heavy into my odyssey and I had been to neither Madrid nor Lisbon. Both were unbackpacked until something like settlement 834.

Basque had been magnificent. Is it a real country? 100% yes. It's the epitome of a real country to the core.

Chapter 24
Gibraltar Ego

Europa Point, GIBRALTAR (April 2015)

"Not sure I understand this role I've been given"
– Robbie Williams.

On the quest to visit 100 countries, along the way I was becoming more and more curious about the lesser recognised countries. My forte was now wacaday republics, restricted zones, micronations, unrecognised countries, autonomous states and anywhere obscure enough for me to visit.

But then again, Gibraltar wasn't quite in that bracket was it? It's a member of UEFA!

Whether it was or not, wasn't the point, the point was that I still hadn't been to Gibraltar. It was high time. I was buzzing at the thought of backpacking in Gibraltar for a load of reasons.

Firstly, I recalled a former Glentoran winger named Colin Ramirez who came from Gibraltar. When he signed for Glentoran in the 1990s there was a buzz around the Oval that this was some new superstar. In the end, Ramirez only played a few games and was ineffective. I don't think he ever scored a goal for the first team. It reminds me of a classic quote from my Dad Joe, who always says *"Northern Irish football fans love a player with an exotic name. Like if he has a name like 'Ramirez,' we will all assume he is absolutely excellent without even watching the guy play! It's so Northern Irish. We just love a good foreign name and no doubt, managers have signed players on the strength of their names in the past."* For me, Dad is totally right here and it makes me laugh everytime he tells me this!

Other reasons for visiting Gibraltar? Curious about a place with native monkeys in Europe. Wanted to see Africa and Europe at the same time. Wanted another FIFA / UEFA country on my list. Wanted to see how much an impact the UK had on Gibraltar. Wanted to have a beer in "Irish Town" to know what on earth "Irish Town" was.

Getting into Gibraltar was easy. I spent quite a while in Madrid though – I visited all three top flight stadiums (at the time) – Atletico Madrid, Real Madrid and Rayo Vallecano. I toured two of them with Anthony, from Blackburn my mate who I met in Ecuador and have also met up with in Brazil and France! Anthony let me stay at the flat he was sleeping in though I also spent nights in two different hostels, reviewing both. In one of those hostels, I met Andrew Janes in – a guy who would later be there on my last week as a resident in the Kong. Full circles were on the brain here.

After leaving Madrid, I headed to Malaga on a fast train. It was brilliant. Then from Malaga, I got a bus towards Algeciras but got out at La Linea De La Concepcion. From there, I simply walked across the land border into Gibraltar. I would be reviewing the Cannon Hotel here and I was very excited. I'd only have a few days in Gibraltar, but on one of those evenings, AFC Bournemouth were away to Reading in the second tier of English football and we whispered it quietly, but a win would have meant we would only need 7 points from our last 9 to gain promotion to the promised land – the top flight, the English Premier League. In Gibraltar, I needed to find a bar showing that match.

As well as that, I wanted to visit Europa Point, the Top of The Rock, Casemates Square and tour the sights. I was very much a tourist here and I felt I'd only ever visit it once in my life. It was now or never, all or nothing.

Gibraltar was great but there was also a realisation that I wasn't travelling with Panny at the moment. She was back in Hong Kong. I hopped on a bus in La Linea De La Concepcion and headed back to Malaga. From Malaga, I was booked on a secret flight direct to Bournemouth on Ryanair. I'd get to Bournemouth in time for the Sheffield Wednesday home match!

Also, of more significance, it was on that bus to Malaga that I finished typing my "Backpacking Centurion" book series. The books were done, officially that was where I wrote all of chapter one/one hundred and closed the door on the "writing." After that, only editing, organising and chapter shifting would be needed.

The next morning, I'd arrive in sunny sunny Bournemouth and we were dreaming of watching our football club in the top flight of the English league system, for the first time ever.

Chapter 25
Your Bacon The Pig

Dean Court, Boscombe, ENGLAND (April 2015)

"Boscombe, back of the net!" – AFC Bournemouth fans.

Nobody's legend has it that I finished writing my book "Backpacking Centurion" on a bus from La Linea de La Concepcion to Malaga. That book was done and dusted and so the timeline from here until the end of this book, is now a part of my life which has never been released in print before. None of it. I was 35 now and the "Backpacking Centurion" series was my life from 0 – 35. It's not like this feels like the real start of the next chapter of my life, but there is a realisation that now, on Chapter 25 I closed the door on 100 countries, I lived in Hong Kong and I still had no clue I would end up living in Poland.

After finishing my book writing on that bus, I then flew from Malaga to Bournemouth. It was a direct flight.

On the Saturday lunchtime, I shocked the lads by turning up in the Harvester Pub by Boscombe Pier. They were all in complete shock except for Austin and Shep. I was staying with Austin, and Shep had lent me his season ticket for that afternoon's match, at home to Sheffield Wednesday. Those two lads knew I was coming – for the others it was a shock visit.

There were so many flashbacks here. Sheffield Wednesday had been my first away win as a Cherry, when we beat them 2-0 at Hillsborough on Saint Patrick's Night in 2004. In 2005, Sheffield Wednesday had fluked their way into the play-offs and got themselves promoted, at our expense. This was because in January 2005 we were 1-0 up (Garreth O'Connor) and dominated the game, before they scored a 95th minute equaliser from a corner. In 2011, while working in Delaney's Irish Pub in Hong Kong, my manager Colin one night printed me the League One (Division Three) scores and brought them to the bar – one of these was an AFC Bournemouth 2-0 home win against Sheffield Wednesday. In 2014, while I was at a travel blogger conference at Doggett's Bar by the River Thames, I sneaked out to watch the final moments of AFC Bournemouth's 2-0 win away to Sheffield Wednesday. That result put us top of the table that night.

Now, Sheffield Wednesday were part of the story again, and we had a chance to go up to the top division of the English pyramid. We had three matches left and on paper, 7 points out of 9 would guarantee us Premier League football in 2015 – 2016 season. It didn't seem real because I had supported Bournemouth through the bad times, including the time when we were in the bottom two teams in the top four divisions and destined for relegation into the Conference (fifth division), and liquidation. Here in April 2015, to gain access to the top tier, all we needed was 7 points to guarantee it!! Zero points could also be enough if other teams lost!!

Now that I was back in Bournemouth, with my team on the brink of Premier League fame, my mind cast back to my days studying and living in Bournemouth. I spent around 6 years living here.

My life went before my eyes.

At university here in Bournemouth, myself, Lock In Lee (Lee Adams), Jody and Millwall Neil used to crack puns together. Lock In Lee was the pun king. He used to say, "that's be cider pint" instead of "that's besides the point." Around the same time, I used to say, "you're bacon the pig" instead of "you're taking the piss." In fact I changed it to "your bacon the pig." Now that we were on the verge of promotion to the football elite, "Premier League – your bacon the pig" completely summarised what my pun had meant all those years prior. There is no grammar error here. I know what "your bacon, the pig" is. It might be an in-joke, but it works.

The Sheffield Wednesday home match proved to be an anti-climax. Despite the fact that Matt Ritchie scored a screamager of a free-kick in the second half to put us 2-1 ahead going into the last minute, Sheffield Wednesday were up to their old tricks. This time, Adam Smith tripped one of their players in the box in injury time. This meant that Sheffield Wednesday nabbed a last gasp McCrum and a 2-2 draw with us.

It felt like our Premier League dream had slid away. The other teams, Norwich City, Middlesbrough and Watford now all had a chance to take the top two spots. We'd have a 9 day break before we played again – our next match was to be at home to Bolton on the Monday week.

On that trip, I had a good time back in Bournemouth. It was the longest duration of time I had spent in the seaside town since leaving in 2009. The ghost of Noemi was well and truly gone, my Polish friends were mostly all now back in Poland and my girlfriend Panny was waiting for me back in Hong Kong. I was only here for my English friends and the AFC Bournemouth football team. On this trip, I stayed at Austin's flat in Westbourne.

Luckily for us, in that nine day period, the other teams around us had failed to capitalise on our draw. This meant that going into the Bolton match on the Monday night, a win of any kind would more or less confirm our promotion. Only a huge goal difference swing could allow Middlesbrough to overtake us, but we had to win.

We only had to beat Bolton Wanderers at home. Meanwhile, in my szalony life, I flew back to Northern Ireland to spend a week with family and be with Dad on his birthday. One of my old haunts in my Bangor hometown, Calico Jack's (a bar I frequented in the late

1990s, and one that my brother Marko used to work in) had a big screen for the football and they showed the AFC Bournemouth v. Bolton Wanderers match that night. I went down to watch it with Dad and Marko.

I actually knew we were going to win that. It just felt right. My plan was to fly back to England in time for the last match of the season (Charlton Athletic away) and maybe, just maybe celebrate promotion or dare I say it – winning the league.

Marc Pugh, then Matt Ritchie, then Callum Wilson and it was AFC Bournemouth 3-0 Bolton. Yann Kermorgant could even afford to sky a McCrum and we still won 3-0. We were as good as promoted. Thanks to my mate Dan Darch, I was able to get a ticket for Charlton Athletic away on the last day of the season. If we could win that and Watford draw, then we would go up to the Premier League as Champions.

We celebrated with champagne on the train from London Victoria to Charlton pre-match. On the day, we swept Charlton aside easily, winning 3-0. This time, Sheffield Wednesday helped us out, equalising late against Watford to ensure that the Championship champions of 2014 – 2015 were AFC Bournemouth. Suddenly my football team were in the top flight. This was all a dream.

We watched our team lift the trophy at the Valley stadium in London before going for a beer at the bar in Victoria Station (Vicky C). Then, we had a bus back to Bournemouth where I'd stay with Austin a while longer before heading to Kuwait. However, from this elation there was a real health scare ahead.

Chapter 26
Queue: Wait

Kuwait City, KUWAIT (May 2015)

"It's a long, long way from here to there" – Paul Van Dyk.

It was time to fly back to Hong Kong and be with Panny again – things would get back to normal pretty soon. Up next, I decided on Kuwait as a stopover on route, and of course a new country.

My first memories of Kuwait stemmed from the Gulf War in 1991 when Saddam Hussein and his Iraqi troops invaded. I was also aware that footballer Michel Platini played for Kuwait (for one match only, in 1988) and that Kuwait had even played against Platini at the 1982 World Cup.

I booked a route from London Luton to Kuwait. I had a few days in Kuwait, then I'd fly to Hong Kong via India. Before all that, there was waiting time in England. And things in my life were not all hunky dory.

In the aftermath of AFC Bournemouth winning the league, I found myself feeling very ill. After winning the league title at the Valley in London, our group headed back to Vicky C to have a pint of beer to celebrate. Then when I drank a beer on the bus from London to Bournemouth, I developed a migraine. I was in agony. Backpacking 100 countries and seeing Bournemouth win the league had taken its toll on me.

This time, I had no idea what was wrong with me. I was staying with my mate Austin in Westbourne. When I got back to his flat that night, I was in the worst pain of my life. I was often screaming.

To this day I still have no idea what the problem was. But I made a sharp decision to give up alcohol and detox, there and then. For as long as I felt was possible. For as long as I felt my body needed a break from it. When I look back on it now, I am convinced that travelling to 100 countries had taken its toll on me. I was knackered that night and rather than head out in sunny sunny Bournemouth to celebrate winning the league, I went to sleep and I didn't waken up until early morning. I either slept or screamed the whole time.

I woke up screaming. On the Monday morning I went straight to the doctor. I had developed a boil on my forehead. I was in agony and I was given strong painkillers and advised to rest. I had no energy to do anything else. That day I couldn't even get a bus to and from the hospital. I had to book a taxi there and back. That was so unusual for me as I was always public transport loyal. The fact that I was booking taxis, rolling into one, falling asleep and wishing I was back in bed said it all. This was a wakeup call to me. Life had to slow down. This extreme pain continued for 3 or 4 days and I didn't leave Austin's flat.

On the Monday when I was at Austin's flat, everyone was asking me if I was heading down to Bournemouth pier and beach to see the team bus and their victory parade. But I had to miss it. I was too ill.

I still had the small matter of heading to London, then to Luton and flying onwards to Kuwait.

I had recovered by the next weekend and suddenly that boil was gone as was the memory of a week lost. I headed up to London and spent a few days with Millwall Neil. We toured hippy Camden Town and for the first time in ages, neither of us were on the rip. We were both teetotal and not drinking alcohol now.

Backpacking in Kuwait passed me by in the blink of an eye. I had just three days and nights there, although I did sleep in two different hotels and review them. Firstly I stayed at the Ibis Salmiya, near the promenade. My room was air conditioned and I spent a lot of time sleeping instead of sightseeing for once. My second hotel was the Ibis Shard in Kuwait City and this was more central. It was a good time to visit Kuwait as I wasn't drinking alcohol and was recovering from my illness, so I didn't need anything crazy.

Kuwait is alcohol free and is a small country with extreme heat. I went for iced coffees in malls, did some typing and chilled out. I was looking forward to returning to Hong Kong now and planning the next chapter of my life.

Those main plans I had in life were to complete the editing of my long awaited book series "Backpacking Centurion" and enjoy living with Panny in Hong Kong.

We made plans for our wedding in Taiwan, Japan or Thailand. Panny wanted Japan and me Taiwan. But we didn't confirm anything. I had previously bought Panny a ring and asked her to marry me on two different occasions – both on her birthday – her 2011 and her 2013 birthdays!

For the time being at least, we'd be back to being in love again, like the early days.

Chapter 27
Magic Whip

Wan Chai, HONG KONG (July 2015)

"Every paper that you read says tomorrow's your lucky day. Well here's your lucky day. It really really really could happen" – Blur.

After Kuwait and a brief stopover in Mumbai, India, I landed back in Hong Kong in late May 2015. All my belongings were here in Panny's flat in Lam Tin. We had a nice double room, in a high rise skyscraper in the east side of Kowloon. It was a great place to live.

I found it easy to settle into life in Hong Kong back in 2011 and now, four years on, I was back here again having now completed that 100 country journey and my entire book about it. However, my next steps were to release that book, to work online and to just enjoy Hong Kong life and cement my relationship with Panny.

Through May, June, July and August 2015 while based in Hong Kong, Panny and I rarely argued. We spent time together at home and in some bars and restaurants in the city. We didn't travel outside of Hong Kong at all. That was so odd and unusual for us, it was four months in Hong Kong.

Looking back now, it's tough to fathom and comprehend for me. My time in Hong Kong was coming to an end. My relationship with my wife to be was coming to an end. We never said it but looking back now, it is clear that this is what was happening. Panny still had her ring of course.

It was here in Hong Pak Yuen (Hong Pak Court), Lam Tin that I first arrived into the Kong in May 2011.

To be honest, and in the sadness of it all, I don't even remember exactly where I was on the 8th of November 2015, the day that Panny and I had been together for 5 years. All I know is that it was over. I was single again.

"It's over. You don't need to tell me" - Damon Albarn.

In those final few months in Hong Kong that I lived with Panny, we didn't do much. Neither of us left Hong Kong. I sat on my computer and worked most of the time. Panny worked. I started to learn Cantonese finally. I now had the time to do that. I studied at the Chinese University of Hong Kong. I was the only male in my class. I was the only non-Asian in my class. It was fun to be learning Cantonese but I was now only a blogger. I wasn't teaching English at all. In my previous life in Hong Kong I was always either a teacher or a barman there. Now, I was only writing, studying and blogging.

"What you had; and what you lost" - Fleetwood Mac.

Curiously, I finally joined Instagram on this stint in Hong Kong – that was actually encouraged by Panny. Panny is responsible for the fact that I am even on Instagram! I am still on there as "jonnydontstopliving." Now that I was working only for myself online, I didn't have an employer. It was weird. I wasn't teaching, I wasn't working in bars. I was waking up at whatever time I wanted. I worked on a hotel project for Hipmunk and put all the chapters together for my book series "Backpacking Centurion." I also released an e-Book on the Inca Trail and contributed to another e-Book on South American borders. It wasn't a lazy time, but it was an odd time of my life. It was still a productive period of life, even though travel was stagnant. Also for 8 weeks of that, I wasn't drinking alcohol and I also don't think I was eating much.

"I hope your tears don't stain the world that waits outside"
– Noel Gallagher.

My first beer in 8 weeks was consumed at Delaney's Irish Pub in
Wan Chai just before the Blur gig. English rock band Blur were
playing a gig in Wan Chai, Hong Kong and I went alone. I bought
a ticket and was really looking forward to this concert. It was my
third Blur concert and in my third different country in my third
different decade. In 1999, I saw Blur in Belfast's Waterfront Hall,
Northern Ireland. In 2003, I saw Blur at the Bournemouth
International Centre in England. Now they had a new album out
called "Magic Whip" and Hong Kong held significance. Blur had
split up years before you see. However, while the band passed
through Hong Kong the previous year, they headed to a studio here
and recorded a song. They were so enthusiastic about it that they
ended up just staying in Hong Kong to record a full album,
complete it and release it!

"It's the last run boat out here tonight, out in the bay" – Blur.

This gig was mind blowing and I also bought their new album at
the gig, "Magic Whip" whilst I was sat next to Taiwanese
gighopper, Tempo Cheng, a highly interesting bloke. It is one of
the best gigs I have ever been to.

Blur's "Magic Whip" is a superb album. The album is drenched in
Kongic twangs and metaphors.

That gig in the Kong when I had my first beer in 2 months was also
the start of the end of my time in Hong Kong, and indeed my time
with Panny. Though neither of us saw it coming. We just didn't
know our relationship was ending, just yet.

Chapter 28
Last Plane Out of Hong Kong

Hair of the Dog Pub, Tsim Sha Tsui, HONG KONG (August 2015)

"I'm leaving on a jet plane" – John Denver.

Time came to leave Hong Kong for a short trip back to Europe. At least that was what was supposed to happen. Life is just really spontaneous and unpredictable.

My last ever two weeks living in the Kong were action jam packed. Looking back, I was living there, it felt like my home now and it had been for over 4 years now, despite the travels in between.

My friend Chris Ragg got married in Northern Ireland in the summer of 2015 and part of their honeymoon was a few days in Hong Kong. So I met Chris and his wife Alison and showed them round some markets and restaurants. At dinner that night, unknown at the time, either Chris or Alison would take the last ever photo of Panny Yu and I together.

"Nothing lasts forever and we both know hearts can change" – Guns 'n' Roses.

My cousin, also called Chris, also happened to be in Hong Kong on those last two weeks. We had a mighty night on the rip in the notorious Lan Kwai Fong. Again, it would be my last time there as a Hong Kong resident. We even had beers called "Evil Cousin" by pure fluke. It meant that my last four meetings with Chris were in four different countries. Northern Ireland, England, Singapore and Hong Kong. Yet oddly in the timeframe, both of us had spent time living in Australia but never met up there.

And so, it was to be that that day I left Hong Kong was to be my last ever day living in Hong Kong.

"The Queen of England – there's no greater anarchist.
But one man's freedom fighter is another man's terrorist"
- Primal Scream.

My last few months in the Kong flew pretty fast. At the time I had no idea that this was my time living in Hong Kong coming to an end. I stayed in Panny's flat at Lam Tin. This was a new flat that she had moved into in 2014 just before we went to Brazil for the World Cup.

In my previous 4 years in the Kong this was the fifth flat I'd live in. Two of those were on the island of Ma Wan (Park Island), one was in Lai Chi Kok and there were two in Lam Tin. In that time, the nationalities I shared with were Hong Kongers, Chinese, Phillipino and Northern Irish.

When I landed in Hong Kong this time, May 2015, I had been teetotal for a few weeks. The plan was to detox, retox, rest and get my book written and released. Panny was working full time in merchandising. I had quit teaching for now and was working only online at this time.

Yet these final few months were fantastic. It was like the best of my time in Asia smuggled calmly into a hattrick of fast months where I stayed only in one country - Hong Kong. In the pub I used to work in, Delaney's Irish Pub in Tsim Sha Tsui I watched AFC Bournemouth's first ever top flight game live. We lost 1-0 to a second half goal to Aston Villa. That was ironically to be Villa's only away win of the season, and in their first match. Months later the tables would turn as a Steve Cook backheel and a nifty Josh King finish in a 2-1 away win at Villa Park would trapdoor Aston, whilst keeping us Cherries in the Prem.

I also headed to a few bars with my mate Neil Armstrong, who hails from Larne but spent years living in Asia. Neil and I watched Liverpool v. AFC Bournemouth together in the Hair Of The Dog Pub and soon, it was time to leave Hong Kong.

When the curtain fell on this part of my life in Hong Kong, I didn't realise that the curtain had fallen on my entire life living in Hong Kong. Later, I would know the consequences of all that.

Meantimmic, I would backpack my weary way through Bangladesh, Singapore (on repeat), United Arab Emirates (on repeat) and Bahrain.

I was simply leaving Hong Kong for a month or so. At the time, I expected to be back soon in Hong Kong.

This of course, never happened. I never moved back.

"The ringmaster's telecaster sings from an empty stage" - Eels.

Chapter 29
Chitty Chitty Gong Gong

Chittagong, BANGLADESH (August 2015)

"I woke up sleeping on a train that was bound for nowhere"
– Noel Gallagher.

After the Bangladesh visa struggle, I wound up back in Singapore for a night. Again, this felt sentimental, special and fateful. For many reasons. For starters, it had been Singapore that I backpacked through with Natalja back in 2009. Here, in 2015 I made the decision to walk the same route that Natalja and I took that hot morning. This time was more calm, more lonely. I had aged. I got my photo taken at the same spot by the Merlion. I copied the entire route, a mere 6 years on. But I had aged more than 6 years. I realised how young I must have been in 2009, even though I was 29 back then. I drank a craft beer at the same bar in Clarke Quay. I hostelled it loyal as before. This time, I reviewed the Green House Hostel, as opposed to the Singapore Backpackers Hostel at Kallang MRT where we stayed before. The magic of Singapore hadn't passed me by.

Believe it or not, I like Singapore. I've actually passed through it loads of times. I think it's 9 times, with 5 of them actually leaving the airport and seeing the city. I also stayed with cousin Chris here in 2011 just before I relocated to the Kong. That was another weird coincidence, given that Chris and I had just been on a night out in Lan Kwai Fong, Hong Kong earlier that month.

But Singapore's time was up on this particular timeshell and off I went back to the airport. The best airport in the world outside Northern Ireland, is Singapore's Changi Airport. It'll never bate George Best or Aldergrove Airport but it's a fantastic airport. Also, when you fly with Singapore Airlines, they used to give you a complimentary Singapore Sling cocktail! I loved that and I have no idea if they still do it (I edit this book in 2021). Almost as cool as going downtown to the Long Bar in the Raffles Hotel to order up a sling in the place where it all began. As I reminisced way too much on the glory days of 2009, the time came to fly out of the Pore again.

I grabbed an iced coffee and a plate of nachos at Changi Airport to use up a coupon I had found from my budget backpacking days, and I boarded a packed flight to Dhaka. That's the capital of Bangladesh so it is.

"Silver spoon? I'm from T-Bay. That's the ghetto mate"
- Carl Frampton.

Bangladesh is no silent sleeper and in my life, this was the busiest and noisiest flight I have ever been on!! In terms of fellow passengers, this hit high decibel levels. If you have ever flown in or out of Bangladesh, you will probably echo my sentiment – these flights are very noisy! I was sandwiched in between a huge family. There were groups of Bangladeshi machos males everywhere. Everyone was talking incessantly for the whole flight. But at least I had my Bangladesh visa (that was very difficult to get in Hong Kong that time), so immigration at the airport went smoothly and I was in. Another country had been swallowed on route to the seemingly easy "200 country mark".

I grabbed some local Bangladeshi Taka and my pre-arranged driver arrived to take me to Uttara. I would be staying here in the Nagar Valley Hotel in Uttara, just north of the capital city, Dhaka. The first few days were spent exploring Dhaka and Uttara. Bangladesh was a new country for me. The strict visa process was probably why I left it late. I had already backpacked through Myanmar,

Laos, Cambodia, Malaysia, Thailand, Vietnam and Singapore before. This trip kind of filled in the gap for that part of the world.

The first thing I did when I got back to the Nagar Valley Hotel was to ask for the Wi-Fi password. The reason? AFC Bournemouth were playing West Ham United away that day and I wanted to watch it or at least keep up with the scores. It was the third top flight (Premier League) match in our history and in that division, we had yet to –
1. Score a goal (Steve Cook's v. Liverpool was disallowed).
2. Gain a point.
3. Win a match.

This, was to be the day when it all changed. As soon as I was given the Wi-Fi, I logged in and our Cherry Chat group on What's App had already confirmed we were winning 2-0!! It was still the first half and we were on course to do all three of the things we hadn't yet done in that division. Callum Wilson struck a hat-trick and we took the three points in the end with a scintillating 4-3 away win at West Ham's Upton Park, The Boleyn Ground. Writing about this now, looking back is tinged with happiness and sadness.

My childhood friend Michael Whitford, Whitty, was a West Ham fan and we messaged each other around the time of those games. I miss Whitty. He died in 2016, after a long fight with cancer. Rest in peace my hero.

Alas, the Cherries had now won a Premier League match and I knew that in September or October I would be personally at a top flight match at Dean Court. For the meantime though, of course I had to backpack through Bangladesh…it's a test of stamina for any gregarious backpacker.

One thing that will never be forgotten is that Bangladeshis are extremely friendly people. They love to talk. I was a rare tourist here and I stuck out like a sore thumb. Remember one thing too - Dhaka is insane. It is as simple as that. The city is a people houser. Streets are crammed and rammed. The tuk-tuks / three wheelers are nuts. Same as the rickshaws. The traffic in Dhaka is complete and utter mayhem. I booked a night train out of Dhaka, bound for the southern city of Chittagong. This journey usually takes around 7 hours and is known as the Turna Express.

"Even innocence has caught the midnight train"
– Jon Bon Jovi.

This was a sad and crazy night on my journeys and one I will never ever ever forget. I could and should have died here. Around the time, I covered it on my blogs. So I arrived at Uttara train station in the north of Dhaka. I had my bought ticket already the day before. I chose second class. There were three classes.

3 Third Class – 300 Taka (cheap, but basic and probably a tad dingy)

2. Second Class – 610 Taka (mid-range, cosy recliner seat, air conditioning)

1.First Class – 1,100 Taka (you get a bed – well beyond my budget though).

I was the only foreigner anywhere in sight. However, rather than being scary, dangerous or daunting, this was incredibly emotional. I cannot even begin to write about this emotional moment in the train station in Bangladesh. Just imagine the scene.

I walk onto the correct platform for my train, the Turna Express was due to leave at 23:30 from Dhaka's Biman Bandar station. I have water, some snacks and two backpacks. I set one backpack down to use as a seat, I often did that. I start to write travel notes into my book. I sip the water. I stare up.

I am surrounded by people. Local Bangladeshis have encircled me fully. They are all around me, 80% of them male. They are staring at me. It is not intimidating. It is emotional.

A shiver wriggles its way through my Northern Irish spine. I'm tingled. More and more people crowd round me. I have an audience. I realise the reason why. They are curious. They cannot believe it. This is not central Dhaka. This is not a popular train station to get a night train from clearly. This is clearly an obscure option that I have chosen.

As more and more people crowd round, the audience has got up to around 50 – 100 people by now. I couldn't have counted it. They're all staring at me. Some smile. I smile back. Nobody speaks.

After a few minutes, one of the Bangladeshis plucks up the courage amidst a trained silence.

"Sir, where are you from?," comes the correct English question. It is clearly spoken from the person in that crowd who speaks the most English and has confidence to ask. The crowd halts in anticipation. They are sure that I will answer. They don't know that I speak or understand English, but probably most foreigners that come here do.

"Northern Ireland," I proudly loftily announce.
"Welcome to Bangladesh" comes the response from the same kind gentleman.

The entire situation is rather moving. Everybody is nervy in anticipation. A few of the Bangladeshis then come over to shake my hand and welcome me. Dhaka houses 13 million people, perhaps I'd be the only backpacker getting this night train, and yes I am sure was – I saw no other foreigners. But it was now almost midnight, the crowd had dispersed slightly and one of the guys,

Masoud introduced himself and we went to sit in the waiting room. He told me trains are often late and just to wait and he asked to join me when the train eventually rolls in.

I take my seat on the train. I'm used to nighttrains the world over. You leave one city when it's dark. You sleep. You wake up in the next city at dawn. It was all too commonplace – nighttrains and nightbuses on my wacaday journey.

What's ahead is alarming. In the middle of the night, the train stops. We don't move anywhere.

It's a slow train to Chittagong for sure and this makes me chuckle at the time due to the fact that the city name starts with "Chi" – there's a "Slow boat to China" as a song, and a "Slow bus to Chingford" as an episode of one of my favourite English sitcoms, "Only Fools and Horses." Here, the slow train is for a sad reason. At 6:30 a.m. it is clear that we are nowhere near Chittagong – we should have been arriving around this time. Something is very wrong. At 7:28 a.m. Masoud alerts me of a four hour delay, meaning we now won't get into Chittagong until the earliest 11:28 a.m. He says there has been some kind of accident but nobody is sure of what.

We are stranded in a place known as Chinki Astana. Then the horrors become clear. We are lucky to survive. The nighttrain that night from Chittagong to Dhaka, it crashed. In other words the same route but coming the other way, it crashed. It went off the tracks. It went off the rails, crashing and people died with others injured. This is scary. I'm told about this fact onboard but it was hard to take in at the time.

As we rolled out of Chinki Astana station, I prayed we would somehow arrive safely in Chittagong. 11:28 a.m. passes and we are still around 100 kilometres from Chittagong. At 2:44 p.m., just after we leave a station called Sitakunda, we saw the horrors for real – the other train on the opposite tracks, off the tracks, crashed. It's horrific. The train derailed.

We now move very slowly and I understand why. At 3:29 p.m., which is 16 hours after leaving my hotel in Uttara, we finally arrive in Chittagong main train station. It has been one of my scariest and worst journeys in life. I am lucky to be alive. From Chittagong train station, I knew I would sleep nearby somewhere and all I wanted was a chilled out bed, some water and a hot shower.

On arrival in Chittagong, I walked straight to the Golden Inn Hotel. I checked in, I toured a bit of the city, had a dinner, took an early night. The next morning when I awaken for breakfast, this hotel gives every guest a newspaper as well as your breakfast. The horror was magnified in its entirety now - the front page of the newspaper has a photo of the train accident and a report on it. I am truly blessed and lucky to survive. God saved me that night.

"If God spares us" – Mary Blair.

Chittagong ended up being a nice city and I backpacked all the sights, made some friends here and celebrated the fact that my travel blog, Don't Stop Living (https://dontstopliving.net/) was now 8 years old. That fact might have astounded me, but I also couldn't wait to leave just to try and ease my mind of the train accident, that luckily I wasn't in. It wasn't my time to die. I am 100% sure that God decided that.

I remember that on the morning that I flew from Chittagong International Airport to Sharjah in the United Arab Emirates I had a gut feeling my time living in Asia had come to an end. To get from my hotel, the Golden Inn Hotel to Chittagong Airport that morning I was in a beat-up tuk-tuk on the verge of falling apart. It was classic. I loved that exit.

Sharjah in the United Arab Emirates was only a short stopover but I got to see another city and add in my second of the seven Emirates. My next dream fell on Bahrain. Again, I was clocking up new countries on handy stopovers, a handy little trick for anyone into visiting multiple countries. It gets too boring always going via Doha, Istanbul and Dubai.

Chapter 30
Manama Na De De Du De Du

Ibis Manama, BAHRAIN (August 2015)

"What light through yonder window breaks? It is the east, and Juliet is the sun" – William Shakespeare.

Everything in life had become too easy for me. Backpacking was no longer a challenge. Backpacking the world lost its charm. It really did and at this point, in Bahrain I didn't even know what number of country it was anymore, or even why I was doing this. But I knew I still wanted, craved and needed to see every country, and write about every country. I needed to see Bahrain and this was actually a cool little country to visit on a three day trip. I actually copied what I had done in Kuwait – use it as a 3 day stopover between Asia and Europe. I even stayed in the Ibis here in Manama too, as I had done braceically in Kuwait.

In Manama I hired a car as it seemed the easiest way to get around. The heat was astonishing for me. Inside every mall and building was air conditioning; outside was a full time sauna, even at sunsink!

I visited the interesting "tree of life," the oil fields in the deserts and the Formula One Grand Prix circuit. I generally believe as a tourist that you don't need more than 3 days to see all the sights in Bahrain. I also visited the Mosques, markets and main sights in Manama, the capital city.

Perhaps my highlight in Manama was making the trip towards Saudi Arabia. On my journeys, the visa for Saudi Arabia had always proved the most difficult as a tourist. In short – Saudi Arabia didn't really do tourist visas before. You had to get invited or to go there on a business visa. On this trip, of course I didn't have a visa for Saudi Arabia but I wanted to head on the bridge that leads from Bahrain to Saudi Arabia just for the adventure, to see how close I could get to Saudi Arabia before being told to head back.

Having hired a car, I headed onto the King Fahd Causeway. This is a road that has been manmade, on bridges over the water. It leads from Bahrain to Saudi Arabia. It's one of the world's coolest borders as far as I am concerned. It also looks great and I was honoured to be driving on it. I was able to get to the border point where you leave Bahrain. The Bahrain and Saudi Arabia flags fly side by side, but to get through the actual border, you'll need a visa for Saudi Arabia. I parked and pondered. I was given a departure ticket at the border point which I kept as a souvenir. In the petrol station by the border, I was also able to get Saudi Arabian Riyals. Down the years, I have flimsys (poly pockets / A4 pockets) with all my travel notes, stories and souvenirs in them. I keep them for every trip and I love looking back at them. I also use them to do my travel writing and indeed, needed them for writing this book! On this occasion, I wouldn't be able to visit Saudi Arabia – a dream for another day.

Bahrain is not mind-blowing but was definitely worth seeing. There are even a few licensed bars here that I had some beers in, watching the AFC Bournemouth v. Leicester City match in one of them.

I flew out of Manama which had a curiously huge Irish Pub at the airport and it was yet another Istanbul layover before I'd be back in Denmark. The reason for being back in Denmark was not to be back in Denmark. It was because the easiest and most regular way to get to the Faroe Islands is from Copenhagen, given that officially the Faroe Islands is part of the Kingdom of Denmark.

Politics aside, I'd be on route to another GAWA outing in the Faroe Islands, Northern Ireland were to play them away in Torshavn in a Euro 2016 qualifier, which handily was also a new country in this growing jigsaw.

"Kiss the girl; she's not behind the door" - Noel Gallagher.

Chapter 31
Freetown Christiania

FREETOWN CHRISTIANIA and Copenhagen, DENMARK (September 2015)

"Life in a rucksack" – Abbi Morrison.

This was actually my second visit to the quirky Freetown of Christiania in the same year and I've not been back since. That's the way the wacky tourist rolls sometimes.

I've only met Abbi Johnson (nee Morrison) 4 times in life, yet we visited 4 countries together in essence – England, Frestonia, Denmark, Christiania. Abbi was also there in my life at two highly significant moments. She was unknowingly there on the exact nights before two flights I took that totally influenced my move to Poland. When I later reflected on such curiosities, I couldn't help but fall into some kind of depression as to why and how my life was full of fool circles, or fool or full circles.

There was an odd sense of freedom here in Christiania. I picked up some souvenirs, such as a flag, a postcard, the local currency (the LÖN), some stamps and a beer. It is a completely separate country here.

Freetown Christiania is not in the EU. Christiania has different laws from Denmark. There are no adverts here, no global excremental companies that litter the street buildings of bordering Denmark. No building can be higher than 3 storeys. No motorised transport is permitted in Christiania. Soft drugs such as marijuana are legal. It's a free spirited country here. It's a utopia, it's a free paradise. While I wouldn't choose to live in Freetown Christiania, it was these quirky places that I now loved the most.

I'm including Christiania here in this part of my story not just because it fits into the chronological timeframe, but because my Hong Kong farewell (which I didn't know at the time) was sandwiched in between these two visits to Freetown Christiania. I was here in February 2015, and I backpacked it again in September 2015. The first time, I was alone. The second time, I was with Abbi Morrison. In the middle of that, I had that final flirt with Hong Kong life and here, in September 2015 whilst in Freetown Christiania, the unknown was that my own freedom would become singledom pretty soon.

In September 2015, as well as delving back into Freetown Christiania, I also visited Denmark, Sweden, Ladonia and the Faroe Islands.

I love the word "delve," let's see if we can forward-chapter delve into Ladonia. Where on earth is Ladonia?

Chapter 32
Ladonia

Nimis, LADONIA (September 2015)

"You're driftwood, floating under water" – Travis.

Having not seen Daniel Evans in 5 years until February 2015, I was suddenly going to meet him twice within 7 months as we clocked up our fourth country together. Weirdly, none of those four countries have been our homelands of England and Northern Ireland.

Daniel Evans and I met in Sydney in Australia in the land down under. We met on a crazy first night there while I was backpacking with Natalja. I covered that story before in *Chapter 13's "Living In A Land Down Under"*. Daniel and I had been flatmates and backpacking buddies in 2009 to 2010. We visited 4 of Australia's 8 provinces together and had some unforgettable memories.

Time had moved on. I finally met up with Daniel again in February 2015, weirdly on the EXACT 5 year anniversary of last seeing him. That meeting happened in the city of Angelholm in Sweden. Why? Because after the Australian adventure, Daniel Evans moved to Sweden! Thanks to fate, Daniel met Swedish chick Sofia in the land down under. If he had stayed with me in Tasmania, the pair would never have met. They are now married with two kids. Fate played such a huge part in their lives, and mine, and yours.

So, I was now back in Copenhagen on route to the Faroe Islands, so I messaged Daniel again to see if he was up for yet another crazy spontaneous meeting. He was. Now that I was a micronations geek, I spied the chance for Daniel and I to visit a wacky less ventured country together. Ladonia. Sorry, where? Ladonia! It's an unrecognised country that borders Sweden. Country? Define country then.

Ladonia is a micronation on the coast of Sweden. It is an area of forest and rocks. It has been self-declared as a micronation since 1996. The country has its own flag, stamps and leader - Queen Carolyn I. Daniel had actually been before but kindly said he could drive us. He didn't mind visiting it twice even though he is not such a micronation geek like me.

The capital city of Ladonia is Nimis – this is basically a huge wooden maze type dwelling structure on the rocks!

It was crazy to be backpacking Ladonia with Daniel Evans, my English flatmate from living in the land down under. The main way to describe Ladonia is that it is a separate country that borders Sweden and is basically a forest and coastal park area with rocks and wooden structures. We toured Nimis before heading back to Sweden, then back to Denmark. I even had a beer and lunch in Nimis, on those wooden structures by the bay, Nimis for all its glory is the Ladonian capital. But there was no passport stamp here, nor a rendezvous with Queen Carolyn I.

After Nimis, we headed back to Angelholm for dinner and beers at Daniel's local pub. Daniel and Sofia both invited me to their wedding, scheduled for 2016. As a regret, I sank into deep depression in 2016 and had to cancel my presence at the wedding. On the table that day, was my name and a note to say that I was Daniel's friend from backpacking in Australia and that I had visited 100 countries. I felt glad to tour Ladonia with Daniel; but ultimately I feel very sad that I missed his wedding. That can never be rewound. Here, still in September 2015, the journey to another remote country continued.

After meeting up with fellow travel blogger Klaus Andersen, I ended up back at Copenhagen Airport for the fourth time. Today, I'd be boarding a direct flight to the Faroe Islands.

Chapter 33
Fare Auld World

Sorvagur, FAROE ISLANDS (September 2015)

**"It's the Ulster boys making all the noise everywhere we go"
- GAWA.**

I arrived into the main airport in the Faroe Islands. This is near the village of Sorvagur on Vagar island and not near the capital city, Torshavn, located on Streymoy. Pre-arrival in the Faroe Islands on a flight from Copenhagen already involved some classic tourism. Firstly, a beer in a Copenhagen hostel with Bangor Boy Michael Lewis as the brace of us prepared for the GAWA madness ensuic. Secondly, epic Faroese beer on the flight was served up with delightful salmon. Oh the joys. Also, at the airport before leaving Denmark, I bumped into Justin Wallace from Ballyclare, John and long term GAWA nut Paul Duffin for a swift Carlsberg. The only time I drink the stuff is in Denmark. My nationalism mixed with localism does that to me. "When in Rome" for me wouldn't even include The Sovereign Military Order of Malta, nor The Vatican City. There's a hat-trick of real countries in that area. Carlsberg – definitely a lager I'd only ever drink in Denmark.

In the Faroe Islands, if truth be told, I was only here for one main reason - to watch Northern Ireland in a Euro 2016 qualifier. This was the main reason I had left Hong Kong that time. It was totally the catalyst and it was easy to see why.

I was killing a few birds on one stone here. I was visiting a new country of course. The Faroe Islands. I could also watch Northern Ireland play live. After that, I could visit my family. It was so handy and the perfect time for me to visit these beautiful islands. What was neglected and a welcome addition is just how stunningly beautiful the Faroe Islands are. This is a country that craves to be backpacked.

After landing in the Faroes, I decided I would walk from the international airport to my guest house for the night. Walking to airports only really happened in a few countries. I walked to the airport in Nauru, Western Sahara and The Seychelles. I can't remember any other places where I walked to the airport. I was staying in the tranquil Guesthouse Hugo in the village of Sorvagur. I arranged my stay here due to the fact that it was one of the closest places to stay near the airport. But also because it was in the west part of the Faroes. This area is beautiful. I flew in a couple of days before match day and could backpack the sights and do some hikes here.

As I walked away from the airport, I noticed another lady walking the same way as me. This was a fellow backpacker Katie, from USA. Katie was also staying in the Guesthouse Hugo.

We walked down the hill and found the village of Sorvagur at the foot. One thing was certain already: The Faroe Islands are beautiful.

We checked in to our super little cosy hotel and decided to meet up and tour the local village and area together. This was a fresh country. The air was clean. People were friendly. Football was the national sport.

In Sorvagur, I even created my own makeshift bar. The local petrol station sold Faroese beer and had a corner where you could sit down. This was my bar! With Katie, we decided to plan two hikes and do some touring together in a car. We aimed to island hop and visit a good chunk of the Faroe's islands. Katie was also here for 6 days like me. This was like I was still in backpacking mode. I wasn't even hanging around with the Northern Ireland fans. In fact, I didn't even see any for the first two days.

We took an early kip after touring Sorvagur and we decided on the hike to Sørvágsvatn the next morning. Up early, breakfast and off we walked to the next village up a hill.

There was a huge lake. There were no other people about. This was pure travel bliss. It was gorgeous here. At the top, there was a marvellous viewpoint over the Atlantic Ocean. The next morning in the wicked wet rain, we did the hike to Gásadalur. It was all too beautiful and Katie was a great backpacking buddy.

After three days and three nights in Sorvagur, it was time to head to the capital city, Torshavn. This was for the big match. It was crazy to think that Northern Ireland were in with a huge chance of qualifying for our first major football tournament since 1986. It would also be our first European Championships. However, we still had 4 games left. Win them all and we would qualify. Lose them all and we wouldn't. In theory though, a mix of wins and draws would be enough. But a win here would be essential.

I was reunited with the GAWA on a corner pub in Torshavn, the capital city. In here I was reunited with Nolers (Nial Coulter), Andrew Milliken, Aaron McCallister and Richard Henry and many others I knew from down the years. Katie came with me and I tried to source her a match ticket, which I managed thanks to Jim Rainey. Jim is a popular figure amongst Northern Ireland fans from his World Cup stories to his days of bringing a megaphone to Windsor Park to his work with the Amalgamation of Northern Ireland football supporters clubs.

After that bar, we headed down to the Glitnir bar, which also has an Irish Pub above or attached to it. On route I was interviewed by

Ruth Gorman of UTV. We popped into another pub on the walk to the stadium and the match began.

Tonight, this was our night. We were inspired. Gareth McAuley scored twice, Kyle Lafferty added a third to make it 3-1 and on as a sub, Josh Magennis smacked the post and almost gave us a 4-1 cushion. Still, we held on for a 3-1 win. We were top of the group. Only a complete collapse in our final 3 matches could prevent us from qualifying for Euro 2016 now. But actually, nothing was going to stop us now.

My final three days in the Faroe Islands were pretty eventful though! Katie and I hired a car and drove all over the islands. We also got the famous "milk boat," visited the historic Old Town of Kirkjubour and watched the sun sink in the simply gorgeous village of Gjogv.

The Faroe Islands were beautiful, my life in Hong Kong had been left behind and I prepared for another epic milestone on my journey. Watching AFC Bournemouth home and away in the top flight. The Premier League.

"Bones sinking like stones, all that we fall for" – Coldplay.

Chapter 34
Back To The Portman

The Portman Hotel, Boscombe, ENGLAND (September 2015)

"The final whistle against Bolton" – Eddie Howe.

If you read *Chapter 25's "Your Bacon The Pig"*, you will be aware that my English football club, AFC Bournemouth lived the dream in May 2015 by finally reaching the top flight of English Football (Division One / The Premier League). I was there for 2 of the last 3 matches (v. Charlton and Sheffield Wednesday) in the second tier (Division Two / The Championship).

But now we had finally made it to the Premier League, I wanted to go back again to Dean Court, and complete my mission as Ulster Cherry in the top 4 divisions of English football. Ulster Cherry is actually a self-made moniker for me, given that I come from one of the 9 Ulster counties (Down, which is also one of the six Northern Irish counties) and I support The Cherries. This is the nickname of AFC Bournemouth, who play in red and black in a town I made my home from 2003 – 2009.

As an AFC Bournemouth fan, I remember where I was for all those early matches in the top tier, I was still travelling and country hopping. I watched the Aston Villa defeat in Delaney's Irish Pub in Hong Kong. I watched the Liverpool defeat in the Hair of the Dog, also in Hong Kong. I followed our West Ham away win from my hotel in Uttara in Bangladesh. I watched our 1-1 draw with Leicester City in JJ's Irish Pub in Manama, Bahrain. Our next match was at home, against Sunderland and I would be there.

The Sunderland game came round pretty fast. I had now managed to juggle my life to the level I had always wanted. Here in September 2015, I had worked only for myself for well over a year.

I was a copywriter for hotel companies, a travel writer and a travel blogger. I didn't need or have any jobs outside of that. I was self-employed and working online. Life was pretty good.

Back to the Portman…

After the euphoria of reaching the top level of English football, I had to pinch myself a few times to check it was all real.

Not only were AFC Bournemouth now in the Premier League (Division One/top flight) but I had been on a journey here with friends. It felt fitting that I could complete that journey at 3 p.m. on a Saturday afternoon at Dean Court in Boscombe, with the same friends.

"Everything's changing but I still feel the same" – Keane.

For the football purists, it was "same old." In other words, nothing had changed for me, for my friends, for my club. It was just friends heading to the pub for lunch and pre-match pints, then to the match, then back to the pub. This pub had endured it all. All four divisions. The ups and downs. The Portman Hotel. The downstairs bar here.

Now, once the dust settled, I found myself back in the sunshine of Bournemouth. I made my Cherries Premier League debut at the Sunderland home match on Saturday 19th September 2015. It felt like I had timed everything perfectly in life, for once.

My books were written, my base was still in Hong Kong (officially) and I was back in Europe watching football and with friends.

On matchday morning of the Sunderland match, it was business as usual. My AFC Bournemouth friends and I acted as we had always done. We woke up early, donned our shirts and scarves and headed for a fried breakfast.

The venue for our fried breakfasts changed down the years. Today, we were in Piggies in Westbourne. Piggies is run by Robert Taylor, a Nottingham Forest fan. Robert wished us well as we munched our fries and headed to The Portman. It was back to The Portman. We got the Yellow Bus to Boscombe. When did we ever not? This time, we got it from Westbourne to Boscombe. I think it was the 1a, or the 1b, or the 1c. At any rate, this was a high in life. I assure you of that. Those smiles were genuine.

This pub, The Portman, had served us well down the years of following AFC Bournemouth. Today would complete the milestone for me. I'd now have been in the Portman before and after a Cherries home match in every domestic competition in England. Division 4, Division 3, Division 2, Division 1, FA Cup, League Cup, Paint Dry Trophy, Friendly, Testimonial.

The town had lived up to its sunny sunny Bournemouth moniker today. We were in the beer garden in The Portman. Pints flowed and we spoke to a few Sunderland fans. They were well natured, one of them felt they would lose that day, saying the club was cursed and they would be relegated that season. In the end, it was to be their north east rivals Newcastle United who would be relegated that year.

We were in the stadium before kick-off. Dean Court, Boscombe. This was a traditional 3 p.m. kick off, the time we all loved. A treat was in store.

After four minutes, our star striker Callum Wilson found himself free and in the area. He smashed in a low shot and suddenly we were in dreamland. We were winning a Premier League match – it was the first time I had personally seen us winning a top flight match. I had missed the West Ham 4-3 away win.

Then, more was to follow. After just nine minutes, from a corner, the ball came to Matt Ritchie on the edge of the box. He chested it down and smashed a twenty yard volley into the top corner. It was sublime. We were 2-0 up after 9 minutes – unbelievable!

Sunderland later had a goal disallowed but we held on for an impressive 2-0 home win. It was the first home top flight win in our club's history and I felt privileged to be there that day. We drank to celebrate in the Portman as always and watched a rock band in O'Neill's Irish Pub at Lansdowne.

Within the next month, I'd also be physically in stadiums to witness a home defeat, an away defeat, an away penalties win and a home draw. I had remarkably now seen AFC Bournemouth win, lose and draw at home in every domestic type of match possible. Only Europe and a top flight away win and draw remained.

In October 2015, I spent a full month in England. As well as watching 4 live AFC Bournemouth matches, I also visited two micronations, Adammia (which borders England in Yorkshire) and The Lagoan Isles (a country housed on a lake within a park in Portsmouth). In the same spell of clock movement, I visited Gloucester and the Forest of Dean. I was whacking a touch of good old English culture in here, working along the way and feeling good amidst the horrors of a background which included a break-up.

8th November 2015 would be five years to the day that Panny and I met. We had met on that day in Barrientos Island in Antarctica. But this was the end of our relationship.

Bournemouth were in the top flight, Glentoran were Irish Cup holders, Northern Ireland were on the brink of qualifying for the European Championships in 2016 and I had backpacked over 100 countries. That all felt less relevant now that I was single.

It was Jonny Blair alone again. I ordered up a pint of beer one night in the Moon in the Square pub in Bournemouth and I cried again. I have cried thrice in that pub down the years as an adult. Twice over a girl – Noemi, and now Panny.

Since my relationship and engagement was now finished, I would have to head back to Hong Kong and move my stuff out of Panny's flat. I wasn't ready for that farewell just yet but I planned my adventure east for December. Northern Ireland to England to Poland and then into the Stans and leave Hong Kong behind.

First though the football would dominate. Low and behold, could Northern Ireland actually do the unthinkable and qualify for Euro 2016?

Chapter 35
Greece Lightning Strikes Twice

Cottesmore Golf and Country Club, Crawley, ENGLAND (October 2015)

"It is Magennis; and that's the moment they've waited a generation for" – Football Commentator.

It actually felt weird for me that the night that Northern Ireland finally qualified for a major football tournament in 30 years, I was alone and in a place in the middle of nowhere. It was typical of my barmy life to have crazy nights for nondescript and unimportant matches and now, when it mattered the most, I was in a hotel all alone in remote countryside! None of that was planned of course. Life had changed for me since leaving Europe in 2009, and now, that I had left Hong Kong behind, I was nomadic again. Me and my backpack.

Of course, I should have been in Belfast that night, at the match, but having lived away from Northern Ireland for so long now, I was only going to a few matches a year now. I gave up my block booking for home matches in 2009, having previously only missed 3 home matches since 1990!

Ten years on from the famous Monopoly Pub Crawl (a story covered *in "Backpacking Centurion Volume 1 - Don't Look Back In Bangor", "Chapter 17"*), I planned it again. This time over a weekend in London.

But this was a magical week. First up, I'd tour the unknown micronation of Lagoan Isles. I arrived at Portsmouth train station and walked past Fratton Park, home of Portsmouth FC. On past it, there's a park called Baffin's Park, and within that park is Baffin's

Pond. It is here at Baffin's Pond that three islands sit, unclaimed by Portsmouth, England or the United Kingdom.

This is a separate country here and it is called The Lagoan Isles.

Next up on my journey, I couldn't have timed this one more bizarrely. For it was tonight, on the day I'd visit The Lagoan Isles that Northern Ireland play Greece at home in a Euro 2016 qualifier. The previous time we played Greece at home, I was there. Keith Gillespie and James Quinn were both sent off and we lost 2-0. As a result, Greece went on to qualify for Euro 2004. A competition they later won despite losing to Poland in a pre-Euros warm up. At that time, Northern Ireland finished bottom of the group. 12 years later, the tide had turned.

Some people who know me from following Northern Ireland down the years will wonder why on earth I wasn't flying back to Belfast for the match. The answer was simple. I wasn't even supposed to be in Europe. I had expected to be in Hong Kong. When things changed, my mind had drifted.

I hadn't even checked the fixture list to know that on the day Northern Ireland play Greece, I'd be in Crawley!! Crawley of all places. I was reviewing a hotel and country club here - the fantastic Cottesmore Golf Club. It was a someway stopover between Bournemouth and London.

Also, when I had decided to stay in Europe longer, it wasn't clear how significant the Greece match would be. But when push came till thon shove, this was to be the crucial match.

Before that, we had a chance to qualify outright by beating Faroe Islands and Hungary. While we did bate the Faroes in a match I was at *(Chapter 34 – Fare Auld World)*, we only scraped a last minute draw with Hungary. That goal by Kyle Lafferty was vital though. It meant that the Greece match was now the important one!! And here I was in Crawley!

At the time, my blogger friend Abbi Morrison, also from Northern Ireland, she lived in Crawley. I got off the train and she picked me up before we headed for dinner and chat at a local harvester on a corner. I asked Abbi if she knew any bars in the area that might possibly show the Northern Ireland v. Greece match. With other matches on that night, it was suddenly very bad timing of me to be stuck in Crawley on what was potentially such a big night for Northern Irish football.

Abbi knew of no bars, nor did I. It suddenly emerged that of course, I'd be watching the match at my hotel. My hotel wasn't even in Crawley. It was a countryside dwelling place about 15 miles from the city. Time was running out and kick off was soon. Thankfully, Abbi was driving and she gave me a lift back to the Cottesmore Hotel.

I dashed straight to reception to inquire if they could show the match for me. The Hotel general manager came in. His name was Johnny, with an h. The answer was *"of course!"* and he showed me to the bar. I had 20 minutes to spare!

I dashed back to my room to check my emails, grab my scarf and laptop bag (in case the bar television didn't actually show the match and I'd have to stream it). I rocked up to the bar, which had Guinness and I ordered a fresh pint. The barman was Bogdan, from Romania and the national anthems were on. I was buzzing.

Part of me also wondered what on earth I was doing here, in the middle of the countryside near Crawley! My Dad was at Windsor Park that night though. All the omens were good here. I wasn't nervous. For once, I was confident we would win this one. I have no idea why. It was a gut feeling. Defeat didn't seem like an option.

As I wrote, the omens were good…I had met Abbi that day. Abbi is from Northern Ireland. The hotel manager was called Johnny. The barman was Romanian and they were in our group. There was Guinness on tap. I was the only football supporter in the bar as a customer!! Bogdan liked football and supported Romania. It had also been Romania who we had beaten 1-0 away in Bucharest in 1985 which basically secured us (in hindsight though it came before the vital 0-0 clincher at Wembley) qualification for Mexico 86.

On the pitch, we didn't have a single striker who had ever scored a full level international goal. Kyle Lafferty was suspended. David Healy and Martin Paterson had retired. Conor Washington wasn't in the squad yet. Will Grigg and Liam Boyce were fringers, both also without an international goal. This meant only one man to rely on. Bangor-born Josh Magennis, also of course without an international goal at full level at the time.

Josh, wearing number 21 started his career as a goalkeeper before deciding to play up front. He had never scored an international goal at full level. This was surely the time to do it. Northern Ireland expected. This was set to be a fairytale. Everything was in our favour, it seemed.

There were no nerves but after having a big dinner that night, I was certainly necking the beers. I was three pints in when our captain Steve Davis slid in the opener. A half-time 1-0 lead was good but nothing is certain in football. At the start of the second half, Oliver Norwood glides a corner in. Big Josh Magennis jumps to meet the ball, heading it into the exact gap between the Greek full back on the post, and the crossbar. It's in the net. It's 2-0!! It's 2-0 to

Northern Ireland, we could now afford to concede a goal and still qualify for Euro 2016!

Belfast goes wild. Here in a bar that I'd never been in before, and would never be in again, I just start crying. I can't contain my emotion. The reason I start crying is because I know that Greece won't score twice. I just know. I cried and finished my Guinness, ordering another one and a shot of Bushmills single malt on ice.

"That's the moment they've waited a generation for" states the commentator. He's absolutely right. As I wipe my tears, Davis nonchalantly heads in a third goal. Now, there was no doubt. We were going to our first ever European Championships. It was high time, given how only a late West Germany goal (v. Albania) in 1983 had kept us from qualifying for Euro 84.

Greece actually scored a consolation goal after that, but nobody remembers that. We won 3-1.

Even though captain Steven Davis scored 2 goals on the night, for some reason, Josh's sandwich goal felt like the clincher.

Tears continued all night while the next day, I headed to London to do the Monopoly Pub Crawl. In the middle of all that, the reality was that I now knew that in June 2016, I'd need to be in France. From now until then, nobody knew my adventures ahead, nor did I know that just after France, I'd end up in Poland. Not to visit, but to end up living here.

More madness would come in between, however.

Chapter 36
Stanislas Is Coming To Town

Dean Court, Boscombe, ENGLAND (December 2015)

"When it's done and all this is gone. Just find a feeling; pass it on" - The Coral.

Amidst all the drama of watching Bournemouth in the Premier League and Northern Ireland qualify for the Euros, I had almost forgotten my purpose. The tourist. Jonny Blair is a tourist. I was once described as a perpetual tourist. My Russian friend, Evgenia (who lives in Kyrgyzstan) echoed this sentiment.

"You are the coolest and cutest tourist I've met, I can't wait to see you again Jonny" - Evgenia.

The big tour was ready to start again. From "Backpacking Centurion" to "This Is The Next Century." The 100 country to 200 country quest had to go on. And on. And Ariston. I was ready to crack the 200 mark.

But I was now single. When the five year mark hit of my anniversary with Panny Yu, 8th November 2015, things were over. Our relationship had ended. I was alone again. I was lost again. Something must have been brewing.

"On the eve of a golden age I'm told. At the end of the rainbow, there's no gold" - Jonny Blair.

There were a few pivotal moments just before I left the UK this time. For only the second time this decade, I went to a Northern Ireland match with my brother Marko. We bate Latvia 1-0 at Windsor Park. I went to a further brace of Cherries games - AFC Bournemouth won away at Preston North End and got smashed 5-1 at Manchester City.

"Where were you when you were sh*t?" - Manchester City fans to AFC Bournemouth fans.
"Playing you at Maine Road [in the third tier]"
- AFC Bournemouth fans retort.

My next journey was Bangor to Belfast to London to Poznań. I was pretty excited to be heading back to Poland again. It had been too long. The reason for that trip back to Poland wasn't even entirely clear to me. As I was on route to the 200, I felt that a cheap flight into Poland before overlanding into Ukraine and then touring "The Stans" would be a good plan for the next few months. Flights from the UK to Poland at the time were always cheaper than direct to Ukraine, whether it was Easyjet, Ryanair or Wizzair. Plus, of course I wanted to visit Poland again after that crazy journey. It was a country I had missed so much – I hadn't ever been to Poznań, Gdańsk, Gdynia, Katowice, Krakow or Auschwitz back then. Now was clearly a great time to do that – and also just before Christmas was a perfect time – I love the magical cold countries in winter and Poznań would also have its ice festival on.

Just before that, the Bournemouth gave me a huge lift by beating Chelsea 1-0 away and then we had to play Manchester United at home. I watched that match with my Mum and Dad in Bangor on television. Junior Stanislas scored direct from a corner and Josh King added a second. We won 2-1. It felt like we finally belonged in the top flight. It was just before Christmas, and Stanislas was coming to town...

On the same night, the draw for the group stage of Euro 2016 was made. Life was moving fast. Northern Ireland were to be in a group with Poland, Ukraine and Germany. We would be playing those teams in that order in three different cities next June. Poland in Nice. Ukraine in Lyon. Germany in Paris.

In the intervening months, to come, by coincidence (but unknown at the time) I'd also visit Poland, Ukraine and Germany in that order. I spent a cosy night in Gatwick Airport's swanky Yotel before boarding my flight to Poznań. That night at Gatwick oddly I also met Abbi Morrison, who again in the freakiness of it all just happened to be there the exact night before the two fateful events in my 2010s that aided my decline and plunged me into depression. Abbi, would of course be blameless and unaware of that. It was just odd though.

I was so excited to be visiting Poland again. I couldn't believe I had left it so long.

My plans for Poland were to visit Poznań, Kraków and Auschwitz, meet some friends and head on the night train to Lviv, Ukraine.

I knew in advance that Pozzie (Poznań) would be something special. It was here, that I'd arranged to meet some travel friends, one of whom was also a global backpacker. This was the third different country we would be in together. It was always good fun with that lady.

All in all, I did meet those friends and enjoyed the charms of one lady in particular. There was something both magical and tragical about that travel contact. I loved the way she muttered the words Gdańsk and Gdynia. She oozed them out of her lips with unmeant sensual charm. There is no doubt in my sky, that my mind fell itself in love with a girl there, from this day forth. Who's going to dwell?

"Waiting for a star to fall" – Boy Meets Girl.

Chapter 37
Grzaniec

Poznań, POLSKA (Grudzień 2015)

"She moves in mysterious ways" - Paul Hewson.

The magic was in the air. I loved it. It was dark, damp, cold and misty when I arrived in Poznań for the second time. But it was really the first time I was here. You can't count a twenty minute train stop ten years previously (March 2005), can you? I added a decade to my lifespan and rolled into this town. It was now 2015.

This time, there was a sensual magic. I felt alive. I was single again. I was alone. I was a backpacking centurion now. I was a professional travel blogger now. A lot of water had passed under the bridge since last I muttered a shy *"dziękuję"* to a Warszawa barmaid. That was summer 2007, two years after my 2005 debut visit. This was now a more mature Jonny Blair, of December 2015 vintage. Eight years and wow how I had neglected Poland. It was high time to return and this trip was a huge influence on my lifeshell. Plus, I was now in Poland as a travel blogger for the first time. When I recheck the dates, I find that I was last in Poland in August 2007, two weeks before my first travel blog post went live on Don't Stop Living. In those intervening 8 years, I had written over 2,000 travel blog articles, visited every continent, footstepped in over 100 countries, been engaged and split up. Here I was, unlooking for answers in Poznań.

As well as backpacking, I was reviewing some hostels and tours here in Poland. I was working from the comfort of my laptop. I flew into Poland from Luton, of all places. Perhaps, the only reason in the whole world that I booked that flight was that it was so cheap and I had neglected Poland for so long. On arrival, I boarded a bus from Poznań airport to the city centre. I was in love with this country again. I had forgotten how much I liked it in the first place. Backpacking in China, living in Australia, feeding hyenas in Ethiopia were all just travel memories now. They couldn't really compete with Poland anymore, as this was a safe and happy haven. I knew from this point, that this could be an easy option of a country to live in. Though I couldn't dwell on that, nor did I plan anything back then, in 2015.

My first night back in Poland was just dreamlike. I remember how I smiled when I heard those church bells ring down by Pozzie's beautiful Stare Miasto. My first sip of ice cold cheap Polish beer was devoured in a bar that showed Leicester City beating Chelsea 2-1. I did a pub crawl on my own the first night. I was single, I was backpacking again in a country I loved. In fact, I realised, it was my first time to tour Poland alone. In 2005, I was with my Northern Irish friends. In 2007, I was with my Polish friends. Now, I was alone. It was liberating. It was a turning point. I was really really happy. I slept in the excellent Poco Loco Hostel and was the first travel blogger to write about it.

Incidentally, this was my first time being both single and outside the British Isles in 5 years. This didn't mean I was flirty or looking for love but somehow, Slavic girls are always the best and Polish girls play a huge part in that opinion I hold. They are educated, smart, knowledgeable. They are often bilingual or trilingual. They are enthusiastic about life. They are eager, they are curious. They are beautiful. But one quality in Polish girls that always shines out... they are approachable, open and welcoming. You can be on your own in a bar and just chat to a group of Polish girls. They are almost always very approachable and delighted to speak to you. Tonight, I am the exotic one. It is a cold winter night. There is snow all around. My hostel is virtually guestless. In the bars, I am the only tourist, the only foreigner. I love it. I always loved that.

I met a couple of nice Polish girls that night, Kasia and Michalina, both in Pijalnia Wódki I Piwa by Poznań's Stary Rynek – they were drinking in there together. "Pijalnia" is one of those old school PRL style bars with cheap drinks (beers and shots were 4 złotych that night - 72 pence), communist newspapers adorn the walls and textbook Polish snacks grace a delightfully cheap menu. In another bar, Bee Jay's, I chat away to the barmaid. This is a great city. Within hours, I loved Poznań. The following few days would feature some reunions. These were reunions with travel and work friends from my wacaday journey.

The next morning I toured Poznań on my own and loved it. I remember posting happy photos on my blog social media pages that day. The Old Town Square in Pozzie (as I had now resigned to calling it) is breathtakingly beautiful. Awash with colour in the cold winter, this was nothing short of a backpacker's paradise.

This time, it was the cafés and bars I was loving. It stuck in my mind. But I was still a nomad, I had no home. Not here in Pozzie, nor anywhere...

I was 35 now. I was wiser. I had no concrete plans. After Poland, I would *probably* go to Ukraine by land and then head to Russia and Kazakhstan. I booked an onward train to Kraków and plotted my journey spontaneously and without any real purpose. Before I swung my *"Dobranocies"* to pulsating Poznań, there was just one significant final reunion that was to take place.

A message from another local friend had confirmed that we would meet that night. It would be yet another in a long list of reunions from my journey. 2015 was brimming with reunions. Here in Poznań , I would meet two travel friends who I had met in my previous backpacking days. We would have a night of travel chat, more Polish culture inductions and some drinks.

This reunion was more memorable and significant than most. It was probably aided due to the fact that I was now single and was meeting up with two very fine single Polish ladies. There was nothing more than a winter warm hug and a cheek kiss of course. But one of those girls, in her vivacious glory had chosen to look and smell attractive tonight. She had a fine aroma that couldn't go unnoticed.

She swept back her golden locks behind ears that had smelt sweetly during the hug. She revealed a surprising low cut top once we had stripped off our winter attire of hats, scarves, gloves and coats. She was closer to me than the other friends I met on this trip. We had messaged each other more often and she was fully aware of my blogs, and upcoming book launch – she wanted to buy my book. But looking back, there was no time for anyone to get excited here. There was no sexual tension in the air either. It's only looking back that I realise what we had and what we lost, possibly. She was born and bred in Poznań, which I liked as it was as local as I could get.

The other lady was from near the Belarus border – from a city called Zamość. This brace of ladies provided me with ammunition which would come in mighty handy later on when I would get round to documenting Poland again. You see, for the first time in my life, I tried grzane piwo (hot beer!). They taught me a few more Polish words, which I jotted down. These included *"Główny"* (Main train station) which I had pronounced very badly wrong in my Northern Irish English as "glau knee." When I look back on that, I chuckle to myself as to how stupid I was.

After checking out Poznań's yearic ice show (by the main square), posing for photos by the iconic Ratusz (City Hall) we headed onto a quiet street and into the "Swiat Bar", which translates as "World Bar." It was here that we had agreed we would all drink grzane piwo together.

"Watch the first light kiss the new world. It's a wonder, baby, like you and I" – Geri Halliwell.

As the ladies checked my requirements barside, I grabbed a table and the ladies ordered a hattrick of hot beers. I asked one of them to tell me all about it...all about Grzaniec. In an almost posh level US influenced accent, she said, *"it is a hot winter Polish drink – basically it's a hot beer called grzane piwo or grzaniec."*

The girls give me details of the ingredients, of which cinnamon makes a surprising appearance. I sip it and am immediately enchanted. I have opened up another new world, in the World Bar! You'll never know unless you try. How had I skipped grzane piwo all these years?? How had I missed hot beer?? We devour this sensation in what is a tranquil and pleasant bar. The girls tell me stories about their journeys. They are impressive young travellers for their age. They are a decade younger than me but none of us noticed that. We are travel friends tonight.

Some of their anecdotes stick in my mind, to this day. One of these girls is very profound in her manner and she details things with precision. The ladies recollect a hostel in Limassol in Cyprus, where they shared a room with a lad called Bob. But Bob was always in bed, under a cover. He didn't ever move. Flies flew round his feet. It was an honest and true story, but not a pleasant one. It felt like Bob had died.

On the same evening in Pozzie, the younger of these two girls recounts a trip to Tbilisi, the Georgian capital city where she "backpacked a country with no money" and had to call her brother. As she tells me this tale, I can't help but think that she is a perfect travel partner for me, as she is the same as me. We were cut from the same tree.

Forget all that, for now though, I would be leaving Pozzie the next day.

These ladies were typical of so many Polish people I had met on my journey, I liked them, they liked me. There was nothing unusual in that was there? After drinks in another Old Town bar (standardzik), they made sure I got back to my hostel safely. As a gentleman, it should be me doing that. But it reminded me of Polish hospitality which impressed me time and time again.

Twenty four hours later, I would board a night train to Kraków...

Chapter 38
A Bit of Krak

Auschwitz German Death Camp, POLAND

"Arbeit Macht Frei" – Germans while erecting death camps in Poland.

"Libraries gave us power, then work came and made us free" - Manic Street Preachers.

After Poznań, this was now my first ever visit to Kraków. That I waited so long to visit this city in life might seem quite unfathomable; and to me, it also is. Love or hate Kraków, it is a very very popular tourist city.

Yet here was me, aged 35. A veteran backpacker. I had been to Suriname three times, to remote unknown villages in deepest China, to Bruny Island, to Yaseh Chah in Iran, to Sulaymaniyah in Iraq. Yet I had never been to Kraków. In the five years since that first visit, astonishingly I have now been back to the city of Kings over twenty times.

All that was in the future, as for now, I strolled as a lonely backpacker off my nighttrain and into the commercial mayhem of Galeria Krakowska. Still, I was here for four days and would be able to visit all the sights of the Old Town, Wawel Castle, Kazimierz, Schindler's Factory and the grim pre-Christmas trip to Auschwitz and Birkenau.

I don't know why it took me so long to finally visit Auschwitz. Travel can be grim sometimes and it needs to be – to remember the horrors of yesteryear.

This was not for the faint hearted. I chose to stay in the Mosquito Hostel, where I had super roommates and new friends and would review the hostel, its tours and entertainment nights on my blog.

There was a further chance to catch up with my friend Ania. I met Ania 10 years earlier in Bournemouth. In Bournemouth, Ania and I worked together in bars, cafés and cheeseburger joints. Ania had also been travelling and had now moved back to her native Poland. We met up two nights in a row and the following night I was booked on a cross border night train till Lviv in Ukraine. Ukraine was another new country for me as I plotted my way back through the Soviet Union jigsaw.

Like a lot of my journeys, there was one truly unforgettable moment here that would send a crazy slice of fate to me some 7 months later. Looking back, the chances of this happening were crazy. But basically before I left Kraków, Bournemouth had just played West Bromwich Albion away in the English Premier League. I had been busy backpacking that day and hadn't been able to check the score. I expected we would lose. In a bar the previous night, I had noticed an advert for a bar called "Football Heaven" and when I checked that bar was located somewhere between my hostel (the Mosquito Hostel) and the train station for my night train to Lviv. So I grabbed my bags from the hostel and left 2 hours before my train, allowing time for a beer or two in this "Football Heaven" bar.

When I arrived in that bar, they were getting ready to close. However, the lady working there was very attractive and very friendly. She served me a beer and I started to chat to her. She introduced herself as Kasia. I then just told her I really just popped in to check the AFC Bournemouth result and have a quick drink. She was so interesting, and just so typical of why I had a fondness for Polish people. This lady, Kasia Brzyk, well she typified what being a nice person is all about. She went online to check the football score for me immediately.

"Bournemouth won 2-1!" she says softly as I sip my "Shawn Jensen", this is the nickname I had given to the Książęce IPA (Polish Real Ale) I was drinking. That's because the pronunciation of "Książęce" to me sounds like "Shawn Jensen"! It was incredible to hear that we had won 2-1. And from Kasia here. A lady I had just met. She served me a second beer, I gave her my business card and we became friends on Facebook and I told her I was heading on the night train to Lviv.

"I might see you again, someday." I hugged her and waved goodbye. It was only in countries like Poland that I could do that. Arrive in a bar I had never been in before, make a new friend, feel close to them when I left, even though I was in Kasia's company for barely more than an hour.

Of course, I never expected to see Kasia again. You will have to read on to see the lunatical way in which I met her again. This is all a game of fate.

One thing is for sure, that this part of my travel life was brilliant. These were glory days.

"It's only Matthew Le Tissier who can score goals like that" – BBC football commentator, 1990s.

Chapter 39
Don't Stop Lviving

Lviv, UKRAINE (December 2015)

"I know who I want to take me home" – Dan Wilson.

When I boarded the train in Polska's Kraków, I was in a three person train dorm for the night, along with one Ukrainian guy and a Japanese tourist, Ikuma Sasamoto. Having drank a few beers in the Football Heaven bar in Kraków, I decided it would be a coffee here on the train and sleep. There was some epic Polish / Ukrainian hospitality to follow.

The conductor came in to check our tickets and I asked him *"masz kawa lub piwo?,"* I was looking for a café or a trolley serving coffee or beer. He replied that they didn't but he was the train conductor and would be making himself a coffee in a few minutes in the staff part of the carriage and he said it would be no problem if I could have a coffee. Brilliant guy.

He poured me a coffee and I updated my travel notes, before drifting to sleep on route back into the former Soviet Union. These dreams were inspired, they were my childhood lusts and wants, aged 6 reading about the USSR in Atlases and Panini sticker books. I awoke after we reached the Polish town of Przemyśl and I was stamped out of Poland, and into Ukraine at "Shiny" (Shehyni). I drifted to sleep again before awaking in the dawn breaking cold of Lviv. I can tell you now that this was damn inspiring.

"I'm out of season all year round" - The Jam.

Remarkably, this was my first ever trip to Ukraine and my aim on this part of my journey was to visit a lot of the former USSR states that I had missed in my 100 country journey. That journey had already included Georgia, Russia, Azerbaijan, Armenia, Nagorno Karabakh, Latvia, Belarus, Lithuania, Uzupis, Estonia, Moldova and Transnistria. I was about half way through my Soviet jigsaw, which was begging me to complete it.

I had three main things to do in Ukraine and then I planned to head to the "Stans" of Central Asia, again part of my quest to get through a chunk of ex-Soviet Union states. In Ukraine, those three things were to tour Lviv and Kiev, and to visit Chernobyl. First up – I was completely shocked by Lviv. I loved this city, and I really never expected that. I basically only put Lviv on my list as I was curious about a city, which was once Polish, was located near the Poland and EU border but also was once in the former USSR.

I arrived at dawn in the freezing cold with Ikuma and we had to part ways here – oddly. I say oddly as we were both backpackers of the same ilk. However, he was the one staying in the cheap backpacker's hostel and here was I living it up by staying in the 5 star Citadel Inn. By this point in my life, all my accommodation was sponsored or free and I was constantly reviewing hostels, hotels and guesthouses for my main travel blog, Don't Stop Living. I'll never know if it was this selfish aspect to my life that resulted in the ending of my relationship with Panny, or not. It's all in the past now, but somehow my travels had become more selfish and blog related since I had become a professional travel blogger. I couldn't dwell now though – that relationship was over and here I was in Lviv! I was only spending 2 nights here in Lviv as I gathered that would be enough for me to see the city and then get the train to Kiev, where also a couple of days would suffice.

The Citadel Inn was fantastic. I was checked in and welcomed with smiles by lovely ladies Oksana and Iwana on reception. I had a huge room, with Wi-Fi. Breakfast was included, the bar had cold beer at the ready and they even let me check in early. Having met

Ikuma on the night train, him and I agreed to backpack the city's sights together.

We grabbed a coffee and some varenyky in a downtown café and then we headed around the sights. I'd have two full days here anyway and yet on day one, we managed to visit most of the places on my list. When I got round to blogging about it that afternoon in a bar in central Lviv, I was surprised to find that a fellow Northern Ireland football fan, Kyle Gallagher, lived locally and was giving me tips on what to see and do. Oddly, Kyle was not actually in Lviv at this point – he was back in Northern Ireland!

However, Kyle's tips came in handy and on my two day stint, I used all his tips including some brilliant bars and restaurants he had mentioned. Lviv, is one of the best cities I have ever been in for bars – there is such a diverse range of bars, cafes, pubs, clubs and restaurants here. Eating out and drinking is cheap here. Of course, as a social geek, there is absolutely no doubt that the cheapness of bars, cafes and restaurants in former Eastern Bloc countries have influenced my decision to live in Poland. I just love it. Bars, cafes, restaurants in countries like Poland, Ukraine, Belarus, Kyrgyzstan are just incredible and I love them.

Themed bars are all the rage in underestimated Lviv. The first of these, is the notorious "Kryivka" Bar. To even get inside this "well known secret bar" requires a password. Ikuma and I head to "number 14" in the main square of Lviv and we mutter the words "Slava Ukrainia" (glory to Ukraine) to a window. The reason? This acts as a password about Ukrainian Glory and is the only way you can enter! Once inside, we are ushered down to the basement accompanied by a dude carrying a gun. We are given a shot of red blood coloured vodka and then I choose blood sausage with chips for dinner. It's all happening in a darkened basement bar. Later, I held a replica gun against the walls of this cellar hangout. I thought of the horrors of gun warfare back in Northern Ireland, growing up.

**"Masked gunmen shouted 'trick or treat,' then opened fire"
– Northern Irish news reporter on the Greysteel tragedy,
Halloween Night, 1993.**

Another bar in Lviv which I loved is the masochistic themed "Cafe Masoch" – this is a unique little darkened bar where attractive waitresses will handcuff you, slap you, and whip you. Why? Because Lviv boasts the home of Leopold Ritter von Sacher-Masoch, founder of sexual masochism and from where the word "masochism" takes its name, Masoch.

A sultry waitress serves me in sexy suspenders. Her name is Valeria. After a few sips of my beer, I ask to get spanked. She brings a pair of handcuffs over and cuffs me to the chair in the corner. She brandishes a whip, pulls up my shirt to reveal my naked back to a crowd of four. She asks me to say "more" and then whips me hard and good five times. My Japanese travel buddy Ikuma is in hysterics. It was all part of the fun. While this was December 2015, I would return to Lviv again in March 2019 for a "Steven Davis Pub Crawl" this time, I'd meet Kyle who lives there. Stuck in the here and now, I loved Lviv, it had been a super city at a wonderful time of my life.

I was revelling in the freedom of backpacking alone again, and after Lviv, I toured the sights of Kiev before the time came for another gory, gruesome experience. This is dark tourism. I'd be heading to Chernobyl and Chapter 40.

Chapter 40
Chernobyl's Witness

Reactor Number 4, Chernobyl Exclusion Zone, UKRAINE (December 2015)

"There's silence in the air, there's silence in the ground. A presence moving through the rivers in the moonlight. Desolation all around. The wind blows through abandoned buildings, photos scattered on the floors, possessions of a vanished population" – Ash (Pripyat).

I always wanted to visit Chernobyl. It had been on a long list of must-sees. I finally was in Ukraine in December 2015 and so it was time to make that a reality. A geography lesson with my old teacher Raymond Mowat back in Bangor Grammar came back into my head here. I remembered Chernobyl, I watched a documentary on it and I did a school essay on it back in the day. The Chernobyl nuclear power plant disaster happened on April 26th 1986. Just under 30 years later, I was here to backpack through the now termed "Chernobyl Exclusion Zone". That zone has parts of it in Ukraine, Belarus and Russia.

All in all, December 2015 was a dark month for me. Firstly, I toured the horrors of Auschwitz and now I found myself in the grim yet unique Chernobyl Exclusion Zone after those dark dingy bar experiences in Lviv. The trip to Chernobyl started early, 7 a.m.. The night before, I had been on a guided tour of Kiev. That tour was conducted by a stunning model, Lyza. While I feasted my eyes on her, I knew the viewpoint the next day would be far from a blonde babe in paradise. It would be a staggering contrast from a golden locked bikini babe to a grey desolate, deserted part of the world. Also that night in Kiev, I tried Borscht soup as well as Ukrainian beer. Passports at the ready, coffee in hand, I meet my two Chernobyl day trip buddies and my tour guide. We are handed a Geiger counter. Throughout the day, we can point it at parts of the terrain and even buildings and items inside the CEZ. At times of course, the radiation levels on it boom.

Essentially, it wasn't the song (opening quote for this chapter) from my favourite Northern Irish rock band Ash that gave me inspiration to visit the sad city of Pripyat. I always meant to visit Pripyat, it was a trip to the Chernobyl Exclusion Zone that I had waited a long time for. Having been to all the countries that surround Ukraine, it wasn't until late 2015 that I finally made it here. For the record Ukraine borders Poland, Belarus, Slovakia, Hungary, Romania, Moldova, Transnistria and Russia. The most notable of those experiences in my personal case was when I toured Bobruisk in Belarus in 2007, at the time I was only 40 kilometres from the Chernobyl Exclusion Zone. Until you've backpacked your way to lonely empty Pripyat, it's pretty hard to understand what really happened at Chernobyl.

Chernobyl is the name of a town in Ukraine, in the former Soviet Union. It is also the name of the power plant. It is also the name of the exclusion zone. The reality hits hard here – Chernobyl is only a two hour drive from Ukraine's capital city – Kiev. The entrance into the Chernobyl Exclusion Zone is at Dytyatky. There are passport and radiation checks here, then we head to the actual town of Chernobyl. The day tour, I had organised with the company Solo East, who have been running these tours for a long time, and were the first company to offer such a tour to tourists.

There are a lot of amusing parts to the tour – you'll never be bored. We head through a forest at one point and spy up at the trees, behind which is the Duga Radar System, this was a special radar system well hidden from view. Aeroplanes flying over would barely spot this. Nearby we see abandoned trucks and items from the aftermath of the tragic event – these include diggers and trucks.

There is a memorial in Chernobyl town itself dedicated to all those settlements that had to evacuate after the tragedy.

We visited two of the most affected cities within the Chernobyl Exclusion Zone – Kopachi, and obviously Pripyat. Kopachi is where we enter a decrepit Ukrainian Primary School. This is a timewarp. This is a timewarp to the Soviet Union of 1986. This is actually a Soviet Union Primary School. Nothing has changed. The school books are as they were back then in 1986. This is a glimpse of a country which doesn't exist anymore. I get a chill through my bones thinking that since the last time children sat here studying, Northern Ireland have been at the World Cup. Those children are older than me now. I also ponder on the reality that Maradona played in 3 World Cups after this disaster. This is definitely a curious vision into the past – for one day only, we are actually "Back in the USSR."

Time comes for us to get up close and personal to the culprit – you know what's coming. We drive past Reactor Number 1. We drive past Reactor Number 2. We drive past Reactor Number 3. So, what's next?

Reactor Number 4.

This is the culprit. This is where the explosion was. We are here.

We get out of the car and walk to a monument that sits in front of a fence. We peek through the fence and we see that sight we all saw on television screens back in the 1980s. We see Chernobyl Nuclear Power Plant Reactor Number 4. A sarcophagus was built to cover it back in the day – to try and maintain the radioactive dangers within. Even that sarcophagus has given way. This meant that the European Union had to help fund another cover, to be rolled over the entire area of the culprit. When I visited in 2015, this was still under construction.

Next it was time to visit the craziest city of the day. Pripyat. This is a truly sad and creepy place. Every part of the day was grim, dark and forlorn. That's to be expected when you backpack your way through the top sights of the Chernobyl Exclusion Zone. This ain't no pleasure cruise. Pripyat was once the beating heart and entrepreneurial cool city in this region.

Pripyat was affluent and all the USSR locals who aspired to have some money and a good standard of living longed to move to Pripyat. There was lots of work nearby of course - at the infamous Chernobyl Nuclear Power Plant and away from that, hotels and local businesses thrived here. It's ironic that Pripyat went from being one of the most sought after places in the former Soviet Union to live to being a place where nobody wanted to live. A place where nobody could live, anymore. The mighty have fallen. Spare a thought for Pripyat's fall from grace. At midnight on the night of the Chernobyl disaster, around 50,000 people lived here. Within days, the city became a ghost town – nobody would live here, ever again.

Pripyat has appeared in the afforequoted Ash song (at the start of this chapter) and in computer games. When I mentioned to friends and family I was going to Chernobyl, they spoke of some computer game I've never heard of that included Pripyat in it. On the way into Pripyat, we pull over to open an "entrance gate" to the city. Here, the name of the city is written in its dialect, it writes itself in Ukrainian: Припꞌятъ, Prýpꞌjatꞌ and Russian: Припять, Prípyat. The fact remains - Pripyat is an abandoned city in northern Ukraine, very close to the border with Belarus. It encompasses all the horrific D-words you can think of: dull, dark, desolate, deserted, dreary, drab, doomed, dead, decrepit, disaster, destitute, deadly, devilish and I could go on...Pripyat was also built from scratch. It was a "Nuclear City" – built for that very purpose.

There is a checkpoint and a gate on the way into Pripyat. You need permission to be here. Our guide Misha hands over the relevant documents and the guard opens the gate and we are now inside the area where the city of Pripyat once blossomed in the morning sun. Today, there are no bright colours in sight; there is no morning sun. The place has all the makings of a disaster zone. The roads remain intact and it looks exactly as it should - like a city where nobody has lived in for thirty years. No "Welcome to Pretty Pripyat" signs, no postcards, no fast food outlets and nothing short of a vacant city with a ghostly ghastly appearance.

Named after the nearby Pripyat River, Pripyat is a custom built city - made from scratch and founded in February 1970. It was the ninth such "Nuclear City" in the Soviet Union, it officially became a city in 1979 and had reached just shy of 50,000 residents by the time it was evacuated, within days after the 26 April 1986 Chernobyl disaster. These days, the city sits in complete ruins and is one of the most horrific places from my travels so far, up there with the German Death Camps in Poland, Saddam Hussein's House of Horrors in Iraq and the Torture Chambers and Killing Fields of Cambodia. Pripyat is currently supervised by Ukraine's Ministry of Emergencies, which manages activities for the entire Chernobyl Exclusion Zone. Visits to the city are strict and few and far between - 35 tourists per day maximum make the sad trip out here. You need a permit, you need to be on a tour. On a cold December day in 2015, there were 3 in our group and 4 in another group and that was it.

We have two different parts of the tour in Pripyat. First of all we are backpacking our way through the downtown area – this is sightseeing at its most grim. Here is where swanky hotels, restaurants, a cinema and a huge cultural building sit. Yes, the buildings are all still here. It's just that they've been looted, abandoned and left to ruin. There are four of us backpacking our way through the main sights of central Pripyat. There is no map and no tourist guide book here. The city of Pripyat doesn't shine in the morning sun. Here in the Chernobyl Exclusion Zone, they've even been deprived the right to sparkle in their midday sun. A grey misty foggy cloudy bombscare sky gapes down on us. Perhaps Oasis were wrong...

"Some might say that we will find a brighter day"
– Noel Gallagher.

Our guide Misha, a local, takes us through the main sights of the city. Whether you like the idea or loathe the idea, this was my adventure in abandoned Pripyat and oddly, I enjoyed it, at least as a tourist three decades after the sorrow. We park on the main street that runs through the city. There is no car park, you can park where you want here. There are also no cars or buses here - they were buried, destroyed, scrapped or even looted and used elsewhere. The main avenue has seen better days, naturally. When I later "Google Search" for the Main Street in Pripyat, there's a deep and sad irony. My tour company, Solo East comes up number one on Google.

The Main Street is (was) named after Lesya Ukrainka, a female activist and well known poet. It's a sad state of affairs and we drive along it, dander within it and ponder on what might have been.

"A hotline, a wanted ad, it's crazy what you could have had"
– Michael Stipe (R.E.M.).

There's no R.E.M., Britney Spears or Freddie Mercury classics belting out as we head to the main disco and dancefloor inside the prominent Palace of Culture, which is also named "Energetik." A hint of double entendre and irony yet again here, a play on words or just due to the proximity of the Nuclear Power Station. Again, Noel Arms and No Sir Prizes, the place is carnage personified.

The Palace of Culture is in the main "Lenin Square" of Pripyat; it looks like it was once the place to be for the Pripyat people, the Soviets, the Ukrainians and the Belarussians back in the day. We walk through the main dance floor. Nobody cuts a Wacko Jacko Moonwalk style bit of rug. At times though, it's as empty as the moon and we walk. Rubble, glass, wires, everywhere.

Again forget whacking your Google page onto "best hotels in Pripyat" and pumping out an Agoda or Booking.com reservation for your war reluctant soul. The city's tallest building is an abandoned hotel called Hotel Polissia. You can't sleep or stay here, permit or not. You may not last the night. Hotel Polissia has to be one of the largest hotels in the world that hasn't had any guest stay overnight for three decades, and counting. There is actually an option to stay overnight in the CEZ if you want. Though not actually in Pripyat, The Hotel Pripyat in Chernobyl has rooms and even a bar. The hotel name of "Pripyat" is only a homage to where you could have stayed. For this lifetime, a day trip sufficed me. But the fact remains - you can stay here and the radiation risk is effectively no different than if you spend the night in Kiev or Kharkiv.

As we enter a completely destroyed and non-intact football court inside the council building at the main square, I cast my mind back to watching Soviet football back in the day. The Soviet Union won the European Championships and reached the World Cup Semi Finals in the 1960s. Two years after the Chernobyl disaster, they'd also be in the European Championship final, where they lost to the Netherlands (1988). My glory days as a footballer might have passed me by, but here, there was a smashed up caser nestled in behind the nets.

I lined it up and scored a goal.

I hit the net in Pripyat. No cause for celebration.

But I did remember how the Soviet heroic goalkeeper Rinat Dasaev (former world number one keeper) once came up against Glentoran's Canadian centre half Terry Moore who scored and my team Glentoran drew 1-1 with Spartak Moscow. Ironically in the 1986 World Cup, the Soviet Union and Canada were in the same World Cup group, and both Terry and Rinat were stickers in my Panini sticker book! Another irony! It was just two months after the Chernobyl disaster that I collected those stickers and two years later would be the Glentoran v. Spartak Moscow match.

We toured Pripyat Park, where trees have grown over where the grass once was, but apart from that, this has all the remnants of what a Soviet Park actually is (was). It's sad of course and apart from some ground moss, there's no bright green colour here. Fallen leaves, barren trees and emptiness all around.

"Under neon loneliness, motorcycle emptiness"
- Manic Street Preachers.

A sadly infamous Ferris Wheel dominates the derelict playground outside. Its rusty mechanisms have lasted the test of time. It hasn't collapsed yet but no kids have been on the full circle for a hat-trick of decades. And nearby some dodgems remain, the way they were in 1986. This is no time to be amused in an amusement park.

They haven't even removed those 1986 Soviet propaganda pillars from the park in the downtown area either. Gorbachev was in control when the Chernobyl disaster occurred. It's all rather grim. No rear end brown coloured solution Mr. Holmes. But yeah, this shit lives on.

Even the revolutionary leader Lenin is still remembered and statues of him inside the Chernobyl Exclusion Zone remain. Here in downtown Pripyat, Lenin Square is nobody's dream here, anymore.

Trees without leaves sway in a wind that can no longer be bothered. Lock away your smiles, preferably in a year before 1986.

We get back in the car, the air still decidedly rough and choky. We drive for a tour of two more spooky buildings now, in a more residential area. Your eyes won't forget what they've seen in central Pripyat.

A swimming pool visit is up next on the backpacking sights ticker. Bring yer togs and let's go skinny dipping in the Soviet Union? No chance, although oddly the swimming pool and leisure centre here in Pripyat were still in use up until 1997, a bit ridiculous really given that the radiation risk has lingered in this city since 1986. That was one of the odd facts that we were told by our guides. Who still used this swimming pool in Pripyat in the 11 years after the disaster?

It's the craziest swimming pool I've ever been to. Diving boards are still on display, trashed changing rooms and smashed up windows all around. Even if the 1997 stat is to be believed, it's still a brace of decades ago since bikini clad babes ever front crawled through waters here.

Next up, and still in Pripyat, we visit Middle School Number 3, the most toured one of the city's remaining schools. This place hits deeper into my heart and gullet than I foresaw. It's truly horrific. Misha, our guide used to attend this school. Maybe that's what's so creepy. One room is full of gas masks. I feel something odd in my mind as I see this room. Gas masks everywhere, like on some kind of display.

You see, under the rule of the Soviet Union every child had to have a gas mask at school. I thought of my time growing up in Northern Ireland and we had bombs going off and sectarian shootings all the time, but we had no need to have gas masks in school. The USSR lived and breathed military ideals. Gas masks even look scary. Put them on the floor of a dusty, dirty, derelict, dis-used, abandoned building in a city that nobody has lived in for thirty years and it's even more scary.

As we backpack through the school, water drips, floorboards creep and Misha tells us this is the scariest place in the world at night. He hasn't seen the world, nor have I and nor have you. But as I pause, I feel that actually he's bound to be right. A day time dander through the school gives me the creeps as it is. It feels like this building will collapse of its own accord within the next decade. When I suggest this to Misha, he agrees. Some buildings in Pripyat have already failed the test of time and crumbled.

When we walked out of the Middle School Number 3, it was time to get back in the car and drive out of the city of Pripyat. This had been a truly sad and moving adventure and as I looked back using the wing mirror in the car, I knew I wouldn't be back here.

We drove through the red forest and would have our lunch appointment next, which would be a perfectly grim blog, "Dining out in Chernobyl: Top 1 Restaurant".

Lunch here, is surprisingly good. For the record, here is what I had for lunch in Chernobyl -

Starter – Borscht (Ukrainian style soup).
Salad – Beetroot, egg, cabbage. Basic but tasty.
Main course – Nice cooked chicken with potatoes, broccoli and carrot.
Dessert/Pudding – Fried dough with cream.
Drinks – 1 cherry juice, 1 berry juice. (kompot)

Love lost aside, this is perhaps the saddest book chapter I have ever written.

After Ukraine, I headed to Kazakhstan for the first time. I had found a cheap flight, a one way ticket from Kiev to Almaty on Christmas Eve. It would be a snowy dreamy Christmas in urban Kazakhstan from where I would make some plans to tour Central Asia. I wanted to crack through most of the Stans, including whackpacking in two lesser recognised countries in that fusion - Gorno Badakhshan and Karakalpakstan.

Chapter 41
One Almaty Decision

Bochonok Bar, Almaty, KAZAKHSTAN (Christmas Eve, 2015)

"I want to dance with somebody" – Whitney Houston.

I arrived on Christmas Eve in the city of Almaty in Kazakhstan. Again, like many randomic choices I made in my life, this one was suitably inspired. Almaty was shrouded in gorgeous snow, it was dreamlike. Plus, after Ukraine, this was another new country on my globe and I checked into the Almaty Backpackers, also known as the Silk Road Hostel. Again, I was doing a review and getting my bearings here before planning my route through the other Stans.

Immediately, I met a girl in the hostel. Her name was Mina. Mina was from Shymkent in Kazakhstan. We agreed to go out for a Christmas Eve drink. Mina was a model and a dancer. She had the looks and the style.

The first bar we went to was in a posh shopping mall. It was too upmarket for me. So we moved on to Bochonok, at least that is how you pronounce it in English, phonetically.

Being single and travelling alone brings up many such encounters. I danced with Mina. We didn't kiss. But I felt that if I stayed longer in her company, I could fall in love with her. Panny and I had split up about a month earlier. It had been girls I met on my journeys that had so much more influence on my life than I thought. I dwelled on it over a beer that night in Kazakhstan. I knew that as a child, I had been influenced by my childhood sweetheart Claire McKee, my teenage crush Vicky Everitt and the ladies that had come and gone before Noemi walked into my life. The Slavic charm of the girl I had met in Moldova was back in Poznań for now, and Mina shone her rays into the kind of spotlight that Michael Stipe once cornered whilst losing his religion.

Mina looked good and we had a great night, but I knew this time not to do anything about it. It was a one night dance. I decided to get up early on Christmas Day, to tour the city on my own before returning to the hostel to call Mum, Dad, Marko, Cathy and Daniel for Christmas Day.

I awoke early on Christmas Day morning with only two plans. Firstly to make sure I Skype call my family that day for an online Christmas chat. Secondly to backpack all the main sights of the city. Luckily, Kazakhstan was many hours ahead of Northern Ireland. I left the hostel around 9 a.m., and mid-morning, on Christmas morning I arrived in the city park near a burning flame. The fire that never goes out. The tomb of the unknown soldier. This was a moving moment. Music and a song began to play. I was alone now.

"Caravan oh caravan. Caravan oh caravan. Caravan oh caravan" – the song that repeated that Christmas morning.

As that song played, it was a really sombre moment. It was a freedom and the realisation that the 100 country journey, the 100 country book and my failed romance with Panny was not the end of my dreams, nor my life. I pondered on some of the Slavic girls I had met. One of them had been messaging that day, and again over the Christmas period. I imagined Paul McCartney mixing "Let It Be" with this random Kazak tune.

"Caravan oh caravan. Whisper words of wisdom. Caravan. Caravan" - Paul McCartney while whackpacking in Kazakhstan.

In Kazakhstan, I also toured the magnificent Ile Alatau National Park. Snow was everywhere and it was ice cold with epic views all around. Freshly cooked barbecued Shashlyk in Ile Alatau National Park was a definite highlight. But my mind was made up to leave Kazakhstan after just four nights and on the fifth morning. It wasn't anything to do with Almaty. I liked Almaty, but the point was that I reckoned I needed at least 4 weeks in Bishkek, Kyrgyzstan to sort visas for the rest of my Central Asian adventure. Bishkek was a better place to get my visas, plus it had a 90 day stay for Northern Irish people. Kazakhstan allowed me only 14 days as a "British" person at the time, and zero as an "Irish" person. Plus, I knew I would be back in Kazakhstan on this tour anyway. The reason would be that Shymkent (Shimmy) would be a perfect back door entrance after leaving Uzbekistan, further down the line. However, I needed the visas.

"Down the line, down the road, another town, another city" – Joe Blair.

In short, my 14 days in Kazakhstan (that my visa entitled me to) wouldn't allow me time to grab visas for all of Tajikistan, Gorno Badakhshan, Uzbekistan, Afghanistan, Turkmenistan and India.

India?

Did you just say India?? I thought Jonny Blair always skipped India!? Something had now changed. But hey that will wait until chapters to come. With a Slavic charm occupying my mind in Poland, former Soviet Union countries began to dominate my life for now.

Kazak dancer Mina, elegantly and thankfully, also passed me by.

Chapter 42
Magnetic Kyrgyzstan

Bishkek / Frunze, KYRGYZSTAN (December 2015 – April 2016)

"I get the strangest feeling you belong" – Fran Healy.

Without meaning to, I spent the best part of 5 months in Kyrgyzstan. I arrived in December 2015, overland from Almaty on Marshrutkas. I booked to stay in Bishkek, initially for three nights in the Apple Hostel. I guess I expected to move on pretty fast after that.

But like many parts of my journey, this was spontaneous and impulsivic.

Despite being in Bishkek during 5 different calendar months, I was really using Bishkek as my base in the Stans (and India region). Embassies here meant I could get a visa for Uzbekistan, Turkmenistan, Afghanistan, China, Tajikistan, India and Gorno Badakhshan all here, within Bishkek.

"Where do you go? Buttoned in your favourite coat, stepping out to a different world. And you might be home late" - Ocean Colour Scene.

It was mostly out of convenience that Kyrgyzstan, and notably Bishkek became my base. It certainly helped that I met a lot of cool people at the excellent Apple Hostel. Yes, the excellent Apple Hostel! This was to be my home for most of my time in Kyrgyzstan.

In the first week in Bishkek, I had become good friends with Aigul Kubatbekova. Aigul is the owner of Apple Hostel – she's a true example of a real hostel owner – the epitome of how hostels should be run. She's a people person, she's fun, she's lively, she's positive. She inspires.

I should mention that as the 31st of December 2015 arrived in Bishkek city, I had no depression. I wasn't sad. I was lonely, yes; but not sad. I had split up with Panny. But I wasn't sad. I was the complete opposite. This was possibly the most inspirational time of my entire backpacking life. I knew that when 2016 arrived, that would be my first calendar year with clear singleton in evidence. I would be single at 00.01 a.m. on 1st January 2016. That felt exciting. I felt alive and ready for something new.

After 3 days in Apple hostel, I told Aigul I was extending my stay for a further 7 days, and probably longer. I loved the hostel, the city, the vibe, the food, the bars, the cafes. I just liked it and felt at home. I didn't even need to change beds. I was in the bottom bunk on the left on the top floor, where I was in the first room on the left. In the first few days, I had already toured the main sights of Bishkek. Bishkek, formerly Frunze, is a textbook juxtaposition between a throwback to the Soviet Union days with its soldiers marching at Ala Too square to its modernity in the breeding apparence of up and coming entrepreneurial ventures. I just loved that fusion. I've always loved that intermixture. It's why I generally detest the way of life in countries like U.S.A. and Germany for their set ways. Those places just don't fit with my ideals of paradise, in any way, shape or format. Here in Kyrgyzstan, I was magnetised.

"Think twice, it's just another day for you and me in paradise" – Phil Collins.

As well as Bishkek, myself and some of the hostel crew also did a tour to Lake Issy Kul, where we toured Petroglyphs and the Ruh Ordo centre where all religions were represented in the beauty overlooking this magnificent lake. One of my hostel buddies there was Nate, from the U.S.A. Nate shared a lot of my opinions on life, he had spent some years living and working in Russia and he was now doing something similar to me. Nate was backpacking the rest of the countries from the former Soviet Union. Nate was also a blogger and we hung out for a few days. Nate was also about to visit Tajikistan, Uzbekistan, Afghanistan and Turkmenistan. It was Nate who inspired me to go to Afghanistan in fact. For some reason, I hadn't realised how easy it could be to get an Afghanistan visa here in Bishkek. More on all that later.

In Bishkek, I soon realised how Kyrgyz people warmed to foreigners very quickly. Bishkek is a wonderful city for making friends in a short timeframe. It was literally brilliant for it. I could walk into cafés and raise curiosity and chat with locals. As Aigul once professed to me, *"Jonny, Kyrgyz people love it when people write about and promote Kyrgyzstan"* and as a blogger that is what I was doing. This place came into my life at the right time.

I did an interview on my 100 country trip with the local newspaper in Bishkek, I toured the cafes and bars of the city daily and nightly, I reviewed the Apple Hostel and the swanky Europa Hotel and I also reviewed some tours. Through a contact, on those tours, I now had met Evgenia who worked with Silk Road Tours. This was another major turning point on my journey. The networking with Evgenia led to me being able to get my visas for Uzbekistan and Tajikistan easier. I could go even deeper into this, to say that later in life (2018), it was through the same connection that I made it to Turkmenistan. And while doing all of those trips, most of my tours would be sponsored, free or heavily discounted. My accommodation would also be either organised through the tours, or done by myself so I'd be planning not to spend any money on tours or beds for the next few weeks. I'd be spending money mostly on visas, food, drink and transport. I spent the first 10 days in Kyrgyzstan immersing myself in the local life, embracing it, networking and then I realised I should stay at least a month here. Bishkek was an easy city to chill out in.

In that month, I organised my visas from the embassies for Tajikistan, Gorno Badakhshan, Afghanistan and Uzbekistan. Turkmenistan was proving a bit trickier, and as I didn't need a visa to enter Kazakhstan, I started to plan my route.

Basically, I was going to tour a few of the Stans, whilst basing myself here at the Apple Hostel in Bishkek, run by Aigul. Aigul's hostel was the perfect base for all of this. In that month, my writing also excelled and I did some more book edits on cold winter days whilst sipping cappuccinos at either Sierra Coffee or Adriano. Sierra and Adriano had become two of my favourite haunts – still two of my favourite cafés from my entire travels.

This time, I was a real perfectionist. I planned every single day to a tee. It was like clockwork. I'd list the exact borders I'd cross, the places I'd sleep, where to tour and everything was ready. When I left Kyrgyzstan for the first time, my days were meticulously planned. My order of countries / disputed regions up next would be Kyrgyzstan – Tajikistan – Gorno Badakhshan – Tajikistan – Uzbekistan – Afghanistan – Uzbekistan – Karakalpakstan – Uzbekistan – Kazakhstan – Kyrgyzstan. I really planned this part of my travels well, it was immaculate. Unlike some of my previous trips. When I'd arrive back in Kyrgyzstan after that trip, I knew I had more time to plan my next adventure.

As I left Kyrgyzstan that time, I had already afforded it the nickname "Magnetic Kyrgyzstan," a moniker which stuck with me. I've been back three times since of course, living it up to its magnetic name. For this timeframe on life's corridor, Dushanbe was calling me…

Chapter 43
Nights Alive On Monday Town

Dushanbe / Stalinabad / Monday Town, TAJIKISTAN
(January 2016)

"The names on the faces in places, they mean nothing to me"
– Noel Gallagher.

Kyrgyzstan was a brilliant base for backpacking in Central Asia and I managed to secure five of the six visas I wanted while I was there. The only one I didn't manage to get was for Turkmenistan. Later on (in 2018, after relocating to Poland), I was able to get it and visit places like Ashgabat, Mary, Merv and Darvaza. The first four visas I got in Kyrgyzstan were for Tajikistan, Gorno Badakhshan, Uzbekistan and Afghanistan. At the time, I didn't require a visa to visit Kyrgyzstan for 3 months, nor for Kazakhstan for 14 days and the Uzbekistan visa sufficed for a visit to the Republic of Karakalpakstan. The fifth of the sixth visas to obtain, would be India but that adventure was to come.

And so I arrived with so much enthusiasm into Tajikistan that day. I knew I was visiting five completely new countries in the next few months. It was all an adventure like my backpacking glory days. Now that I was single, it gave me time to ponder. While I liked this region, I still didn't think I would fall in love or find a girl here. Then again, I wasn't looking for love, but something inside me told me that I had already met some girls that would later play a part in my journey. They would, and they did, but first up was "Monday Town."

Now for a quiz question. How many football teams have a day of the week in their name? Well you've got Sheffield Wednesday (England), Polonia Środa (Poland), Abergavenny Thursdays (Wales), any "Domingo" Sunday) teams in Spanish speaking countries and then…there's all the Monday clubs in Dushanbe such as CSKA Pamir Dushanbe (Tajikistan). Amongst other "Dushanbe / Monday" teams of course such as Gwardia Dushanbe, FC Istiklol Dushanbe, Dinamo Dushanbe and Hima Dushanbe. As a Bournemouth fan, and a football geek, I happened to know that Aleksei Cherednyk, one of the first USSR footballers to play in England, was at our rival club, Southampton FC. Cherednyk, was also some kind of a legend here in Dushanbe. Dushanbe translates as "Monday." Dushanbe for all its love and vibrancy, was also once called Stalinabad. Ouch.

To be honest, Dushanbe didn't blow my mind – it certainly wasn't in the same league as Bishkek, or Lviv, or Poznań. Those three cities from my recent tour had all been cities I knew I would like to live in. But Dushanbe allowed more time for me to be myself. To be my tourist lonely self, as I didn't have any friends here, except for the travel guide contacts I built up. I had a guided tour of Dushanbe, and a day trip to Hisor, where I toured the castle. I slept at Marian's Guesthouse in Dushanbe, which was really homely and I enjoyed the walk from here down to the city centre, where the world's largest teahouse and second highest national flag on a flagpole were the stand out sights.

What I didn't yet mention is that these countries have disputed regions and yet more "wacaday republics" as I like to call them. Basically the Tajikistan visa only allows you access to the west part of what is generally classed as "Tajikistan." Gorno Badakhshan, the eastern region that borders China requires an extra visa or permit that takes up a full page in your passport. I managed to secure this permit at the Tajikistan embassy in Bishkek. This meant, I would be visiting both countries housed within what many class as Tajikistan. Up next, with my backpack loaded, I went on a truly crazy overland adventure to the city of Khorog. Khorog sits on the Afghanistan border and is the capital of the Gorno Badakhshan Autonomous Oblast, often referred to as "The Pamirs." Hold on tight, this was a death road.

Chapter 44
Death Road

Khorog, GORNO BADAKHSHAN / PAMIRS (January 2016)

"Let me take my chances on the wall of death" –
Richard Thompson.

After touring Hisor and Monday Town (Dushanbe), I headed on the long journey east to Gorno Badakhshan. Sorry where? I had my GBAO visa and I was heading to GBAO. Gorno Badakhshan Autonomous Region, a mountainous separate state often known as "The Pamirs."

I didn't know it then, but I needed to be ready for a death trip - 22 hours of mayhem lay ahead. This was no pleasure cruise, this was an absolute backpacking journey from a lunatic asylum. How about a border crossing within the same country? Is it possible? Yes, kind of. I remember crossing the land border in the DMZ between South and North Korea some five years ago. I also crossed from Ukraine into the Chernobyl Exclusion Zone, which is still inside Ukraine of course but needs a special permit. Some buck eejits class Scotland and England as the same country, others disturbingly do the same with Northern Ireland, Podjistan and the Irish Republic. The same has to be said about these two places - Tajikistan and Gorno Badakhshan.

Tajikistan is clearly the name of the entire country, yet within Tajikistan this is a separate autonomous region and oblast - the Gorno Badakhshan Autonomous Oblast (GBAO).

Before I decided to head from Dushanbe to Khorog, I was advised to contact the authorities in Gorno Badakhshan to ask about traffic issues. Basically in the winter time, every day they issue warnings based on weather. I got myself signed up for these warnings as it helps plan your trip better, and safer. I registered for the GBAO Daily Situation Report and map and they emailed me daily updates so that I knew when it was safe to go. Weather and landslides are a big issue here. With hindsight, I'd also blame the roads.

Okay so the route I personally took to get to Gorno Badakhshan was overland, in winter from Dushanbe, the capital of Tajikistan and I planned to go all the way to Khorog, capital of Gorno Badakhshan. The roads are a disaster in winter so if you ever decide to follow my journeys, you need to be aware that this is not that safe. There are flights to Khorog's tiny airport but they're not really for a budget backpacker, coming in at around $100 US one way. In hindsight, though, such a flight would have saved me a lot of stress and effort, not to mention I wouldn't have nearly died. Plus, if I had booked the flight, this chapter of "I Went To Gdańsk With Somebody" wouldn't exist.

After receiving the email update to say the roads seemed to be open the next day, and that my overland venture would work, I got up early the next morning and headed to the bus station, near the old green market in Dushanbe. I had been told that this journey would take me 8 hours. That felt quite long to me, but it would be worth it. However, if only it was only 8 hours.

Here is my timeline of that day in my life, which was a day of pure lunacy.

6:30 a.m. - I awoke and munched my breakfast at the excellent Marian's Guesthouse in Dushanbe, Tajikistan, already packed for my journey.

7:45 a.m. - I got a lift from Said at Travel in Tajikistan - he took me from the guesthouse to the bus station. Said was also my tour guide for Hisor and Monday Town.

7:55 a.m. - I am already inside my 4 x 4! I am so early. I can't wait, so if it's around 8 a.m. now, then we should be in Khorog at 16.00 or 4 p.m. at the latest right? This jeep is an 8 seat Range Rover. There is one other Tajik girl inside. We agree on a price of 280 Somoni to take me from Dushanbe to Khorog. This is about £28 so not too cheap, but saving a lot on the flight and some adventure lay ahead! I can't wait to leave and hope the car fills up soon. Another guy from Afghanistan gets in at 8:10 a.m. Now there are 3 of us, waiting to have 8 people in the jeep so we can set off.

8:55 a.m. - The car is still not filled up. I'm going a bit crazy as some people get in, then get out again. It looked at one point we were ready to go. Nothing is happening. We are going nowhere. I have been here for one hour, no issue hopefully.

9:55 a.m. - The car is still not filled up. I'm still going a bit crazy as some people get in, then get out again. It looked at one point we were ready to go. Nothing is happening. We are still going nowhere. I have been here for two hours, no issue hopefully.

10:39 a.m. - The car is still not filled up, but we actually move about 5 metres! There are now two new passengers, but the first girl has now gone. We are back to having 4 out of the 8 we need. It's becoming quite lonely and infuriating. If I had known it would take this long, I would have left my backpack on the seat and gone to have coffee for 3 hours! I did do some writing, but as each second ticked by, I had no idea when we would leave. The entire place is static. I guess I was still new to Central Asia at the time, but this was slower than most places I had been in Africa, notoriously the slowest continent for overlanding.

10:43 a.m. - We have 4 passengers now and we move to the front of the Autovagzal (Bus Station). However, I still have no idea if we will be leaving soon. It has been almost 5 hours since I awoke and

I am still in Dushanbe!! The lads start loading loads of stuff onto the roof rack. I don't know if this is a good sign or a bad sign!!

11:10 a.m. - Two girls arrive and they just hang around chatting. At various points, they get in the car, then out again, in again, out again. I can only assume this is normal here and everybody in Dushanbe except for me knows what is happening! We have a random document check with our driver and move again, a few more metres. There are now only 3 empty seats. I have been here for over three hours now, no issue hopefully.

11:12 a.m. - Just as I think we are making progress, we move a further 20 metres and stop again. I assume each time we are somehow crawling towards the exit of the bus station and at some point today, we will finally leave Dushanbe.

Now the driver gets out, and so does one of the passengers. It's becoming frustrating and infuriating. I use my book to translate and try to ask what is going on, but nobody here has an issue with it. To me - it would have just made sense to have a car with "Khorog - leaving when full" (in Tajik) written on it. But it seems that there are 20 - 30 cars the same as the one I am in, all waiting to fill up. There is no first come, first served system. I am sure I have just been unlucky and picked the slowest moving car in history. Since I awoke some five hours ago, I have moved about 1 mile from the Guesthouse, about 23 metres of that was probably in the bus station bus park. The only positives I can think of is that I haven't had to pay yet or hand over any passport. I feel safe but I am itching to get on the adventure to Khorog!

I could just up and leave but my plan is to backpack the sights of Khorog, head to the Afghanistan border and to stay in the awesome Pamir Lodge for three nights. I knew all the time, that the final destination of this trip would be worth it. And of course, later it would prove to be worth it. However on this morning, at 11:13

a.m. I was still stuck in Dushanbe, former name - Stalinabad. Great.

11:14 a.m. - A Frontera pulls up in front of us now. We are told to get out of the vehicle. What the fuck is going on??? We are now ushered into the Frontera, a smaller vehicle. I don't speak Russian, Tajik, Farsi or Dari and nobody else speaks English so it has been tough. And of course there are no other tourists or backpackers in sight here. It's really frustrating.

11:31 a.m. - Hold on, what's happening, are we actually leaving??? We have now managed to fill the car then had to all get out again for some reason. I never worked out why. But we get back in and by 11:32 a.m. we have finally left Dushanbe Bus Station. Is it too good to be true?

Sadly yes! Then the driver gets quizzed on the way out of the station, then we stop for petrol. I have been awake for almost 6 hours and I am still in the same city! This is backpacking travel in a nutshell but at least I knew I was trying, I was doing my best to be heading overland to Khorog. I think.

11:41 a.m. - We stop for "black market petrol" by the side of the road on the edge of Dushanbe, presumably it's cheaper than a petrol station, or its the driver's mate. The price of the trip to Khorog is now 300 Somoni. I reluctantly pay the extra 20, I was told it was 280 Somoni earlier. But the others all pay 300 Somoni too so I know I haven't been ripped off as a tourist. The extra price was presumably because we were now in a smaller car and we couldn't fill the original 8 seats. I whack some music on and put my headphones in. I'm content.

11:46 a.m. – The car is now full of people, full of petrol and I've been awake for 6 hours. We still haven't left the periphery of

Dushanbe, but are on the road out of the city finally. Wow, what a relief! Yee ha!

2 p.m. - After a long drive through drab scenery and a few villages, we pass a fort called Hulbuk, before the town of Kurbon Shaid / Kurban Said.

2:31 p.m. - We arrive in Kulob, this is Tajikistan's third biggest city.

2:41 p.m. - We stop for lunch in Kulob. I pay 12 Somoni in a nice restaurant for a good pilov of rice, beef and carrots and 7 Somoni for a lemon juice. That's less than 2 US Dollars. There was no time for sightseeing but a sports arena out the back had a photo of a football team on it. I still love those random moments on my travels where I see something quickly and then leave, never to return to that town.

3:12 p.m. - We leave Kulob and are now on route to the border checkpoint with Gorno Badakhshan region, which of course requires the special permit. I find out that my Afghan friend on board is called Faruk and he actually speaks better English than the Tajik guys. Not that any of them should of course – it's their country. I should be speaking their language, not vice versa. I ain't no travel snob; though similarly I ain't no polyglot, sadly.

3:49 p.m. - After some epic driving up icy roads and bumpy corners of snow, we arrive at the entry point for Gorno Badakhshan! It becomes exciting now!

There is a hut on the right, a double gate in front and a Tajikistan flag on the left. It is cold, icy, snowy and windy. We stop. This is the border.

The soldier at the checkpoint takes the foreigners passports - mine and Faruk's Afghanistan passport to check the documents are all in order. He is away for about 3 - 4 minutes checking. I get slightly nervous about what he is doing. I'm alone here, something I often seemed to forget on all my backpacking days.

In the meantime however, there is bad news…we have broken down!!!

We cannot get the car to start, madness!! Plus it's already 8 hours into the trip, and we haven't even crossed into Gorno Badakhshan yet so the predictions that the entire journey would be 8 hours were very very wrong.

Here at the checkpoint, no passport stamps are given, but the permits were checked and our passports are handed back. They noticed my Afghanistan visa in the passport but they didn't ask me if I was going there, or what border I would be using. Incidentally, my route to Afghanistan would be later - via Termiz in southern Uzbekistan, rather than the common market border options here in Gorno Badakhshan.

I help with the engine and we have to push the car to get it started through deep mud in the bitter cold winter. It was actually lucky we broke down **here**, as there are soldiers to help, and huts for shelter from the now heavy snow and unsightly roads ahead. There is a quick chance for photos too, as it's the border and I meet a guy from Khorog here.

The car breaks down again and sheep come passing through in a herd. With the army guys, we push the car and get it started again and we are all good to go now! I'm still worried about the car though – it has broken down twice, roads are icy, slippy and rocky. Snow is falling heavily. This whole adventure doesn't feel safe anymore.

4:02 p.m. - But we are not yet there, in Gorno Badakhshan. We have another checkpoint and stop on the Gorno Badakhshan side and passports are checked again. This time, bags are checked too. When this blurred barrier goes back up, we are finally officially in the autonomous region of Gorno Badakhshan, entering in the Dashtijum area. It is Dashtijum, however there isn't really a village here that I notice, despite maps saying that Shohon-i Poin is the first city on this side of the checkpoint. Even that in itself sounds like a different language, a different world.

4:20 p.m. - We now head down some mud roads and valleys, there is one village with a Mosque on our side and then we get lower onto the Shurabad Pass. The Pyanj River is to the right. Beyond and behind this, lies Afghanistan. It looks magical. This is my debut glimpse of Afghanistan. It's misty, tranquil and peaceful. All is quiet.

"It's oh so quiet, it's oh so still" – Björk.

4:53 p.m. - We arrive in daylight in the village of Zigar. It is a small village, which is muddy and obscure. We stop for petrol and it feels like this could be the last petrol station for miles and miles. We break down again here, but we push and off we go! It sometimes feels like we are rolling from one village to the next, praying we get there. However, daylight, nor weather, nor road conditions are on our side. We are in the hands of God.

5:31 p.m. - Daylight is starting to fade and we have a quick stop by gorgeous valleys. It's basically a cigarette stop for the others. For me though, it is a chance to make a video and take some photos of Afghanistan, which is across the river from us, only about 50 metres away. I just find it inspiring, and worth the money and time so far for the views that I savour. However, the breakdowns still make it a scary time.

5:51 p.m. - I was surprised that we have another checkpoint here. We are well into the wilderness by now, daylight has faded completely and darkness and heavy rain is all around. It's really lonely and remote here. It's a tad eerie. I haven't been to many places as ridiculous as this. It is a checkpoint at Kalai Khum – in the Darvaz region, so I'm told. After this, the road is tarmacked (for the first time since leaving Kulob) so we go a bit faster. Then it just becomes mud roads again and we slide through the rain. None of these roads feel safe.

6:55 p.m. - We stop at the town of Kalai Khum (definitely this time). This is supposed to be a dinner stop, but I don't want to eat - I had food with me already. Clever tourists eat on the move, to save time. Even the driver is fast – he munches as he drives and grabs quick bites. Me - I just want to get to the destination, but the two ladies on board need a full meal up. We waste half an hour waiting here for them to eat at a table. The thing is – this is their culture and sometimes as a tourist, I'm too selfish and too eager to keep moving. In the meantime, I buy some mallows and wafers in the local shop and have a beer. I needed that. I felt a bit stressed but it also felt good to have made it into another wacaday country on my journey - Gorno Badakhshan, the Pamir Region and celebrate somehow with a beer. It's a lonely life sometimes. In fact, I shouldn't have been moaning or upset here. I had cracked open a beer in the darkness of country 130 or something.

7:20 p.m. - The ladies were faster at dinner than expected and we leave Kalai Khum with a road sign saying we are 240 kilometres from Khorog!! 240 kilometres still?? At this speed and at this rate, it will be early morning before we are there. If we ever get there. I'm pretty scared now.

8:40 p.m. - There is another checkpoint now at Vanj Valley and passports are checked again. This is the fourth and final checkpoint. Sometimes I think these checkpoints are here for safety rather than checking passports. It's just so they know how many passengers there are heading that way, and what countries they are from. I'm thinking it's so that they can call the Afghanistan and Northern Ireland embassies in the event of a likely accident.

We are in isolation - if we break down, these checkpoints might be the only shelter on a cold winter night. I'm actually glad of the checkpoints by this point – they are presumably there to track the traffic. Since these roads are so dangerous and everything to the right is a death valley, they are probably just noting the cars that come through, safely. I calm my mind to that thought.

12:05 a.m. – It's another day now. This is really scary. Out the window to my right, almost the whole journey, I'm aware there is a huge drop down to the valley and river. If we fall, if the car slides, we'll all die. I fear for my life, every second. It's really scary and probably the only time I felt that scared on a land vehicle since the death buses in Ethiopia in 2013. Then, this happens…

We have an accident.

It could have been fatal.

We are lucky to be alive.

It's that simple. We are so lucky. I can't begin to explain this luck. I was scared. We were done for. The entire last four hours of driving, the roads are icy, slippy and we are basically driving alongside a huge cliff, to the right of me (in the passenger seat) a river. One nasty swerve and we are done for. And that almost happened here.

This is the best way I can describe it.

The car swivelled in the ice a full 180 degrees, with the back part of the vehicle hanging over the cliff. It was hanging over the cliff edge. We daren't look down. It was one of those moments, we were saved by a huge rock that stopped the car. There was no barrier. Without that rock, we were surely all dead. We had been saved by the grace of God. As I looked down beyond that rock, from the back lights of the car, I saw the border river with Afghanistan once again and we all knew how lucky we had been. Nobody was injured. It was just lucky that we were not driving fast and the car had swerved before nestling onto that rock.

I prayed a lot and couldn't now sleep - we had to be careful. Our driver slowed down even more after that.

We had diced with death and survived.

2 a.m. - I got a text message on my mobile phone, saying "Welcome to Afghanistan" because we were now right at the border bridge. I certainly wasn't counting my chickens or celebrating. We weren't there yet. This was a death road. I was scared the whole way.

There was a mini checkpoint of the car again, but not of passports. Again, I think it was road safety. Our driver reported the swerving and the accident to the officials here. All accidents had to be noted. We were also extremely lucky that no cars were coming the opposite way when we crashed. It was a dangerous night. The sleet, hail, snow, rain, ice and wind, didn't stop. It's easily one of the scariest nights of my travels so far.

3:10 a.m. - We seem to have got through the worst part of the road. The roads are now only snow and less ice. We drop one of the ladies off at Porshnev town (I believe) and the driver asks me where I am staying. I feel great relief in him asking me this.

I told him I was sleeping at Pamir Lodge. He didn't understand, but luckily I had Said's number, the owner of the guesthouse and I expected my driver would have a local mobile phone. Though in this deep mountainous region, I didn't keep my hopes up.

3:30 a.m. - We are finally in Khorog and we drop Faruk off at his mates house and the other passengers stay on, to get off after me. My driver was advised by Faruk as to where he thought Pamir Lodge might be. Faruk was spot on.

4 a.m. - Up a steep hill in darkness, we arrive at Pamir Lodge. Yes! We have made it. I have a cosy room, I am welcomed in by Said, my host at 4 a.m.!!! He says I can get some sleep then come for my breakfast at 8 - 10 a.m.! I am so happy I have made it. 22 hours from door to door! We are safe.

This was an absolute crazy trip on my journey. One of the oddest borders I have ever crossed, one of the scariest journeys and I was happy to be here safe and sound in Khorog. Please be aware of the road hazards and risks of travelling in this region in winter - it is not easy. Take it from me. Phew!

Little did I know that I would cross about 5 more land borders in the next 3 weeks including the Uzbekistan to Afghanistan border across Friendship Bridge and a truly Timmy Mallet inspired Wacaday trip to Nukus, capital of Karakalpakstan. In the meantime in Khorog, I toured the sights, met up with a volunteer group and enjoyed the hospitality of the Pamir Lodge. I knew that up next would be Uzbekistan and Afghanistan.

To date, I have no idea where that alleged "8 hour trip no problem" idea came from, this trip took almost 24 hours door to door, and I almost died, but somehow I made it! We are truly blessed.

"I am blessed" – Eternal.

Chapter 45
Ruud Bullet

Friendship Bridge, Termiz, UZBEKISTAN (February 2016)
Hayratan, AFGHANISTAN (February 2016)

"There's a bullet in the gun. There's a fire in your heart"
– Planet Perfecto.

Make no mistake about it. This was a backpacker's paradise. A dream inspired. This was the dream. This was the reason why I loved to travel. This won't be a short chapter. It's probably the longest one in this book, though I won't have time to check that. I awoke early morning in the Sorxan Atlantic Hotel. I headed for coffee and breakfast in what was a textbook communist style hotel. This was once the southernmost hotel in the former Soviet Union. I was backpacking in the city of Termiz. Where the helicopter is that?

Two months earlier, I'd have asked myself the same question. My journeys were long, crazy, off the wall and unpredictable. I ended up in villages without shops, towns without hotels and cities I had simply never heard of. I stepped out of a taxi share all alone in the wild city of Termiz.

Termiz was wacaday. It is as simple as that. When I arrived in Termiz, I had nowhere booked to stay. It was the only city on this trip that I hadn't made precise plans for.

Question: Why was I even in Termiz?

Answer: I was in Termiz because it is the southernmost city in Uzbekistan and serves as an entrance point to Afghanistan. There is a remote land and river border here. From Termiz, I would be crossing on Friendship Bridge from Uzbekistan to Hayratan in

Afghanistan. That was a dream for tomorrow. For today, I wanted a bed, some food, some money, a spot of sightseeing and maybe some Wi-Fi. 4 out of 5 wasn't bad. The Wi-Fi was not forthcoming.

On arrival in Termiz, I was dumped shyly and solitudinally out in a small car park. My shared taxi mates headed on their merry way. Like many times in my life, I was the only tourist here. As far as I could tell.

I had a small backpack with me and I had a visa for Afghanistan in my passport. I also, thankfully had a second visa for Uzbekistan. I wrote thankfully, because I was landbordering myself into Afghanistan and then back across the same border into Uzbekistan. Three weeks before this trip, I had neither visa. Five weeks before this trip, I didn't expect to be doing this trip!

Here in Termiz, the sky was undark but it was late afternoon. It was dry and cold. I knew of only two hotels in Termiz. I would first head to the most expensive one. I would bargain with them for a cheap no frills room for the night if I would be able to review them on my website.

Security was tight and my bags were checked on the way in. There was no bargain awaiting me here. They barely budged with discount. I declined the offer of their room but grabbed a beer in their lobby bar as they actually had Wi-Fi! What?!

To my non surprise, the Wi-Fi didn't work of course. After that drink, I headed back onto a main boulevard to find the other hotel. This was the Sorxan Atlantic Hotel. They gave me a discount. It's the sort of place I'd want to write about anyway, but they were kind. Breakfast was included.

I got into my incredible room late afternoon. Views were magnificent. There was of course no Wi-Fi here.

After dumping my bags off in my room, I headed straight for the city market. This wasn't actually for sightseeing or to buy food, but to change money. Not only would I need money for Afghanistan, but Uzbekistan is ridiculously strict on its borders. I heard many scare stories. Of course, later on I learnt that such scare stories were untrue and mostly concocted by newbie travellers.

The scare stories were that on arrival into Uzbekistan at any border (be it land, sea, bridge or air) you need to declare the EXACT amount of money that you have on your possession. In every currency! And I was also told by many different sources (including fellow whackpackers and Uzbekistan Embassy staff) that when you leave the country you must have the exact same amount of money on your departure as you had on your arrival!!

When I heard that, I really couldn't believe it. It just felt ridiculous to me. I was an experienced backpacker of 120+ countries and I had never heard of any country ever doing that. I remember sitting in Marian's Guesthouse in Dushanbe the night before leaving Tajikistan and thinking it cannot be true. I simply refused to believe the money rumours. I had a double entry visa for Uzbekistan you see and I knew I would enter by land twice, at Tursunzoda and Hayratan. I would also leave by land twice, at Hayratan and Chernyaevka / Zhibek Zholy.

That night in Dushanbe, I checked my currencies. I had ten different currencies in my possession!! Wow – how on earth are they actually going to force me to come and go with exactly the same amount of cash – it makes no sense! What if I lose some of it? What if I give some of it away? On me, I had Northern Irish pounds, English pounds, Polish złotych, European "no country" Euros, USA Dollars, Ukrainian Hvarna, Kazakhstan Tenge, Kyrgyz Som, Tajikistan Somoni and Uzbekistan Som.

So if the scare tactics were to be believed, I would have to write every single coin and banknote on the immigration entry form to Uzbekistan and on the immigration departure form. So I did that! If they want to play that game, I play that game. It felt ridiculous and I was pretty sure that all those scare tactics would be proved wrong at the border. I filled pages just documenting my coins and banknotes!

When you travel you meet many other travellers and you often ask them for tips and advice about places they have just been. But this fact about the money kept being told to me - I just noticed a ridiculous trend of people telling me the same thing about Uzbekistan. I just couldn't believe it could be true.

The truth?

I was, of course, right – it was completely untrue!! They did not want to check the exact amount of multiple currencies you were bringing into the country at all. I knew it. I just wondered where on earth all those fellow tourists got that information from. It's a baffler!

In retrospect, what they told me was cow excrement and untrue completely. Yet more than 6 people told me this – "When you arrive and exit Uzbekistan you must have the exact same amount of money on you, you must declare every single cent of every single currency. No less, no more. It is that strict. They count every penny, so declare every currency." The first time I heard this, I laughed and said it was a lie, but more and more people told me the same thing, so stupidly I believed it.

However, as all those fellow tourists had told me that, I did what they said on my first border entry to Uzbekistan, from Tajikistan. As I mentioned, at the time, I had about 10 different currencies on me and if those rumours from fellow tourists were to be believed, it meant that I would have to write them all down, spend nothing in the country and leave with the same amount of cash to the exact penny. I was trying to work out why this had to be done and what was it all about. Uzbekistan was probably something like my 124th country and I had never had any country that strict about money so far. So...the night before I left Tajikistan, I was in Dushanbe in Marianne's Guesthouse and I counted EVERY single penny / cent of every single currency. I collect banknotes and coins, so for example at the time, I'd probably only 5 Polish złotych in coins and about 6 in groszy. I did the same for all the other currencies. Some of this was simply my banknote collection. I wrote everything down to be exact. The list was long – I had every penny accounted for.

However, I was also told that at the border entry to Uzbekistan they would check everything in my backpack, laptop, camera, phone etc. It was time to see if these rumours were true or not.

The next morning, I crossed from Tajikistan into Uzbekistan and some of what those rumours said were correct - the border guys at the bag checks searched everything - every file on my computer and hard drive (which they almost broke), they looked at the money thing, asked to see some of that money, but when the guy saw I had written down like 5 or 6 Polish złotych he basically ignored it, saying it wasn't important. They didn't care about any of that at all! It was complete excrement what others had told me. However, maybe I thought, this was because I had so far only entered Uzbekistan. Perhaps when I go to leave the country, that might change. I pondered on that and thought that was maybe what all those fellow travellers meant – leaving the country would be different.

So now, I tried to do that that night in Termiz, the day before I was due to leave Uzbekistan and enter Afghanistan. I checked my banknotes - Polish złotych - the same, Ukrainian Hvarna - the same, Euros - the same, Kazakhstan Tenge - the same, Kyrgyz Som - the same, Tajikistan Somoni - the same, British pounds - the same, Northern Irish pounds - the same.

All good so far. I entered with the same, I'd leave with the same. Except for these two currencies -

Uzbek Som and US Dollars.

It was now that I realised what the drama might be all about – the black market.

I cannot remember how much Uzbek Som I changed at the border, or in Samarkand, or in Bukhara but I did it all on the black market. I am not sure how many US Dollars I had when I entered the country. Let's say it was $425 (for example).

At the time, the black market meant that swapping say $100 US would get you double the rate that a bank would give you in Som. But I did all my changing on the black market – it's what you do in Uzbekistan. You find a guy in a market and you swap the money there, often round the back of a market or a shop so that nobody sees it happening.

So if I had $425 US and if I believed all those people that told me the money had to be exactly level (or less) when leaving, I would have to leave the country to Afghanistan with the exact amount that I arrived there in. That seemed impossible to do now. Now I saw the problem – I would be leaving the country with MORE money than when I came in.

Let me make up the figures for the example - I think in Samarkand I swapped $100 US of that, so I currently had $325 US and $100 US worth of Som, which was actually $200 US due to the black market rate. So in other words, **I was now up by $100 US**. I was richer in four days in the country, even though I had bought food and paid for transport (my hotels and tours were free). All my tours and accommodation was sponsored as part of being a blogger so I'd have no outgoings in that sense, but then again, I couldn't exactly tell the police or border guys that could I? They'd think I was a spy or a journalist or something. And I wasn't - I was just a tourist, who happened to love tourism and writing, and therefore I was also a blogger and a writer.

Also in 2016, when I visited, you needed to have a document as proof of where you slept every night! Yes that is true and at the time they checked it very very strictly. Even though my accommodation was sponsored, all my homestays provided me with the relevant document that proved I slept there.

For whatever reason, I decided to swap another $100 US for Uzbek Som in the market/bazaar in Termiz. At one point, I declared this as the "biggest mistake of my entire travels," but looking back now, it seems more minor than that. I still can't remember why I changed that extra $100 US, but it meant I clearly now had much more money after 4/5 days in the country than I did when I arrived. This would be so suspicious, and I was worried would they arrest me, fine me, rob me, imprison me, but most of all would they stop me from living my dream and backpacking across the border into Afghanistan. My biggest worry here was that I wouldn't get into Afghanistan because of this extra money.

When I got back to the hotel I realised I now had way too much money for the border crossing so I thought of 3 options -

1. Spend loads of money on one night (hard to do in Uzbekistan).
2. Leave some of that money hidden under a bed in my room in this hotel and demand to stay in the same hotel and same room when I returned in three or four days' time - this would be tricky. Someone could find the money, check that I was in that room and

tell the police. Or someone could move into that room and I'd never see my money again. Or the hotel would get suspicious and would check the room themselves to find the money.
3. Cross into Afghanistan with more money than I had 4 days ago when I entered from Tajikistan (They'd probably ask for ATM/payment receipt etc.).

Even though, this seems like a ridiculous worry, I was genuinely really scared. It felt like a scene from the movie "Brewster's Millions" but I didn't know what to do.

That's right – I was about to go backpacking in Afghanistan and my biggest fear was that I'd be arrested in Uzbekistan for having more money on me now than when I arrived. Would they think I was a drug smuggler or something. And then I realised – the only reason I was worrying was because of what others had told me. I didn't believe them, so why was I worrying?

I was being an idiot. I was always more selfish than that. I always trusted myself more than others and so, I stuck with trusting myself. Just take all the money across the border. In the end then, I thankfully chose option 3 and just hid all those millions of Uzbek Som all over my body - in my socks, pants, shoes, coat pockets etc. I expected paper money wouldn't bleep in the scanner. And I'd have the exact money on leaving as what I had when I entered.

When I was leaving Uzbekistan, the border checks were crazy, I was there for 2-3 hours I think, they checked everything, but they never checked the money. Weird that, right? Everything else was checked. Laptop, hard drives, even condom packets and anything those guards just wanted to check.

On the same trip, I left and entered Uzbekistan 4 times and actually - it was all a big lie. They don't need the money to match up and be the same. They don't care - it was a huge lie. I still have no idea why many other fellow tourists started spreading those rumours, but they just weren't true...at least they weren't in February 2016.

However, the drama at the border was a lot more crazy than that. Firstly, when I arrived at the border that morning, I was told that strictly "the border is closed Sir." My dream to backpack into Afghanistan seemed over before it all began. All this drama.

Then, while stood at the guard post in Termiz, one of the guys speaks a bit of English and he explains to me that the guy was just telling me that the border is closed at the moment. In other words – now! Because it was only 8 a.m.!!

It closes at night for security reasons but not to worry, it will open soon. Brilliant! He was right. At 8.25 a.m. the soldier signalled for myself and four others – all Afghanis or Uzbeks to come through the gate. The five of us are ushered to show our passports, mine takes longer to check given that I'm not from either Afghanistan or Uzbekistan. The sweat is over.

"I sold ma soul with ma cigarettes to the black market men" – Don Walker.

However, if the money thing wasn't an issue - I'll say this now as you need to know it – after United States of America, Uzbekistan is the strictest country I have ever been to for border checks, bags and belongings searches. They check everything. They check your wallet, every sim card, memory card, hard drive including all the images on it. Pornography is forbidden in the country so delete any photos of Carol Vorderman's tits or Brad Pitt's willy before you get to the border checks. I had photos of me naked in Finland (sauna), Antarctica (polar plunge), my willy after circumcision (ouch!) and I had to delete ALL those photos and email them to myself! After leaving Uzbekistan for the last time, I could then download them from my emails and put them all back on my hard drive!

At the first passport check, one Uzbek soldier calls on his radio to alert his mates that there is one tourist from (Northern) Ireland (I used my Irish passport for this trip) on route to Afghanistan. It's a novelty for them and a brace of equally childish Uzbek peelers crowd round to check my visas are in order. They ask me a few quick questions and then show me to a bus. I have to get on this bus and take it the further 800 metres to the next passport control check. I was going to walk it but I assumed the bus was free as it was within the border zone. I fired my backpack onto the bus and we drove the 3 minute journey to the next gate. The other 4 guys got on the bus with me. There's a catch. The bus costs 5,000 Som (just over $1USD). At least that's $1 USD less when leaving the country just in case that money issue was a problem, I was actually happy to pay it! I pay it and get off. It's now 8.35 a.m.

I filled in the forms in detail. I left no stone un-turned and I headed into the security check room. The officer confirmed all my details are correct. He also asked me where I went in Uzbekistan and if I had registered every night. I told him Denau, Samarkand, Bukhara and Termiz and I had all the necessary proof. When backpacking in Uzbekistan I had made sure to get a registration slip from my hotel / accommodation every night. As a travel writer, I was getting free stays in most hotels but even then, I could still always get a registration slip so no worries there.

He checked my Afghanistan TOURIST visa and asks why I am going there. *"Tourism"* I replied, smugly and obviously – *"it's what it says on the visa mate."* I proceeded to bombard him with a list of backpacking sights I aim to tick off in Afghanistan. Masar e Sharif, Takht e Rostam, Balkh, Tashkurgan, Samangan. At this point he was satisfied with my paper work and passport so it's time for the bag and body check.

"Propaganda as a substitute for action was the essence of fascism" – Mac Smith.

Everything was checked. With scanners, with scanning devices and there was a separate room which is private. One for males, one for females. In here they can ask you to get naked if they suspect anything. I had heard of one girl that had to show her boobies at the Uzbek to Tajik border, she had to show them to another female. But he just body checked me – I had hid Uzbek Som in my socks and pockets.

All the time he was checking my bag I kept thinking of the extra money I had. I hid 200,000 of it in a side pocket of my winter coat! Yes, I was carrying 600 grand on me and I hid 200 grand from him! He checked my camera, my phone, my laptop, my hard drive. It took ages. Uzbeks don't care about time. They love to waste their time and yours and they laugh immaturely as they do it. So my laptop was checked thoroughly.

**"You're wasting your time, and my time as well" –
The Seahorses.**

After the strict border bag search, I was free but as I tried to leave the final exit point of Uzbekistan, the soldier reminds me in local lingo *"here mate ye forgot till get yer Uzbekistan exit stamp"* and he was right!! I had my exit document and he saw me coming from baggage control so he knew I'd had my bag checked. But I hadn't yet got my exit stamp. I feared another long delay here but he ushered me to a booth and within thirty seconds I have that exit stamp and the soldier opens the door. I'm out of Uzbekistan. Yee-ha! And the buzz comes back. I adjust my watch back by 30 minutes – Afghanistan is 30 minutes behind.

An odd feeling enters my mind now. As I backpack from Uzbekistan to Afghanistan, I ask into myself "what country are you in?." The answer is simply "none." I'm standing on planet earth, on land, but I am officially in no country. I have my exit stamp for Uzbekistan. This means I am no longer in Uzbekistan. But I have no entry stamp yet for Afghanistan. I am in no country. I am in no-man's land. Nobody will protect me here. Neither Uzbekistan nor Afghanistan can take care of me here. The feeling is an odd release. From the moment I said goodbye to the last Uzbek soldier, I am walking alone down a road to Friendship Bridge.

My backpacking buddy Nate Jacobs wrote about his experience here too – he felt the loneliness as well and I remember reading his blog just before my trip. Now I was in his shoes and I knew exactly how he felt. The way was long and lonesome. It's pretty remote. I couldn't help be inspired though.

"You come in on your own and you leave on your own" – Richard Ashcroft.

There is nobody else on the bridge. Not a soul. No Uzbek soldiers. No Afghan soldiers. The bridge is over a river and I walk onto it alone. The other four guys that I met at the first control point are gone. They're already in Afghanistan. They were faster than me through immigration since they are local. I cross the bridge alone. Of course I do. On the "Uzbek side" of the bridge there are videos cameras. I know for a fact some Uzbek lunatic is watching me. That's what they're like. Halfway across the bridge the cameras stop.

There are no cameras visible on the "Afghan side." To all intents and purposes, I am in Afghanistan.

As a dull cloud clears and a winter sun smiles down on me, I am in Afghanistan. At this moment, a freight train energises its way past me, just to remind me there are other people around. I briefly envisage Ringo Starr belting out a shit Thomas the Tank Engine line. This is truly off the rails though. This is one of the happiest memories of my entire life.

I'm already at the entry point for Afghanistan. A hat-trick of Afghan flags are here on my right, it's exciting. And a "Welcome to Afghanistan" sign is in front of me!!

I'm here. I have done it! I have crossed Friendship Bridge. The land I'm standing on is Afghanistan. There is nobody else about, the train has long since passed. Oddly, the sun now shines, the clouds clear. Shame on you, Uzbekistan. This was a subliminal message, the sun's out for me here, in Afghanistan – your rival. There's a Northern Irishman in town.

An Afghan soldier raises his non-gun arm to greet me, he looks friendly and is saying hello. "Salam Alekum" I say to him. He shakes my hand, smiles, opens the gate and lets me in. I'm sent to room 204, Passport Control. The building is small, I doubt there are 203 rooms before this one. But it is room 204, nonetheless. As well as my mate Nate Jacobs, we appear to be the only two tourists who have crossed this border in the last few months. I mean backpacking tourists. The list of names in the book is small and apart from those 4 Afghan/Uzbek guys, there was nobody else. It's normally just Uzbeks and Afghans crossing here.

I head into the room where an equally friendly Afghan guy takes my passport, fingerprints and a photo.

"What's in your bag?" the border guard asks.
"Books, clothes, toiletries and passion," I reply.
"Irlandi?" he says, meaning Ireland, *"capital city?."*
"Belfast," I smurkily and deliberately lied back at him, reiterating *"Belfast City. That's our capital."*
"Dublin?" he asks. He's educated, this dude. I do a Mickey Mouse impression and he laughs with me. He stamps my passport and welcomes me in. *"Belfast, North Ireland"* he says, looking into my eyes. He knows what I meant; and I smile.

There are no issues here whatsoever. He's happy to see me. I am delighted to be here. See the blue sky? That's Afghanistan. I'm in. I'm in Afghanistan! I walk past some barbed wire, some sandbags and a few barricades that wouldn't look out of place in Belfast. I am now in Hayratan, Afghanistan!

Due to the 30 minute difference in Afghan time, it's now 9:17 a.m. I was on tour here in Afghanistan with Untamed Borders and was due to meet my contact Noor, at 9 a.m. I'm 17 minutes late, but no worries as he is a bit late too! Excellent timing actually!

I talk to the friendly border guards, they're all armed and I turn down a taxi driver who offered to take me to Masar e Sharif. *"I'm waiting on a friend,"* I told him. Within 5 minutes, Noor is here, along with his mate Mohammed Reza and our driver Sakhi! They pull up in a car near the border. It has been an exciting journey, but now I'm in Afghanistan, the fun really begins! It was off to tour Masar e Sharif, Balkh, Tashkurgan, Aybak, Samangan, eat some Mantoo and smoke some Shisha over the next few days!

Time taken at Uzbekistan exit point: 1 hour, 2 minutes.
Time taken at Afghanistan entry point: 6 minutes.

Okay so there was one final passport check. After driving away from the border, the exit gate for Hayratan town is armed and manned by soldiers.

On the way I spoke to Mohammed Reza who was once an under-19 international footballer for Afghanistan. "Ever heard of Belfast Glentoran?" I venture at him. Of course he hasn't but when I show him the top that has green, red and black colours we notice it's the same as the Afghanistan flag! I snapped a photo of it as we slide through the security gate.

They ask to see my passport at this checkpoint and that's it. Off we go, heading to Masar e Sharif, my first proper stop in the country – to check into my hotel! There is no doubt that when I look back on all of my travels, the time in Termiz and the border crossing and subsequent arrival in Afghanistan was by far the most representative 24 hours of what travel is all about. It had ups and downs; scares and jokes; loneliness and camaraderie; knowns and unknowns; friends and foes; lies and truths.

There were many highlights in Afghanistan, but for me the standout memory will always be the day we went to the old Buddhist Monastery at Samangan. At that Buddhist Monastery, we toured a Buddhist Stupa atop a hill in the wilderness.

Noor gives me a tour and insight into the history here, before glancing at the ground and spotting a bullet.

"Jonny, here's a present for you" he says in pure honesty *"it's a bullet, it's a remnant from the civil war. Keep it. Keep it for good luck."*

Down below, I spot a load of kids playing football. I ask Mohammed Reza if we can go and chat to them, maybe even play football with them. We hop in Sakhi's car and off we go. Mohammed steps out and asks the oldest of these kids if we can play football with them. The pitch is superb. It's a hot winter's day in the shade of a cave monastery. On one side, the rocky road marks the touchline of the football pitch. On the other side, the edge of the pitch is where the cave monastery starts.

Stones for goalposts. Flynets. Goal the winner. This was Northern Irish Bangor's Linear Park of 1990. Same world, everywhere you go.

If the ball falls down a hole, we must climb into the monastery to retrieve. We use desert stones for goal posts and a line of pebbled stones mark the byline. There are 18 of us, so it's exactly a 9 a side match. Mohammed Reza is the captain of one team. I'm the captain of the other team.

The match is not a classic for Match of the Day. In fact, after about 40 minutes, it finishes as a 0-0 stalemate. But that doesn't tell the whole story. My team won 1-0, in my opinion. A throw-in came to me 30 yards out and the ball bounced in front of me, I controlled and trapped it on my left foot, moving the ball on a bounce to my right. I was 30 yards from goal. I lobbed it high and dangerously.

The ball rose, Wimbledon style and then fell brisky just above the goalkeeper in the middle of the nets. It was a goal. I had scored a fluke lob from 30 yards in Afghanistan and won the match for my team. It was similar to Jason Cundy's screamager for Tottenham Hotspur v. Ipswich Town in 1992. Jason scored from a freak lob. Here, in Samangan, I felt I had scored. But the entire other team claimed it was too high for the goalkeeper to reach and wasn't a goal. It was not given. There were no goalposts of course, no crossbar. Therefore there was no proof that I had scored. After the 0-0 stalemate, we posed for photos with the children with my Northern Ireland flag and AFC Bournemouth scarf. There was emotion here.

I knew it was a one off match and experience in life, and as I waved goodbye to the children and we drove back to the town of Haibak, I felt a hint of sad emotion. I felt a hollow feeling in my stomach in the knowledge that I would never be back there. That was it. That was my moment of glory. That was their moment too.

"We may never meet again so shed your skin and let's get started" – Hunters and Collectors.

Also in Afghanistan, I watched a live football match in Masar e Sharif, in the Sina Stadium. This was a stadium once used by the Taliban for torturing. I also watched Afghanistan's national sport, Buzkashi – men on horses chasing after a goat's head.

Two days later, when I had to make the return trip back into Uzbekistan, I left Afghanistan easily, again in less than 6 minutes without so much as a bag check. It was a simple passport stamp and an emotional goodbye to Noor, Sakhi and Mohammed Reza.

And then – the reality hit me again, on friendship bridge. Hold on a moment – I was previously worried about leaving Uzbekistan with too much money. Now here I was heading back into Uzbekistan with a bullet from Afghanistan. There was no way I was smuggling a bullet across the border, was there? I didn't know what to do. This was impossible.

I put the bullet in my shoe. I had remembered that they asked for shoe removal at the scanner. I also remembered that at this point, after the coat check, you could grab your coat as it had already gone through. So I took my shoes off. I put the bullet into my coat which was already scanned and I walked through the scanner.

I was safely out of Afghanistan and was now back in Uzbekistan.

Yet in my possession, I now had a bullet from Afghanistan. Wasn't I the lucky one? Would the wish work? What wish? Read on...

Chapter 46
The Wish Worked

Nukus, KARAKALPAKSTAN (February 2016)

"You're so rehearsed because some wise guy built you pretty so you'd get away with it" – Louise Wener.

When I look back on my days, it was actually the transition from my split with Panny in November 2015 to my arrivation into Poland in July 2016 (which would turn into staying here) that was the BEST period of my entire travel life. That might seem odd, when clearly we had just ended a 5 year relationship. But the freedom of being alone again had me buoyant and my blog articles from that period (November 2015 to July 2016) were some of my best blog writings ever. I love them and I look back with pride.

"Let's play mallet's mallet" - Timmy Mallet, Wacaday (1980s).

I thought I'd experienced some crazy journeys in life but this one topped them all for ridiculous wackiness. I half expected Timmy Mallet to come out and whack me on the head at any moment and shout "Wacaday" at me! This could be lunacy on its head, with a 1990s Television thrown into the mix for good measure and a theme that links back to a 1980s TV show – Mallet's Mallet.

Welcome to the Republic of Karakalpakstan!

Seriously mate, where the duck is that? It's real, it's very real and I spent 24 hours in its capital city Nukus, which was as obscure as they come, this place turns the word "ridiculous" on its head. An odd place to linger maybe but let's hear about the journey that took me there. Again, this was insane, having just crossed into Uzbekistan from Afghanistan as well, some trip!

If you ever want to visit a "Stan within a Stan," a good option is the autonomous region of Karakalpakstan. You don't require any special visa or permit to enter this region. My Uzbekistan visa covered me for Karakalpakstan and I guess yours will (at the time of this book's release, 2022). But this region is pretty damn remote and obscure.

Although it houses a similar population to Northern Ireland, it covers a much wider area. It borders Kazakhstan and Turkmenistan and has its own language, flag and government. I had to get this place on my list so I headed here from the city of Bukhara. Bukhara is a popular tourist haunt in Uzbekistan, though oddly the place was a ghost town on my visit!

I stayed in Madina and Ali's Guesthouse in Bukhara but I left Bukhara early in the day as by now I was used to the ridiculous culture of some of the lazy and slow Uzbeks. Time means nothing in Uzbekistan. In my life, it's the most important thing we have - we must make the most of our time. In Uzbekistan, forget that, they steal your time here for useless things. It will just annoy me if I list all the stupid time wasting involved in Uzbek culture. People spend hours doing nothing. It's the first country I have ever seen this happen in. Everybody has some money due to the military dictatorship, so people get lazy. Green Day would have reported them till the peelers.

"Time grabs ye by the wrists, directs ye where till go" – Green Day.

We stopped for petrol about 3 times. Once at the start would have done to fill the car up. Not rocket science, or bring a spare petrol container, as I did in Australia. A severe lack of common sense exists when you backpack in Uzbekistan! My driver speaks to his mate for about two hours at one point. I just sit in the same seat doing nothing, waiting to go.

We stopped for smoke breaks and for the driver to chat to random people he knows in multiple towns. You end up sitting in the car for hours on end doing nothing. There is no urgency in the country, which is so ironic as we were heading to a city called Urgench!

Half way through the afternoon, we stop at a roadside hut and I'm not that hungry - I always carry food with me to eat in the car as I like to save time. Uzbeks love to waste time, so I ended up eating here as well. I won't waste time writing about what we did here.

I had just over an hour in Urgench but most of that time was spent arguing with taxi drivers. It's an old school Soviet era city with leafy parks, wide boulevards and massive buildings that will never be used. Urgench is the gateway to Khiva as well as being the transport hub for overlanders to Turkmenistan and Karakalpakstan.

Urgench is in the Khorezm region of Karakalpakstan, and my route to Nukus was via Beruni rather than Gurlen and Mangit. Incidentally Mangit sits on the Turkmenistan border, so my UK mobile phone changed networks. It wrote, remarkably, "Welcome to Turkmenistan."

Urgench has too many bus stations so it gets confusing. I didn't even ever stay a night in Urgench, but I was able to tour the city by default on my two trips in and out - mostly I was seeking bus stations, taxi shares and any onward connection from a driver that wasn't rude or a rip off merchant. Good luck. Urgench is nothing to write home about. But it is the last stop in mainland Uzbekistan before the wacaday drive to the Republic of Karakalpakstan, so you're very likely to stop in Urgench on route.

I decided to head to Nukus in Karakalpakstan for quite a few main reasons:
1. It is the capital city of Karakalpakstan
2. It houses the Karakalpakstan government

3. My Uzbekistan visa time was limited to 11days and in a slow, lazy country time was running out so I didn't have time to travel further into Karakalpakstan. Nukus is only a 3hour drive from Urgench.

4. It's well connected by train, bus and shared taxi.

5. It houses the Savitsky Museum. The world's best art museum apparently. Number one.

When leaving Urgench I try to bargain with the taxi drivers. You need patience and a harsh verbal tone when chatting to these guys. Finally we agree on 25,000 Som ($4USD) per person from Urgench to Nukus. The problem is the car isn't full and I want to leave soon. Daylight is fading so the chances of making it to Nukus for sunset have gone. Again, not my fault, it's the slowness of travelling in time wasting Uzbekistan that steals your sunshine here. But still, $4 US seems a bargain now when I look back at how Wacaday this journey was!

Then the driver gets a phone call and at the same time a dude with a bottle of whiskey joins us. It seems he is a mate of the driver! He swigs whiskey direct from the bottle like there's no tomorrow. This is pure lunacy! Wacaday! We leave the Olympic Stadium area behind and are soon in a side street in what to me is a Soviet style equivalent of a British council estate. With whiskey boy swigging away in the front and Northern Irish backpacker eagerly anticipating the border crossing, a man carrying a huge grey TV saunters down towards the car!! I snapped a photo of him as he carried it. This is classic backpacking at its best.

The TV doesn't fit in the boot so we sandwich it in the middle seat between him and I and off we go. My travel buddy for today is a 16 inch 1990s TV!! A TV that the dude is exporting into the Republic of Karakalpakstan! Corker of a time even if we are wedged in!

We have only one stop on the road to Karakalpakstan and one thing stands out straight away – it's deserted and relaxed here. It's so remote. It's so much more deserted and remote than the rest of Uzbekistan.

The other three guys in the car are all from Karakalpakstan. They are Karakalpaks. The Television is Japanese but licensed in Uzbekistan. I am Northern Irish with a visa on my Irish passport.

There are no visas or border checks except one car check leaving Urgench and one on arrival in Nukus, Karakalpakstan. That's right - no visa needed, no passport to be shown and no bag check. This is a different world from the rest of Uzbekistan where my passport would be checked about 5-6 times on average a day for what reason I don't know. Here, I felt free again.

"Freedom, I won't let you down" - George Michael.

Whiskey boy takes another swig, offers me some. I decline. His mate bullets on some pumping Karakalpak jazz music, the TV is still in between myself and TV export boy, and we endure the bumpy ride through Karakalpakstan. It is bumpy but before the sun sets, I'm glad I could sample some of the Karakalpakstan countryside. The Karakalpak guys only speak Karakalpak, Uzbek and some Russian. We try to chat in broken English and at least they understand I'm a tourist and where I'm from - Severn Irlandia, Northern Ireland. Knowing I'm excited about travel, the driver points out a narrow stretch of road which has the Turkmenistan border behind it. I didn't feel sad to see this. I will go there someday. But on this trip, I didn't fancy the cheating option of popping in and out on a transit visa to tick it off. Even a Turkmenistan Transit visa is hard to come by. When we make the stop, Turkmenistan lies in the distance, only a few kilometres away from me.

The only time we get out of the car is a bit after the checkpoint departure from Urgench. It is here we top up with petrol and I breathe in my first sample of Karakalpak air. There is a sign with something about Uzbekistan on it on a hill, everything beyond this is wilderness. We are now in Karakalpakstan.

We get out of the car and our driver fills it up. In Uzbekistan (and therefore Karakalpakstan) it is illegal for a passenger to sit in a car while petrol, gas or oil is being added to it. At this point, I talk to whiskey boy and he takes a photo of me. Jubilant and standing in the wilderness here in Karakalpakstan, nearest I have ever been to Turkmenistan in my life. And another new Wacaday Republic to add to my travel repertoire.

We get a selfie together and the daylight has begun to fade, it must be around 6.23 pm.

The next part of the road is bumpy, straight and direct. There is only one obvious road here all the way to Nukus. It's pitch dark when we arrive in the low lighted city of Nukus. It seems so desolate, lonely, deserted. I'm completely inspired and overaud by this. I felt a sensation of joy here. Something good was happening in my life.

We arrive in Nukus, sometime after 7.30 pm, I'll be honest I don't really know the exact time. I didn't take any notes, or check my watch or work out if it has the time set to the same as Uzbekistan. But I was in Nukus and it was dark. First up we drop off the TV smuggler to another random house in a Soviet era council estate. It's too dark to see anything, but he leaves. I bid my farewell to him and I have a back seat all to myself.

Admittedly my bum and left leg are a bit sore from the bumpy TV ride all the way here so it was nice to have the whole back seat again.

We make a further stop for the driver and his mate to buy some beer! The city at night is deserted. It reminded me of nowhere specific I had ever seen before but a mix of places. It kind of felt like a mixture between a Soviet era Ghost Town, a desert village in Iran and a remote city in China. The beer they chose was Uzbek made but with a German name and recipe - München. I preferred to wait until later as I wanted to try some authentic Karakalpak beer.

My journeys in life are pretty spontaneous. If you had asked me in December 2015 if I would have backpacked through Afghanistan, Gorno Badakhshan and Uzbekistan by mid-February, I would not have believed you. For this reason, I hadn't booked any hotels or hostels to stay in here. I planned the trip the day after I came back from Afghanistan. So I hadn't booked anywhere to stay in Nukus. I knew there wouldn't be a shortage of beds though. In 6 of the previous 7 places I had slept in Central Asia, I was the ONLY tourist in that hostel/hotel or guesthouse! I spied out two potential places and my driver agreed to take me to Jipek Joli Hotel, to drop me off right at the door. This place was advertised as the best budget hotel for tourists. I didn't expect much. I expected cold water showers, no WiFi, average breakfast and at best a smile from the staff. I was completely wrong. The Jipek Joli Hotel was superb and a great deal - one of the best hotels I stayed in in Central Asia.

I said goodbye to my driver, paid him and got a photo outside my hotel with the famous Karakalpak boozing boy. I had arrived safely and happily in the capital of the Republic of Karakalpakstan ready for a night on the rip, a bit of blogging and a day of backpacking the sights of Nukus. Yes, this was a wacaday journey!

And finally, why is this Chapter called "The Wish Worked"? It is simple. When I was backpacking in Samarkand in Uzbekistan, there is a holy Mosque there which has a courtyard famous for making wishes and prayers come true. When I was there, I decided to do what the locals do – you walk clockwise around the courtyard three times making a wish and that wish comes true.

What I wished for was tickets for every Northern Ireland match at Euro 2016. On arrival into my hotel in Nukus in Karakalpakstan, less than 7 days after making the wish, I received an email confirmation that I was successful in applying for those tickets! The wish worked and I knew that in a few months, I'd be heading to France with the GAWA. There was a little more travel to do beforehand though.

Chapter 47
Dashkent

Tashkent, UZBEKISTAN (February 2016)

"I have got to find the river. Bergamot and vetiver"
– Michael Stipe.

My final escape from Uzbekistan was "tight as a nun's crack." This was an idiom often used by my former university flatmate Jody Casey. It means that something was close to happening and did happen but almost didn't. Basically with Uzbekistan only granting me an 11 day double entry visa, I milked it. I milked it to the point that I virtually left right before my visa ended, in the final hour of its validity. When I arrived back into Kazakhstan, it was already one minute past midnight on the day when my Uzbekistan visa was no longer valid. It was a mad dash through Tashkent to see all the sights, enjoy good food and beer in the sight and still get out and safely back in Kazakhstan.

"Too much pressure pushing down on me" - Freddie Mercury.

With Uzbekistan only giving me an 11 day visa (despite my request for a 30 day triple entry), it was time to leave that country trailing in my wake. But I left it tight. I had to. I had no option but to.

In those 11 days, I barely slept. Time was of the essence and I maximised it to the hilt. This was my backpacking experience and wisdom now at play. I traversed my weary soul through dreary Deniz, topsy turvy Termiz, solemn Samarkand, kabbalistic Khiva, uninspiring Urgench and boverrated Bukhara. Not forgetting my side visit to the Republic of Karakalpakstan. Along the way, I tried to see as much as I could.

That left me with 24 hours in the capital city Tashkent...on a Saturday. It meant that extending my Uzbekistan visa would not be possible as the embassy was closed, but then again it was nice to be dashing through Kent and closing on a door that I country that I didn't have any love for. I didn't sleep much and milked this 24 hours in the capital.

"I can't sleep because the world won't wait" – Noel Gallagher.

I planned my self-guided tour of the capital city, Tashkent. It was something like...
5 a.m. Waken up, shower and have my bags ready to leave in haste later on.
6 a.m. Grab an early coffee and breakfast and out to tour the sights, posting my brother a postcard.
12 p.m. Back to the hostel for lunch and have my bags ready to be grabbed later on.
1 p.m. Finish the whackpacking, pint in a brace of bars and try to catch a football match in one of them.
6 p.m. Dinner, a video call to Mum on her birthday and a last beer in Uzbekistan.
8 p.m. Taxi share to the border.

I realised that once I was back in Kazakhstan again, I could chill out here. I was not under as much pressure to leave there, as I was here, in unwelcoming Uzbekistan. I dashed through Tashkent before it was time for another Kent – Shymkent.

Chapter 48
Turkistan, not Turkmenistan

Shymkent, KAZAKHSTAN (February 2016)

"Walking through this changing season, sorrow spreads its wings. We can't keep a hold on time, just receive what it will bring" - Tim Wheeler.

I was glad to have left Uzbekistan and Karakalpakstan behind. They were two parts of the world that I didn't really want to visit again. That's just the way life is sometimes. I don't expect to ever be back there. This was now my second time in Kazakhstan and I chose Shymkent as my base. I had heard about Shymkent from Mina, the Kazak dancer I had met in Almaty at Christmas. She bigged up Shymkent and I had also been told about a place called Turkistan nearby – a superb UNESCO World Heritage site in a little known village. Yes it is called Turkistan, not Turkmenistan. Turkmenistan, would have to wait its turn.

Turkistan is a UNESCO World Heritage Site in Kazakhstan and I planned to visit whilst based in Shymkent. I just loved the name of this city, Shymkent, which I nicknamed "Shimmy." I was here for a 4 day, 4 night stint, all of which I slept in the simply excellent Orbita Boutique Hotel.

From Shimmy, it was a simple decision for me to make as to where I would head next. I would overland via Taras back to Bishkek in Kyrgyzstan and most likely stay there and work online for about 3 to 4 months.

A spanner was thrown into the works when an email out of the blue invited me on a Bloggers Trip to India to take place in March 2016. Despite never having any burning desire to visit India soon, I realised that it was now time for me to go there. The visa was paid for and the company agreed to pay everything for two full weeks of my trip.

When I arrived back in Bishkek, I finally made my first ever attempt at getting an Indian visa. By chance, the Indian Embassy was very close to my hostel, Apple Hostel. The visa would be a 90 day visa so I quickly decided that I would stay longer in India than the two sponsored weeks. I would also like to have three weeks there on my own, so 5 in total.

My visa was accepted and I had a bit of time in Bishkek to prepare for the India adventure and plan my trip. My Brazilian friend Katia would happen to be in Mumbai at the same time as me so we agreed to meet there and do some overland backpacking together.

My plan for India would also incorporate two regions that I deemed to be different (Gujarat and Andaman Islands). As well as some of the main Provinces of India, I added in the special alcohol free province of Gujarat. I basically wanted to "do the Palin."

As a teenager, I had watched Michael Palin travel documentaries. In one of them, Palin had gone to Gujarat province in India and got his alcohol permit. Foreigners or non-Muslims can apply for a special permit to allow them to buy alcohol. This is exactly the type of adventure I enjoy. The whole process of it. The research, the getting there, the arrival, the struggle, the paperwork, the satisfaction and writing about it. I wanted to write about getting that permit to share my story and to help other future tourists.

On top of that, I would later visit the Andaman and Nicobar Islands. Again, this was a region of India but one with a separate visa and entry stamp. The visa would be easy to get but another charm lay ahead in Port Blair. I would literally be spending a night in my town!

After leaving Kazakhstan that time, I haven't since returned. I knew I'd be back in magnetic Kyrgyzstan again though. In the meantime, India now lay ahead.

Chapter 49
Get It India (Get It Intill Ye)

"Will your anchor hold in the storms of life, when the clouds unfold their wings of strife?" – Robin Mark.

On my travels I often became too judgemental and I hated myself for it. Looking back, we all make mistakes.

To put it mildly, neither Thailand nor India had any real attraction for me. Thailand was country 68 on my journey. India didn't even squeeze its way into my first 120 countries. Why?

Because I abhorred the common, the over trodden, the hyped and the popular. 98% of backpackers I had met in Asia in my life, they had been to either Thailand or India. It made me sick. I got really judgemental over it. For that reason I skipped those countries time and time again. In the end, I only really used Thailand as a springboard till Laos, Cambodia and the countries in that region. Despite 8 visits to Thailand now, it still don't rank highly with me.

The more I tried to avoid India, the more it kept cropping up as an option.

While whackpacking in Bishkek, I met up with fellow travel blogger Stephen Lioy (who runs the Monk Bought Lunch blog). Stephen knows Central Asia well. He suggested we meet in one of his favourite Indian restaurants in Bishkek. Weirdly, despite loving Mexican food and spicy food in general, Indian cuisine was not one I tried often. In fact, I rarely ate Indian food at the time. That day, the food was good, the chat was good and then I simply returned back to the Apple Hostel. I logged into my computer and a brace of wacaday Indian references awaited me to complete an Indian hattrick on the same day.

Firstly, the Indian lunch of course.

Secondly, my Brazilian friend Katia had messaged having noted that I was in Bishkek. She was heading for 3 months to Asia, kicking off in India.

Thirdly, I had an email from a travel company in India offering to sponsor me on a two week trip through India. This time, they'd even pay for my flights and visa.

I had never been to India. Now everything was telling me that the time was right for it now. I knew I had to go. The next morning I woke up early and went straight to the Indian Embassy in Bishkek. It wasn't an easy visa process and I was shocked at how busy the Embassy was. There were huge queues. Loads of Kyrgyz people were getting visas for India.

Within a week, I had my visa for India and was going on a direct flight from Manas International Airport to New Delhi in India. I spent my first 3 days in New Delhi before getting a nighttrain to Mumbai on the west coast.

"Down in a den in Bombay. Slack jaw, not much to say" – Men At Work.

In Mumbai, I met up with Katia and we toured some of the west coast together. This included going inland to Gujarat to get our alcohol permits in Ahmedabad. Ahmedabad still ranks as one of the wildest and most chaotic cities I have ever been to. We were fined on the way out of the city! Not for alcohol, as we had our permits but for boarding the wrong nighttrain to Vagator! This was mad as we had bought the tickets for a bed on a nighttrain. But the sneaky vendor had known that train was fully booked and he had deliberately given us tickets for the same train the next month. We had to pay the fine and I had to sit on the floor for 15 hours on that train, while luckily Katia had a seat, kindly given to her by an Indian lady.

I spent over a week in Goa, moved inland to Hampi and then from Hospet, myself and a Polish travel buddy, Ilona and I decided to backpack together. We got yet another nighttrain. This time from Hospet to Chennai.

Chapter 50
A Night In My Town

Port Blair, ANDAMAN ISLANDS (17th March 2016)

"This is my town and I am world leader pretend"
– Michael Stipe.

While India feels like one huge country, there is deeper politics at work. I spent 5 weeks on Indian soil, but twice I left the mainland and on another occasion I visited "alcohol free India". Wacaday Gujarat was mentioned briefly in the previous chapter's *"Get It Intill Ye / Get It India."* I simply won't have time on these pages to cover all those mental times. In a future book, perhaps.

In the madness of all that happened in India, I visited Andaman Islands just because my surname is BLAIR! I remember seeing them on my old Atlas as a kid. I remembered them for one distinct reason - Port Blair is here. Blair is my surname. But surely I would never visit these remote islands in life? I wouldn't actually ever visit Port Blair would I?

Suddenly I realised it was a now or never. Having backpacked overland with the wonderful Ilona (my Polish friend), we found ourselves in Chennai. Again, memories of Michael Palin documentaries came rolling back to me here as Palin was also once in Chennai. Getting to Chennai for Ilona and I was weary, tiring and far from inspiring.

Ilona had been bitten by a monkey and we needed to get her injections. We did that in a town called Anegundi and then we backpacked through Hampi. At dusk in central India we shared a bumpy tuk-tuk from Hampi to Hospet. From there I had been able to secure us both a night bed on a nighttrain all the way to Chennai. My original plan was actually to spend a few days in Bangalore, overland it to coastal Chennai and from there head north towards Calcutta. That, all changed.

Ilona and I were good backpacking buddies. I liked her, I respected her and I cared for her. I was single now too. She spoke of a boyfriend back in Bournemouth. Yes, Bournemouth. It was all signs. A Polish girl living in Bournemouth now backpacking in India with me. So much of my life was fate and chance and coincidence. But there was no date with the pretty Ilona. This isn't another love story you craved.

17th March is always a special day for me. Saint Patrick (who will never be dubbed "Paddy") is buried in Downpatrick in Northern Ireland and this is his special day. It was to prove to be a crazy Saint Patrick's day on my life cannon, my craziest Saint Patrick's Day of my life.

There were only two cool things I liked about choky smoky Chennai. One was the excellent hostel we stayed in - The Elements Hostel. Staff there were very kind to me and Ilona. Ilona liked to sleep alone in a room with nobody else. Not only did they allow her to do this, but as she was with me, they gave her two nights on discount, with a late checkout. And my dorm bed was free of charge, as of course I was reviewing it. The second cool thing was that we found a nearby cafe which had this really excellent Indian Spiced Ginger drink. Ilona took a photo of me when we were in that cafe. I still love that photo. It was the first time I was beardless in India. I paid a street vendor in Hampi to unbeard my bake. Ilona took of me, the perfect photo.

Now that we were in Chennai, Ilona and I decided to tour the city together. On my journeys around the world, this was one of the least inspiring cities I have ever visited. We both agreed with this sentiment.

After dreaming of a glorious sunrise or sunset sipping shocktails on Chennai beach, the reality was far from that. This beach was a shithole. It was dirty, smelly. Really, it was an eyesore. Rubbish, litter, garbage, trash, dog turd everywhere. I am not a posh stuck up twat as I have lived and loved some less than clean locations on my journey. But there was me looking after the gracious Ilona who was ill. It just wasn't healthy for us. We made a great joint decision to "get the fuck back to the hostel."

Then I decided to sleep in the afternoon, having a nap for a change. It wasn't something I did often on my travels. This time, I had such a clean shower and a cosy nap and I woke up with a brainwave. I had to get the hell out of here.

I had only three travel commitments at the time. One was to meet Katia, my Brazilian friend, in Vrindavan for Holifest at the end of March. Two was to be in Salzburg and Grödig to meet Lock In Lee by the end of April. Three was to be in France for the whole of June 2016 for the Euro 2016 tournament.

The next morning Ilona was travelling back home anyway, from Chennai International Airport. I decided I wanted to go the airport with her and get the hell out of here together. She would be on a long connection back to Heathrow in London. But I would just book a random flight somewhere. I just didn't know where to. Before midnight on 16th March, I booked the "Chennai Blair" (Jonny Blair) journey. Saint Patrick's Day would be spent in my town.

At Chennai Airport, there is an Irish Pub! So I had a Saint Patrick's Day beer here, then boarded my flight to Port Blair! I landed in Port Blair and spent the first night in the centre of the city itself, where I backpacked the sights and walked up the coast. There was a separate entry permit needed and independent passport stamps for the Andaman Islands. My last 3 days in the Andaman Islands were spent reviewing a paradise on the coast – The Peerless Sarovar Portico Resort, Corbyn's Cove.

Something incredibly crazy happened here in this swanky resort. My two nights were sponsored and I would write about it. I knew that. However, each night, I was ordering beers from the bar and I had some great meals here. All of that wasn't covered so I put it on my room tab to pay when I went to check out. It was a paradise and without fast Wi-Fi, I ended up writing my books and blogs offline here, over a lot of beers. When I checked out and went to pay, I had racked up quite a few beers, lunches, dinners and other food and drink. The hotel had a problem with their card machine. They couldn't accept credit cards! That time, I was in a huge rush to get to Port Blair airport for my flight out and I had only a few Indian Rupees in cash – just about enough for a lift to the airport! So I basically had no way to pay my bill. I told the manager I would pay it online via PayPal after the trip. I estimate it was around $60 US. I flashed and splashed out there! To my surprise, he said *"don't worry about it Mr. Blair, it's on us. It was a pleasure having you here!"*

I realised right here, right now that life was really really good now and had been worth it. This was good karma for me for my hard work. When I blogged about that hotel, it of course got a great review. The customer service was superb! But good things come to an end and it was back to mainland Indian in time for Holifest and to see the Taj Mahal.

Chapter 51
Holifest And The First Ever Pub Crawl In Bishkek

Vrindavan, INDIA (March 2016)

"Pleasure at the fairground on the way" – Simply Red.

After The Andaman Islands, it was time for Holifest in India. My Brazilian friend Katia and I met up again for this trip and we stayed in both Mathura and Vrindavan for the colourful "Holifest." However, this Holifest festival was disgusting. It's not the promised festival you dreamt of. I spent the entire two days stopping sleazy Indian guys from touching Katia's breasts and vagina. That's the brutal nature of it. Girls are not safe during Holifest. We should have gone to the police. People have been imprisoned for much pettier crimes than touching girls private parts, myself included – I have done jail time on my travels for a totally petty reason compared with what these guys were doing. I was completely disgusted by it. Holifest was basically Indian guys throwing coloured powder at mine and Katia's eyes just so they could blind us and grab her boobs. I was shocked and saddened by it all and we couldn't wait to get out of Vrindavan.

We did enjoy the Taj Mahal though and the food in our last week or so in India. But Holifest – please take care. I was delighted to finally land back in Bishkek in time for my birthday and some pub crawling in a safe, non-sexist country, Kyrgyzstan.

The Kek, KYRGYZSTAN (April 2016)

In my two last weeks in Bishkek, I inaugurated the city's first two officially organised "pub crawls." The thing is that pub crawls were my forte from the age of seventeen. The first pub crawl I ever did was on Saint Patrick's Day 1998. Me and my mate Gavin simply visited five pubs in my hometown of Bangor on the same night. It was The Steamer, The Crown, The Windsor, See Jax and Wolsey's. A beer in each. I abhorr repitivity. I cannot stand mundanity, boredom or banalness. I need change. I crave diversity.

Northern Irish High Streets are good for pub crawls. It is beer to beer and bar to bar. When I moved to England, I continued my crazy fascination for pub crawls. In Bournemouth and Poole over a course of 6 years, I visited over 200 drinking venues in those towns, often ticking off multiples on the same night. In London, I did the Monopoly Pub Crawl. And when I whackpacked the world, I often joined pub crawls or invented my own. It is a culture. An energy. A feel good vibe. A challenge.

Myself and Millwall Neil always spoke about running the Monopoly Pub Crawl in London as a business. We knew it would work. Our travel skills, teaching experience, drinking passion and my social media outreach would have made it **an easy business**. Neil and I spoke about it at length some days. Of course we never started that business and it was obvious why.

Alcohol. We didn't really want to be travelling all over London every single day hopping in and out of bars, ticking off boxes on a piece of paper, looking after guests who had consumed excess quantities of alcohol. On the ground level, it was a goldmine. Yet in reality it was a life ruiner, so we shelved our plans.

Here in Bishkek, I was into my fifth month of exploring the city. I knew all the bars. I knew a lot about the cafés, bars and restaurants. I was an expert. Together with Aigul, who manages Apple Hostel, we devised a new pub crawl. We visited about over ten bars trying to negotiate deals with them, and we chose the top six, then we shared it in groups. It was a blast. It was good fun.

All the while though, my mind was on other things. 2016 was a crazy year. I had been messaging a Slavic girl who I met in

Chisinau, again. We were getting a bit close, with words and thoughts. My next few months of life would take me on a journey I could never have envisaged. That girl from Chisinau would later end up in Gdańsk with me in chapters that had to be deleted.

After Bishkek, some of my plans were known. But of course, I was a nomad now. I didn't have a home. I had left behind my life in Hong Kong. I was now merely a homeless backpacker. But I had all of these aspirations ahead in a concrete-ish plan...

1. To visit Munich to review a bicycle tour, review a hostel, review a beer night out and to go naked at the nudist garden.
2. To visit Salzburg to review the city, the Sound of Music tour, a hostel and to watch SV Grödig with Lock in Lee Adams.
3. To watch 2 AFC Bournemouth matches before the season ends (Everton away and West Bromwich Albion at home).
4. To go to Senegal and The Gambia on a fully paid for trip with Money Supermarket. com.
5. To visit my brother Daniel in Liverpool and my family in Northern Ireland.
6. To edit and release our Northern Ireland football fanzine Here We Go... Again
7. To go to France for Euro 2016 to support Northern Ireland. I had tickets for every Northern Ireland match at the tournament including the final.

After that, the only plans I had in my head, but not concrete were:
1. To visit Gdańsk in Poland and tour the Solidarność and Westerplatte history. (At the time of course, I had no idea how much I would love the city of Gdańsk!)
2. To visit Kaliningrad, and write about the visa process (two years before World Cup 2018).
3. To finish my book series "Backpacking Centurion". (I initially just planned to return to Kyrgyzstan to complete the writing and editing there).

4. To return to Hong Kong merely for a fleeting visit to collect my belongings and close the door on life in Asia.

Life was good again. I was ready for the time of my life. But somehow, depression was just around the chimney corner. When I finally closed the curtain on wacaday Bishkek, I was on route to SV Grodig Baby.

Chapter 69
Left Out For A Reason, (I'm) All Nude

Bishkek, KYRGYZSTAN (April 2016)

"I'm so excited, I can't wait to meet you there. And just maybe, I'm to blame for all I heard" – Kurt Cobain.

As much as I wanted to prolong my stay in magnetic Kyrgyzstan, time was up for me in this town, for now. I had plans to watch SV Grödig in Austria with Lock In Lee Adams and then head to Euro 2016 to support Northern Ireland.

Bishkek is a fantastic city and a superb base. It will probably always rank in my favourite 10 cities in the world. And one of the main reasons for this was mirrored in conversation with my Swiss backpacking buddy Lukas. Lukas has a blog and goes by the nickname Luke Junglewalker. I met Lukas while staying at the excellent Apple Hostel in the Kek. Lukas, one day was musing on how him and I could just nonchalantly dander through the city and be virtually unnoticed. We were anonymous. It was brilliant. Nobody notices you. You're left in peace in Bishkek. It is such a liveable city.

"You're anonymous here" - Luke Junglewalker.

Almost daily, I'd head to my favourite Wi-Fi cafés in the city and get my blogging done. I was working a lot back then and I also finished a lot of my book writing and editing there. My favourite cafés were Sierra Cafe and Adriano Cafe. Both were a leisurely walk from the hostel and I would make those journeys daily. I'd sit in both cafés for hours, until it was dark. I was known to stay there all day. I got to know the bargirls. They were really friendly and pretty. My favourite was Sagynai from Adriano. She'd serve me many coffees, cakes and pizzas in there. And of an early evening, she'd serve me up a beer.

Sagynai had a decent grasp of English, she was very cute. Curious and breaking her shyness barrier, she once said to me *"Jonny what do you do all day, in here, writing on your laptop?."*

"I'm a blogger. I'm a travel blogger. I'm writing blogs, articles and books. But I'm also a teacher and a barman," I told Sagynai. Nothing happened between us. I wanted to kiss her a few times. We never did anything together. But if I had stayed there longer, in her town, maybe this was a romance that would have worked. Neither of us will ever know. I missed her when I left Bishkek behind.

I left my mark on magnetic Kyrgyzstan in the end. I promoted Bishkek for the best part of five months and during my final two weeks, started organised pub crawls. Pub Crawls weren't a thing in ex-Soviet Union countries like Kyrgyzstan. They also aren't really a thing in Poland. I often introduced pub crawls to my friends, and to others when I travelled.

The pub crawls were coorganised by Aigul Kubatbekova and I. Using the power of Aigul's contacts from Apple Hostel, we selected 6 Bishkek bars all with a difference. The pub crawl would start at Apple Hostel with a local beer, we'd head to Greenwich pub for a British style football twist, go local at Jalalabad Restaurant where we try the quirky horse milk alcohol concoction, Bozo and Beshbarmak – horse meat noodle soup. The night ended with beers, shisha, chat and football in the ironically called Johnny's Pub. It was in here, on that epic pub crawl where I'd learn that AFC Bournemouth had beaten Aston Villa 2-1 away, thus virtually relegating Aston.

I packed my backpacks and walked to the morning airport marshrutky. From Manas airport, I'd board a flight to Moscow's Sheremetyevo Airport, where I'd connect to Munich.

This would be my first time in Munich. As my plane went airborne and I left Kyrgyzstan with a tear, I expected I'd be back there in a few months, after the European Championships. Was it bye-bye Bishkek just for now?

"As the day was dawning my plane flew away, with all the things caught in my mind" - Noel Gallagher.

Nudist Park, Munich, BAVARIA (April 2016)

"I can't believe you sent me a nude!" – My Secret Love.

It looks like I couldn't follow even my own advice in life. Days gone by of love, wanderlust and zest were covered in the *Backpacking Centurion* trilogy. Now I was naked in public and caught up in true madness. I even changed the Chapter title to 69, while Chapter 52 will not even be in this book. A reason for this book's delay is the editing and deleting of multiple chapters and flashpoints along the way.

Munich threw up all kinds of odd oxymorons at me. It did feel weird that I hadn't yet been to this city. On previous trips to Germany, I had been to Köln, Osterweddingen, Magdeburg, Berlin, Bremen, Hannover, Leipzig, Dresden and Hamburg. I'd never had any real desire to be in Munich. However, as I was meeting Lock In Lee Adams across the border in Salzburg in a few days, this made a handy new stopover for me.

I organised two nights in the excellent 4 You Hostel. I would be reviewing a bicycle tour and a beer hall tour. Plus there was the uniquement of an "English Garden" in a Bavarian Park where it was legal to be fully naked in public and drink a beer. This was right up my street.

I went alone to the English Garden. It's a huge central Park in Munich. I found a spot, I put my Northern Ireland flag down as a towel and I went fully naked. Willy out loyal. Within an hour I had sizzled a different type of sausage and embarked on an epic beerhall tour.

I had sent a hungover text message to a friend asking if she wanted to see my photo from the nudist park. I had written in a text *"I can send you my nude from the nudist garden for fun, though I am not sure you want to know the size of my willy."* Her reply was surprising, a curious, cheeky *"of course I want – show me it."* It was an unexpected response and I pondered on it too much, but I was meeting Lock In Lee Adams in Salzburg. There was no time to dwell on my nudity antics. Let's leave it at that, for this lifetime.

Chapter 53
SV Grödig Baby

SV Grödig, AUSTRIA (April 2016)

"SV Grödig Baby, SV Grödig Woah Hoah"
– Jonny Blair and Lee Adams.

We didn't just make the "Grödig Bet" and win the Grödig Bet. We went even further than that…we ended up in the barely known village of Grödig in Austria.

This chapter will never be long enough to explain what Grödig Bet is all about. It's not a chapter story, it's a book of its own but to cut a long story short here is all I can do. This chapter is all about Lock In Lee. Who is Lock In Lee? Lock in Lee is Lock in Lee Adams who is Lee Adams. Lee has been a friend of mine since 2003.

I first met Lee Adams at an audition for the Lock In. The Lock In was a Big Brother spoof organised by The Students Union at Bournemouth University. They were locking 12 students in a custom-made house in a secret location for a weekend. They invited people to audition. I totally wanted to be in there. I needed to be in there. We did the auditions. I passed the first round of auditions in D2 Bar. I passed the second round of auditions in The Commodore Hotel. That venue itself spooky enough, as Noemi Linzenbold once worked there. Then there was a public vote for the contestants to actually enter the house. Aka The Lock In.

Lee Adams and I both got voted in. The Lock In took place in February 2004. Lee won The Lock In. I came third. Bronze medal for me. However, it was the house on fire friendship that developed that would lead Lock In Lee and I to Grödig in Austria. In 2016. So the gap of 12 years since 2004 just cannot be fitted into this chapter but I have covered some of it in the *"Backpacking Centurion"* book series in chapters known as *"The Lock In"* and *"Nicky Barmby"* and on my blogs.

In short, not only did Lock In Lee and I become best friends but everytime we meet, **we encounter a spate of freaky events.** We were meant to meet and we were meant to be friends forever.

In March 2015, just before I visited my 100th country, Tunisia, I was back in Birmingham to meet up with Lock In Lee. Down the years, Lock In Lee has also lived in Bournemouth, Oxford and West Bromwich, plus Australia. We often do football bets for fun. It's freaky. We won ridiculous bets. That's also why we ended up in Grödig.

We did two random football bets in March 2015. The first was that Nottingham Forest would beat Rotherham United 2-0 at home. We were going to that match. We both knew it would end 2-0. **It ended 2-0 with a double freak.** Firstly, Daniel Lafferty played for Rotherham United that night. I had met Daniel Lafferty in Turkey in 2013. Secondly, Jack Barmby was on the bench for Rotherham United. That was freaky as the first bet that Lock In Lee and I ever won was about his Dad, Nicky Barmby. So we were at the match and Nottingham Forest won 2-0 and we won the bet.

But it was the second bet that was even more freaky and it won us around £300 on an accumulator. The problem was we were pushed for time to pick the last match on the accumulator as Lee's mate had to drive us to the stadium. Lee had mentioned Gardiner, a player for Nottingham Forest at some point in the conversation. We couldn't decide on the last result to predict and then we spotted what a gardener does. He grows and he digs. Grow. Dig. There it was. SV Grödig. SV Grödig in the Austrian top flight. SV Grödig were at home to Wolfsberger AC (Pellets WAC) that night and they were our final team. It was the last result to come in.

On the way to the stadium, The City Ground in Nottingham, Lee and I were curious who SV Grödig were. We looked them up. They hadn't won a match in about 3 months. They were in the relegation places and had basically no chance of winning. We thought the bet was pointless now. However, Nottingham Forest won 2-0, SV Grödig won 2-1 and the rest is history.

In the pub that night, Lee and I decided that our next random trip would be to Austria to watch SV Grödig. We just follow the randomness of life, and fate. As Grödig had clinched our bet, we were going to watch them live!

13 months later, my train from München (where I had done the nude striptease in the central nudist park) rolled into Salzburg. Lee and I were reunited again.

Two days later we boarded a bus in Salzburg to Anif Zoo. We toured Anif Zoo and then headed to the tiny village of Grödig in the madness of life.

For one day only, we were SV Grödig fans. On the day though, SV Grödig lost 1-0 and got relegated from the top flight. So we were now bad luck omens. So much happened in the next two months of my life, most of it was brilliant and very positive. I was happily single again and with no base. I didn't know where I'd end up. What I did know that I was off to Africa again in May 2016.

Chapter 54
7 Seconds Away

Hotel Baraka, Dakar, SENEGAL (May 2016)

"7 seconds away, just as long as I stay, I'll be waiting"
- Youssou N'Dour.

I had a bath in my hotel room. It was a pleasant surprise. It had been a long time since I had a bath. Or had time to use a bath that was in a hotel room of mine, so this one was used. In total, I spent 5 days in Dakar and even this "easy trip" was full of mayhem.

In the end, a 2002 World Cup performance by Senegal might not have been the reason for my trip here to this east African nation. I had been a backpacking centurion for 14 months now but when I glanced at world maps I still got travel hungry and wanted to fill in the gaps. When you have been to 100 countries, it sounds like a lot but it's really not, it's just a slight dent on the globe. You could visit 100 countries without ever leaving Africa or Europe. Nobody will ever backpack all of the 627 countries on my ultimate list. In fact, in a hattrick of those countries I was their first tourist. In a brace of them, I'm still the only tourist (Podjistan and Adammia).

The Bournemouth had successfully stayed up. When the final whistle went at Dean Court on May 8th 2016, there was a round of applause for the team but I had to act fast as I was on a mission of my own.

At the end of my time in magnetic Kyrgyzstan, I had been invited by a British company called Money Supermarket on a sponsored trip. This was a trip I didn't want to miss as the timing suited me, it was a tailored trip and involved a challenge.

Money Supermarket dot com (http://www.moneysupermarket.com) had chosen about 10 bloggers to be part of a "Lost luggage challenge" under the hashtag #MSMlostluggage. It meant you'd have to visit a random country (or two) without luggage.

The trips timing fitted nicely into my schedule. It was to be in May 2016, in between my wacaday SV Grodig baby trip and my adventure to Euro 2016 to finally watch Northern Ireland at a major tournament. As a bonus, I got to visit two new countries and the entire trip was paid for. I felt blessed again.

"I am blessed; every time I look at you my baby's eyes" - Eternal.

The challenge was to land at an airport in a country far away with no luggage at all. No hand luggage and no hold baggage. I chose Senegal and The Gambia. By no mean coincidence these were also two new countries on my odyssey.

The reason for this choice was most probably as the trip was organised at short notice and those were two countries that I hadn't been to and that I didn't require an advance visa for. Specifically Senegal in this regard, as they had just eased their entry requirements.

The trip was all organised and it felt weird to be travelling without any luggage this time. Down the years though, I had so much experience travelling without luggage that this would be a doddle for me. Airlines have lost my bag 9 times in total now. I named and shamed those airlines on my blog as they owed me thousands of dollars. They still haven't paid me. It seems they love the bad publicity and potential bankruptcy. Pay up please. Years and decades on they remain silent.

The most notable bag losses I had were on arrival in Tbilisi in 2013 and Algeria in 2015. The Algeria one I predicted they would lose my bag and they did. That one was horrific and I said I was done with travel that time. I backpacked for 4 weeks wearing the same Glentoran shirt and blue jeans. I had the same socks and pants for 4 weeks. The airline refused to admit they lost my bag, they refused to pay for me to buy new clothes, they refused to pay for a new battery and laptop charger and I lost thousands of dollars due to it.

So surely this challenge would be easy for me. The biggest difference between the Money Supermarket challenge and the previous bag losses was that this time I'd have no luggage at all!! No toiletries, no change of clothes, no laptop, no books, no chargers. I only had what I was wearing.

In my pockets I had my wallet, passport, camera, phone, chewing gum. I didn't even have any keys as I didn't have a home! My bags were at my mate Austin's flat in Bournemouth, England! However I needed a Smartphone as I had to document my journey on social media. It's difficult to get online in many parts of Africa anyway. But on the challenge, that lasted 12 days, I would be posting on Instagram (@jonnydontstopliving) and Facebook (Don't Stop Living) from my phone only.

On my flight in to Senegal a rarity happened. We made a stop at an airport in a country I had never been to and we didn't leave the aeroplane. This was a stopover at the main airport in Nouakchott in Mauritania. We touched down in Mauritania, some passengers got off and some passengers got on. We had left the country within an hour. As I make the final edits to this book in 2021, Mauritania is the only country I have physically been to without ever leaving the aeroplane. All the other countries I have flown into, I left the aeroplane. If you check the list of places I have visited at the rear of this book, you will notice Mauritania is the only one I listed at the end in brackets. It's also the only country I have been to that I don't personally include in my country or city count. A nice little accolade but soon, I had landed in Dakar, capital of 2002 World Cup quarter finalists Senegal.

My first base in Senegal was a stay by the gorgeous beach at Maison Abaka. I found a peace and a tranquility here. While based in Senegal, I toured the pink lake called Lac Rosa. Of course this "pink lake" wasn't that impressive or even that pink or red. It was one of those clever marketing trick photos where they make it look fantastic on photos, but it's just not.

"No alarms and no surprises, poproszę" - Radio Głowa.

My overland adventure to The Gambia where I was to stroke alive crocodiles was the highlight of this trip.

Chapter 55
Crocodile Drumcree

Kachikally Crocodile Farm, THE GAMBIA (May 2016)

"My smile as real as a hyena's" - Nicky Wire.

If I am ever asked to describe the continent of Africa in one word, it's easy. Animals. I always have extreme animal experiences here. This venture into The Gambia (note the "The" - grammatical English articles on the brain) mirrored that theme.

In Ethiopia it was feeding wild hyenas face to face. In Zambia it was seeing the rhino in its natural habitat and completing the "Big 5" wild animals in Africa. In Swaziland / Eswatini it was waterfall monkeys. In Tanzania it was elephants. In Namibia it was cheetahs. And so on and so eighth. More animals meandered themselfs intill my backpacking ambience but it was here in The Gambia that I touched a crocodile in amongst a sadness that would end in the Polish seaside resort of Gdańsk less than two months later. You can't sleep because the world won't wait.

Life deals you brutal cards. Think of the fate. The chances. Split decisions of other people change your lives. I emailed 10 hotels in The Gambia telling them about my challenge. The first two that replied would be the first two I would choose to sleep in.

I would have two nights of pure fire luxury at The Coco Ocean Beach Resort. When I look back on all the places I slept, this is in the top ten. It's an absolutely gorgeous, modern resort of relaxation by the beach. I had everything here.

Yet I didn't.

I didn't have the girl.

"Missing" - Everything But The Girl.

Here I was sleeping in a Palace of Dreams where they provided me with dinners, breakfasts, and a huge suite with a private swimming pool. It was the kind of resort I should have been with a wife and family. It was perfect for that. On this challenge, I had no laptop, no backpack, no books. I'd waken up and watch the sunrise then get breakfast and go for a swim. In my private pool and in the Atlantic Ocean.

The resort also provided me with a full body massage. As this lady thrust her hands through all my parts, I knew I couldn't feel real arousal or any love for her. I felt sad to be here alone.

On the first afternoon here, I realised I was actually in love with that girl I had met in Moldova. This was clear now. I thought about her every day in the morning and every night in bed before I slept. It was a stronger love than I had felt for Claire, for Vicky, for Lauren, for Noemi, for Panny. This was strong and I was confused. I knew I loved a girl far away now but I was here to backpack the sights and work online.

"Water's running in the wrong direction; got a feeling it's a mixed up sign" – Girls Aloud.

I was here on a mission to survive 12 days without any backpack or luggage. In essence, The Gambia and Senegal are the only two countries from my journey that I wasn't "backpacking" in. I couldn't go backpacking there on this trip because I wasn't permitted a backpack or any luggage. So I didn't backpack in The Gambia because I didn't have a backpack! And I didn't suitcase it either but I certainly travelled in both countries, double land bordering the brace.

There is also a deep irony editing this now. My lucky number is related to "2". I grew up at 2 Marlo Drive, Bangor before we moved to a number 12. My Granny and Granda Blair lived at 22 Drumragh End in Belfast. My Granny Scott lived at 32 Balloo Walk in Bangor. Here, the number 12 was relevant as I spent 12 days without luggage on that trip. Years later, I'd spend 12 days in more brutal circumstances and the lucky number doesn't aim to haunt as the day I awoke in a room numbered 222 proved to be lucky. In my life cannon, number TWO has always seemed to come into play in a happy time.

After Africa, there was only one country I wanted to be in at that time. Northern Ireland. I was going "home" for a week!

"She's got it. Yeah baby she's got it" - Robbie van Leeuwen.

Chapter 56
Blarney Rumble

Belfast City, NORTHERN IRELAND (May 2016)

"One day we'll return here. When the Belfast Child sings again" - Simple Minds.

In May 2016 I landed back in Belfast City. My flight back was from Southampton to George Best Belfast City Airport. There was a realisation that I hadn't made that trip in 7 years, since I last lived in nearby Bournemouth. On this occasion I would be here for a week in my native Northern Ireland before heading south to Dublin, Cashel, Blarney and Cork. Those were only the stepping stones towards France, and Euro 2016.

I was able to go for coffees with Mum, go to the Northern Ireland v. Belarus friendly match with my Dad and brother Marko and catch up with friends.

Indeed, lifelong friends Michael and Gavin McClelland and I brought back our Northern Ireland football fanzine, "Here We Go... Again" after 12 years. We first wrote that fanzine as 16 year olds back in early 1997! Here, 19 years later, we finished the final edits in Gavin's House in The Braniel before selling the publication before the Belarus home match at Windsor Park and the Poland match in Nice. Writing was always easy for me. It's natural. I think I churned all my fanzine articles out in the space of 48 hours.

It felt good to finally have achieved another childhood dream by qualifying for a major tournament with Northern Ireland. This Ireland trip was the prelude to that. It was the calm before the storm.

Northern Ireland beat Belarus 3-0, with three different strikers scoring including Will Grigg. Will Grigg had become a cult hero for club and country due to his prolific goalscoring record on the pitch for Wigan Athletic. However, it was actually all about the song. Gala's 1997 hit "Freed From Desire" had been reworded to "Will Grigg's on fire, your defence is terrified" and this became some kind of hit for that summer.

It wasn't even just Northern Ireland fans that were singing it – other nation's supporters were also belting the tune out!

"Will Grigg's on fire, your defence is terrified, Will Grigg's on fire" – Wigan Athletic and Northern Ireland fans.

I boarded a bus to Dublin from Belfast. At the time, I was still nomadic without any home, or any plans. That was to be my last time in Northern Ireland before moving to Poland. I had no idea of that then.

Dublin to Cashel to Blarney Castle to Cork City, REPUBLIC OF IRELAND (June 2016)

On that trip, after Dublin, I toured the marvellous Cashel and Blarney. As a 36 year old Northern Irishman, here in 2016, this was my first time to visit either of those places. Both felt holy. Both felt wildly significant. At both places, I prayed.

Cashel is a beautiful village in rural Irish countryside. As well as the rock and church, I prayed and stared out in beauty at the fields around. A Celtic cross was shining in the morning sun. Later that day, I joined the tourist crowd at Blarney Castle. It was here that I kissed The Blarney Stone finally.

Looking back now, I had more luck and was more "gift of the gab" before I kissed it than after. I walked down the lucky steps in

Blarney too, making a wish. In Blarney I also had my first beer in the Republic of Ireland for a few years. I chose a Beamish Stout of course – the local brew here. Before I did that, I went to the bookies to put some bets on at the upcoming Euros. I banked on Northern Ireland to win the tournament and would receive £5000 if we did it!

The final leg of this Irish trip was a hat-trick of nights in Cork City!! This was completely sentimental and the timing was fitting! Back in 1996, I had visited Cork with Keith Freel and Colin Walker, two of my mates as a teenager. The reason for that trip was to watch Oasis at their absolute peak. It still ranks as the best ever concert I was at. We saw Oasis at their peak on Wednesday 14th of August 1996 at Pairc Ui Chaoimh in Cork city. Until 2016, it was my only visit to that city.

Exactly 20 years on, I made this fitting return. I walked alone all the way back to Pairc Ui Chaoimh, the same way that Colin, Keith and I would have done in 1996. It was really sentimental. I loved Cork city too – the central part of the city is on an island and I did a pub crawl with my local mate Pol, who I met in New Zealand in 2010.

In life's speedy capsule, this visit in 2016 and my first visit in 1996 remain my only two visits to Cork. I left a nice part of my heart there. It's a top-notch city. Who knows if I'll ever be back again, as I was off to the Euros now, to live an even bigger dream.

Chapter 57
Zielone Ogórki (Green Gherkins)

Milan, ITALIA to Nice, FRANCE (June 2016)

"They can come true yeah. They can come true" – Gabrielle.

The road to my first ever major tournament supporting Northern Ireland was an unusual one. I went Belfast to Dublin, then to Cork. From Cork, I flew to Bergamo. It was a direct flight by Ryanair and I was seemingly the only Northern Ireland supporter on that flight. My brother Marko and my Dad Joe had flown into Bergamo on a flight just before me and the plan was to meet at the airport and get a bus direct to Milan. We would have 3 days in Milan and then get the overland train direct to Nice.

Nice was the venue for Northern Ireland's first tournament match in 30 years. The opposition was – you guessed it Poland. Poland had come in and out of my life all the time down the years.

- My first Northern Ireland win was against Poland.
- Northern Ireland's last goal in 2002 before the goal drought was against Poland.
- My first mainland Europe away match was against Poland in 2005.
- Northern Ireland's last match in mainland Europe while I lived in Europe, was a 1-1 draw in Poland in 2009.

Ironically, we hadn't played them since, nor had I lived in Europe since then. It was now 7 years for me of not living in Europe. Oddly, that was about to change but I certainly didn't know it then.

AFC Bournemouth's current goalkeeper at the time was also Polish – Artur Boruc. Artur is actually a bit of a legend amongst Northern Ireland fans and is nicknamed "Ulster's Number One" *(see*

Chapter 10's "Ulster's Number One"). The game in question, where he earned that nickname was at Windsor Park in March 2009 and I was stood with my mates behind the nets he was staffing that half of the match. He was getting dog's abuse from the fans and then Damien Johnson our midfielder goes in for a challenge and puts a Polish defender under pressure. The defender knocks the ball back to Boruc. Boruc goes to kick it, but the ball hits a divot, passes over his foot and goes into the net! Boruc is embarrassed and enraged right in front of our eyes. Northern Ireland won the match 3-2 yet neither country qualified for World Cup 2010. Slovenia and Slovakia made it from our group.

The journey to Nice and to my first ever major tournament match began around 5 a.m. in Milan. I awoke in my hostel and headed to Milan central train station. I had booked us three tickets on a direct train from Milan to Nice. Dad Joe, brother Marko and I. We had time to grab coffee, sandwiches and beer ready for the overland adventure. I still love the magic of train travel, and this would be the first train journey in a two month period where I'd be taking trains in six different countries.

We arrived in Nice, checked into our hotel, then headed straight to town for beers. We mingled and drank with a mixture of Northern Ireland and Poland fans. Some I knew, some I didn't know. It was lively and fun.

I was inside the stadium well before kick-off and sampled in the atmosphere as the match started and I was now watching Northern Ireland at a major tournament. On the pitch, we looked nervous. I remembered that we had never lost the first match at a major tournament before. In 1958,we had beaten Czechoslovakia 1-0. In 1982,we drew 0-0 with Yugoslavia. In 1986,we drew 1-1 with Algeria. I would have settled for a draw with Poland.

The day was more important than the match though. It had been the euphoria of finally being at a major tournament as a fan. It was a milestone ticked off for me. I met up with so many Northern Ireland fans down the years and finally we were all together here, the GAWA at a major tournament. Some of those supporters I met by chance that day too - Owen Millar, Graham Anderson, Garreth Todd and so on. I also met an old school friend, Darren Loughrey, who I hadn't seen since leaving Bangor Grammar School in 1997.

At half time, it was goalless. We had held our own and were up against Poland's highly regarded Robert Lewangolski. The deadlock was finally breached. It was gutting.

Arkadiusz Milik drilled in a low shot past Michael McGovern. 1-0 to Poland. We struggled to make a real impact on the pitch that day, and deservedly lost 1-0. Germany beat Ukraine 2-0 though, to ensure we weren't bottom of the group.

There were no tears at losing to Poland. It was no shame. In fact, the vibe was happy and upbeat. We had seen Northern Ireland at the European Championships for the first time. The next match would be in Lyon, against Ukraine.

Before that, we toured Nice and Monte Carlo. Both were places I had skipped on my travel odyssey. Monte Carlo is the capital city of Monaco, itself a separate country from France. That was a cool adventure. Outside the British Isles, it was my first land border I remember crossing with my brother Marko. We got a red and white train from Nice Central to Monte Carlo in Monaco.

We got our passports stamped on arrival, visited the harbour and saw the famous chicane known as the most dangerous bend in Formula One grand prixs. We had a few beers and lunch there also, while we caught the live matches that day.

The following day, Marko, Dad and I boarded the train from Nice to Avignon and then a connection to central Lyon. On arrival in Lyon, there was a reunion with my youngest brother Daniel who had come to France for the middle match in the group, against Ukraine. It was crunch time.

Chapter 58
Kings of Lyon

Lyon, FRANCE (June 2016)

"While we're living, the dreams we have as children fade away" - Noel Gallagher.

Memories of Lyon will last forever. For me, for my Dad, for my brothers Marko and Daniel, for the GAWA. After the match against Poland in Nice, our second match against Ukraine was basically a must win. The loser would be out of the tournament. Having waited 30 years to get to a major tournament again, we certainly didn't want to finish bottom of our group. We have never finished bottom of a major tournament group. Either top (1982), second (1958) or third (1986, 2016).

Spirits were high in Lyon and I arrived here by train with Marko and Dad. At the main train station in Lyon, my youngest brother Daniel came to meet us. At this match there would be four Blairs. It was also curious that at all four Northern Ireland Euro 2016 matches, our Blair group contained a different mix of such Blairs!

The first match, a 1-0 defeat to Poland would be me, Marko and Dad. The second match, a 2-0 win over Ukraine would be me, Marko, Daniel and Dad. The third match, a 1-0 defeat to Germany would be just Dad and I. The fourth match, a 1-0 defeat to Wales, was just me. My Dad and both brothers had left France by then.

Everything about the Ukraine match felt right. The GAWA had truly taken over central Lyon. Green Northern Ireland shirts were everywhere. Ukrainians were few and far between. We arrived in Lyon two nights before the match. This was our second group match, and a must win.

In Lyon, the vibe was electric. I met so many old friends from down the years of supporting Northern Ireland. I met Stephen Rowley in a local bar in the Square. I asked him one question, *"What will the score be?."* Stephen Rowley is a veteran Northern Ireland fan who was at both the 1980s World Cups. Espana 82 and Mexico 86. Stephen answered my question without hesitation, *"2-0 to Northern Ireland"*. Stephen, would be completely right.

In the same bar, actor James Nesbitt, radio DJ Colin Murray and former Northern Ireland international Keith Gillespie all mingled with the GAWA. A feel good factor had arrived in Lyon.

On match day, I also had lunch with Michael and Gavin McClelland, lifelong friends. In the afternoon, it was me and Dad and Marko and Daniel. Us four Blairs were together for this. It was the moment in life we had all been waiting for.

From central Lyon, we boarded a GAWA party bus to the stadium. It was just a regular, Lyon public bus of course. But today, songs were being belted out by the GAWA.

For this match, I had extra tickets. Due to the fact that Daniel was only going to one match, I gave him my seat as it was in the heart of the GAWA. Marko and Daniel were in the hardcore GAWA for this one. But Dad and I took the dearer tickets for a change. We would be in a more mixed zone, by the side of the pitch, rather than behind the nets or above the corner flag. This just meant that the 4 of us weren't sat together for the match but no worries.

I was beside Dad and the match got underway. The first half was tight and we battled hard to go in at half-time goalless. Torrential rain began to beat down in Lyon as we won a free kick on the far side near the touchline.

Up into the box goes the cavalry.

Oliver Norwood sail binds a free kick towards the back post. Running in to meet it with a textbook bullet like header is Gareth McAuley. Ukraine have no chance here. The ball is in the back of the net before the goalkeeper even knows it. Bang.

"Oooh Gareth McAuley" – GAWA.

This is our first ever goal at a European Championships. This is our first major tournament goal this millennium, this century, this decade, this year, this month, this week, this day, this hour, this minute, EVER! This is our first major tournament goal since 1986; we waited 30 years for this moment.

The previous goal was a header from Newry lad Colin Clarke against Spain in Guadalajara. This time, Larner G Mac did the job. Gareth McAuley cemented his place in Northern Irish football folklore with this goal.

Then, the unthinkable happens, the torrential rain is too strong. The referee orders the players off the pitch. We are 1-0 up and looking good. The last things we wanted was a break, an interruption or the game to be postponed. I fear the worst. This was elation to anxiety.

The game is stopped. The players are off the field for now. I start to think of the consequences. Will the match restart today? Will it be cancelled and we have to play again tomorrow? Will the match restart with the score still at 1-0 to us? Will the referee abandon the match? If the referee abandons the match, does the score get reset to 0-0? I get so worried. Dad assures me the game will restart and everything will be okay. I trust my Dad.

The wait is worrying. Eventually, the players re-emerge despite the rain. It's a huge relief, but of course the time froze. It made it difficult to work out how long was left. There would easily be time for Ukraine to score two goals. If they win 2-1, that would have eliminated us due to the head to head. On the flipside, a second goal for us, would knock them out. A draw would be no use to either side – we'd probably both go out.

It was nervy and tense. We make two substitutions. Josh Magennis and Niall McGinn both come on. They will be influential, later on. First, are a few moments to sweat over.

Ukraine fire in a few efforts. In the slippy conditions and torrential rain, Michael McGovern remains strong, making a few saves and grasping the ball when he is called upon. It's nervy.

Time is ticking and the nerves are unstoppable. The fourth official indicates a minimum of 6 minutes stoppage time. At the time, it felt like the last thing we needed.

Into that sixth minute of stoppage time, our captain Steve Davis has the ball on the edge on their penalty area. He passes it right to Josh Magennis who isn't far from the corner flag. We yell at big Josh to take the ball into the corner to waste time. If he does that, we will hopefully hang on to win 1-0.

However, Josh has other plans. He beats his man and swings in a low cross. It's a Billy Hamilton-esque teaser. Niall McGinn cleverly dummies that ball, leaving it for Stuart Dallas to fire a shot on goal. Stuart's shot is parried by the Ukraine goalkeeper and running in quickly is wee McGinn to slot it in. We are in dreamland. Northern Ireland 2-0 Ukraine!! The GAWA go wild. I'm in tears. Emotions are sky high.

As it's the last minute, the final whistle blows soon after. Niall McGinn's goal was timed at 90+6. We have won.

It is Northern Ireland's first ever goals at a European Championships. It is Northern Ireland's first ever win at a

European Championships. In terms of goal difference, it is our biggest ever major tournament win. As well as all of that, we have scored 2 and conceded 1 in the group, giving us a strong position to be one of the highest ranked third place teams. Without counting chickens and going by history, we are likely to progress to the knockout stage!

Post-match celebrations are predictably insane. At the stadium itself, we meet a load more friends from down the years of supporting Northern Ireland, including Scott Gordon, Chris Gordon, Sammy Gordon, Bean, Nolers (Nial Coulter), Scott Williamson, Daryl Freel, Neil Millar, Robert Millar and Brucie. It's madness. It was a party bus back till downtown Lyon.

We grab a large cumulative carryout – the Blair lads! We drink in the main square and party most of the night. It's a wild night. Nursing hangovers the following day, my brothers Marko and Daniel head to Lyon airport at the same time that Dad and I head by bus to Paris.

We bid a fond farewell to Lyon. Que sera sera. Whatever will be will be, we're going to gay Paris, where even a 1-0 defeat to Germany will prove enough to be into the second stage (hindsight used).

Que sera sera.

"The greatest thing you can do in life is contribute to something which makes people happy" - Kenny Shiels.

Chapter 59
Bruges That Won't Heal

Ghent, BELGIUM (June 2016)

"And she's looking at youuhu . You Uhu. Uhu" – Calvin Harris.

After the Ukraine euphoria, we lost 1-0 to the World Champions Germany in Paris. That was an expected result, but not scoreline. Many thought we would get smashed 3 or 4 nil. It was all thanks to Michael "10 German bombers in the box" McGovern who kept the Germans at bay. Due to not having a negative goal difference and having 3 points, we went through to the second round as one of the best third placed teams in the group stage. At the time, we knew it would either be a second round match against France or Wales. I had tickets for every match including the final, were Northern Ireland to get there. I hung around in Paris and planned to do so until we won the tournament. Or in an odd universe, until we were knocked out. In the end, we scored the winner for Wales and went out. Gareth McAuley the hero against Ukraine, put the ball into his own net as we lost 1-0 to Wales. It was a tense game and sadly Will Grigg was never brung on to show his worth and light up the stage with his song. McAuley remains a hero to the GAWA though, despite that own goal that ended our Euro 2016 campaign. He's a legend to us!

"It's just a dropped stitch in life's tapestry" – Del Boy's Ma (Only Fools and Horses).

That day, when Northern Ireland lost 1-0 to Wales at Euro 2016, my plan was instinctive and impulsive. I wanted to get out of France as fast as I could. If we were no longer in the tournament, I had no desire to linger there. Au revoir.

In foresight, I hadn't booked a bed that night at my hostel, the trendy Young And Happy Hostel in Paris's quirky Latin quarter, on

Rue Mouffetard. Perhaps in my heart, I knew we were trapdooring it. I didn't want to risk wasting another night in unromantic Paris if my football team had trapdoored a major. It was time to get the fuck out of France.

On the pitch, trapdooring was exactly what happened. Northern Ireland lost 1-0 to Wales to a Gareth McAuley own goal and we were out. A journey that had begun for me on Madonna's Island in Belize was over. I watched the first match of that campaign, a 2-1 comeback win in Hungary on La Isla Bonita (San Pedro), Madonna Town in September 2014. But the dream was over. There wasn't much time to ponder.

"Some might say that we should never ponder on our thoughts today because they hold sway over time" – Noel Gallagher.

When the final whistle went, I didn't even cry. I shook the hands of a few GAWA friends from down the years, I said goodbye to Andrew and Matthew McInnes. I sat (stood) beside Andrew and Matthew at the Wales match and spent most of the tournament with them. That was all fun, but for now we parted, and off I went into the green and white Paris crowds. Solitudinal.

As soon as I got to the hostel, I went online and booked the first bus out of Paris that I found on one condition. It was going to somewhere I'd never been before. I needed to clear my head.

My country were out of Euro 2016. My engagement with Panny was never to become marriage. I was single. I was travel weary. I was lost, tired, homeless and lonely. I had no bed booked for tonight, nor tomorrow night, nor any night.

The bus I chose was the 2:22 a. m. Megabus to Brussels. Weirdly on my journey around the world where I swallowed over 100 capital cities, the EU HQ Brussels wasn't one of them. I had only been to Belgium once before, for one day. That was on a road trip from Germany to France in 2007. This was now my perfect chance to backpack Belgium and shut the door on it. Plus Belgium were still in the tournament and I knew I could watch a Belgium match in Belgium. Big deal.

The bus was booked and I emailed a few hostels in Brussels quickly asking to review them. I had a bit of time before that bus, so I headed to a small and quiet corner restaurant in the Latin Quarter of Paris near the metro. In there, I ordered a beer and a pasta dish and I sat alone. The Croatia v. Portugal match was on the television and I watched it all, bringing myself to tears at what my life had become. I was nowhere. I was a nomad. I had no home. I had no life. I had no wife. I had no flat. I had no car. I had no kids. I had no girlfriend. It was now that I realised my biggest asset was a fucking travel blog. Just as well, as it granted me free accommodation for the next while…at least until there would be a better solution.

"There will be an answer, let it be" – Paul McCartney.

I boarded my Megabus at 2 a.m. and got the fuck out of Paris. For like the 4th time or something. I fell asleep immediately and woke up in the Belgian capital. These days, European Union border crossings bore the hell out of me as they don't exist. There was no passport stamp between France and Belgium, no "Welcome to Belgium" sign. There wasn't even a currency or language change. As a Northern Irish nationalist, I detest such fake lovein excrement. Cultures and countries deserve to be bordered and distinguished. Otherwise they are lost, forevermore. Arguably I wasn't even in a country called Belgium, I was in a country called "European Union." Thankfully, the Soviets tried that and failed. But it took them years to recover and become separatist and nationalist again…

However, I was in Belgium in my own mind at least and I had a friend here in Brussels, well a few. Pol and Boris who I met in North Korea. I messaged them about meeting for lunch or dinner. The YHA hostel had replied to say I could stay the night and even better - I had my own private room. Cosy and quiet. I spent the day touring the sights of Brussels and met Pol for a beer.

I did all the textbook sightseeing. I ate Belgian chocolate, fries and waffles. I had a beer in the famous Delirium Bar and I checked out Manekin Pis male and female. I saw the EU Parliament Headquarters, without even brace fingering it. But simply put - Brussels wasn't my type of city so I decided a day was enough and I booked a train to Ghent the next day. In the meantime, I emailed a hostel there asking to review them. On that first and last night in the capital, from the YHA hostel bar, I watched Belgium smash Hungary 4-0 and went for an early night.

Even now, aged 36 and lonely, my travel days were crazy, unpredictable and spontaneous. I was booking beds night by night and had no clue where I'd be the next day, never mind the next week or month, or year. Something had to change.

I backpacked through Ghent and wound up in Bruges. Whence I made it to this canalic city of Bruges, I sat in the city's oldest restaurant and carved out a plan. I would head back to Kyrgyzstan and finish my book in Bishkek and work out life from there. My travel blog network was still bringing in ample cash for me to travel but now, I felt like having a base for another few months. Maybe I could teach English again in Bishkek – it was a job I actually liked even though I used to hate teachers as a kid. Plus, I knew in my heart of hearts that my book series *Backpacking Centurion* deserved to see the light of day now. The books were finished but I had no idea how to release them. I was certain Bishkek would be the place I could base myself in again to work all that out. Maybe I'd even get my dream kiss with Sagynai.

However, on route to Bishkek I of course wanted to nab a final bit of exploring and my mind was made up. I would visit Gdańsk and Kaliningrad. Both places had been high on my hitlist for years yet I hadn't been to that region of the world before.

My previous days in Poland had been central or south. I had friends in and around Gdańsk and as a student in Northern Ireland, I had studied the "Free City of Danzig" with intrigue. Plus, I had never seen the Polish Baltic coast at that point in my life. As a footballic bonus, Poland were still in Euro 2016 so maybe I'd even be there for the final with Poland in it. If Greece won it in 2004, Poland could win it in 2016 having bate Northern Ireland in the first match.

The same day, a flight company sent me a flight voucher. I found a perfect flight ticket. Amsterdam to Warszawa, with a day in Warszawa then an internal flight to Gdańsk. For the record, not that it matters anymore but those flights were free thanks to my travel blog. The spy who loved me. The blog that ruined me.

From Gdańsk I could then work out my route back to Bishkek. I was suddenly excited about life again. I knew my destiny didn't belong here in Benelux.

Belgium had been average I guess. Brussels was all I despised about the "EU." Ghent was nice to party in, just. Bruges was a pretty little town. But it didn't heal me. I didn't belong here. There was no way I could be in love with countries that adopted a fake "Euro currency." Even the Republic of Ireland succumbed to the dreaded Euro and left the beautiful Punt in history's dustbin. Oh the shame. Alas, it wasn't my problem and after a half day in Antwerp, I was back in The Netherlands.

Chapter 60
Amsterdammed

*Saint Christophers Inn, Amsterdam, THE NETHERLANDS
(July 2016)*

**"This could be Rotterdam or anywhere. Liverpool or Rome"
- The Beautiful South.**

It was now early July 2016 when I arrived in Amsterdam for the third time. I had met a Chilean Air hostess, Maria, in Belgium. Maria was backpacking in Europe and we agreed to meet up in the Dutch capital.

I felt a change coming here. I was looking forward to Gdańsk. I messaged a few of my Polish friends, inviting one of them on a food tour to Gdynia with me and telling another Polish friend we'd meet for Polish craft beers.

When I arrived overland by train into The Netherlands, I knew it would be two quick nights here and then on to Gdańsk. My train left Belgian Antwerp and had a brief stop in Rotterdam. Or anywhere. My backpacking friend Maria from Chile arrived in the Dam almost at the same time as me. We agreed to meet up. Like many such reunions in my life, Maria would become a multiple country ticker friend.

After checking into the Saint Christopher's Inn in the poky streets of The Dam, I headed downstairs to the bar to watch the next Euro 2016 quarter final. The previous night, Portugal had beaten Poland on penalties to reach the semi-finals. This ruled out my dream of watching Poland in the final in Poland. Here in the Dutch bar, I was watching Wales against Belgium. Oddly, the bar was packed with Welsh people. There were Welsh jerseys everywhere. That was a bit of a shock.

As I sipped my beer I realised I shouldn't even have been here. Football matches had changed my fate. I was supposed to be in

Paris that night as it should have been Northern Ireland against Belgium. But Wales had knocked us out. I decided to support Belgium that night as I thought Wales were jammy to bate us.

Belgium lost. Wales were semi-finalists! In their first major tournament since 1958, they were in the last four – crazy, though inspired of course by Gareth Bale and ex-Bournemouth player Sam Vokes weighed in with one of the goals that knocked out the Belgians. Sightseeing wise, I just couldn't be bothered anymore. I had been to Amsterdam in 1991, and again in 2014. I had done all the sightseeing I craved in this city. But really, I was only here to fly to Poland. It was a transition period in a transition country.

Instead of sightseeing, it was bar crawls and the quirky Brouwerij De Prael Craft Beer Bar had a beer called Johnny, almost my name. The second day, I got my haircut in Amsterdam. Haircuts around the world on my journeys had been sporadic, unplanned and all over the place. For a period of 13 years, I don't recall EVER using the same barber twice. This trend continues into 2022...

That night was another quarter final knockout match. Germany v. Italy. I watched it with Maria and her friend, Evan from the USA, whom she had met in the hostel. The next morning, I had a flight to Poland...early riser.

I caught a train from central Amsterdam to Schiphol Airport. It was just a regular trip that was typical of my journeys around the world. I'd be flying to Poland again. This time with no onward flights, trains or buses out booked, but I'd done that before so many times, including with Bishkek. Surely I wouldn't end up moving to Poland? Just another dot on my globe. Nobody could predict what lay ahead. Lastly, not me.

"If there's a God, would he give another chancer an hour to sing for his soul?" - Noel Gallagher.

Chapter 61
I Went To Gdańsk With Somebody

Stare Miasto, Gdańsk, POLAND (July 2016)

"All in all, the world is small enough for both of us" – Grant Lee Buffalo.

This was supposed to be different. I sometimes don't know what to say. I sometimes don't know what to write. It was weird being in Gdańsk that time and not everything can be written in this book. Some good and bad things happened around this time. As I typed it all up to put in the book and release the truth, there was a problem. It wasn't legally possible for me to include certain details in here. Whatever happened, happened. But it's too late now to change all that. It has been and gone. There will be a sequel to this book *(spoiler – it's already written, almost finished).*

"You'll never change what's been and gone" – Noel Gallagher.

On Sunday the 3rd of July 2016, for the first time in my life, I landed in Gdańsk in Poland. I was supposed to be here for a week to meet some Polish friends, tour the sights, review a hostel, a bike tour and a food tour. After that, my plan was to get a visa for Kaliningrad. This is the enclave of Russia in Europe which I had longed to visit for years. I planned to overland into Kaliningrad, head back to Warszawa to visit some friends and then, (probably) I had fully expected to fly from Warszawa to Bishkek and to settle in Kyrgyzstan to edit my books and start life from there. That was the rough plan anyway.

In the circle of life...that never happened.

I stayed in Gdańsk!!

"I wanna dance with somebody" – Whitney Houston.

Yes, on this trip, after I arrived in Gdańsk on Sunday 3rd July 2016, I stayed there. I stayed here. Apart from a few trips, I've basically been in Poland ever since. But why did I stay? Is that what this book was supposed to be all about? If you bought, borrowed, pinched or read this book only to get that answer, then keep looking as I also don't have a concrete answer. It just felt right that I was here now. It was fate taking me to a place I belong in. It was my destiny to live in Poland. I believe it had been written in the stars. We never know what can happen in life – sometimes we just can't predict it.

"I went to Gdańsk with somebody" – Jonny Blair.

If there was a simple answer to the question why I moved to Gdańsk, I would write it here. I would tell it. But there is no simple answer. In life, if you like a place and you have nothing pulling you to somewhere else, and nothing suggesting you should leave, then why should you leave? You shouldn't. And that was exactly what did it with Gdańsk for me. I knew I needed to stay here. I knew I belonged here. This city was what I had been waiting for. Everything glew with a gleam.

"Bo bez ciebie nie ma nic z tobą jedną mogę być. Jeśli tylko chcesz" - Paweł Kukiz & Jan Borysewicz.
[Without you, there is nothing. I can be with you, if you only want]

In the end, no flight to Bishkek was ever booked. I extended my stay in the Cycle On Hostel and then, I started touring the province that Gdańsk is in – Pomorskie / Pomerania. This was some of my best travel writing for a long time. I toured the northern town of Łeba with Marina and Giacomo from the hostel. I toured Sopot and Gdańsk with popular Taiwanese travel blogger Mika on the Road. I strolled on the gorgeous sands of Poland's "desert" - Słowiński National Park. I was loving life again. Every day I was exploring Gdańsk and I started to love three streets in particular – Ulica Piwna, Ulica Mariacka and Ulica Długa. Over the next two months, July and August 2016, I must have visited 90% of the bars, cafes and restaurants on those streets. I was truly loving it.

I moved into a flat in Gdańsk in August 2016, after a few side trips. On my last morning in the Cycle On Hostel, another freaky coincidence occurred. Kasia from Kraków was in the same dorm room as me! Yes, Kasia Brzyk who I had met in Football Heaven bar in Kraków, the December before, as mentioned way back in Chapter 38.

Also in Gdańsk, I took a local girl out for dinner on a fine date. I dined her out in style and she was amazed by it, later she felt me up and kissed me as a huge surprise. She did that in full view of the public, on a main thoroughfare in Gdańsk old town. Everything was feeling incredible here in this seaside town. I'm a seaside boy remember. I grew up in Bangor, Northern Ireland.

"It's written in the starlight and every line on your palm"
- Mark Knopfler.

For the first few weeks of staying in Gdańsk, almost every bar or cafe I was in had Wi-Fi. But it was much much more than just that. Those bars and cafés were local and quirky, with super staff, with a calm atmosphere. In central Gdańsk, I frequented Józef K, No to CYK, Red Light, Café Factotum, Lookier Café... I worked in all of them, the same way I had worked online for about 5 months in Central Asia. I was able to get a lot of writing done in this town, Gdańsk was inspirational.

As I write this book and prepare to release it six years on, my favourite writers bar in the world, remains Józef K. It's the bar where I finally finished my Backpacking Centurion series. Gdańsk felt like it was where I belonged. I had missed a trick for the last 4 years of working from my laptop. This was the perfect city for a digital nomad. I had landed. Please head to Józef K in Gdańsk! I love it. It's my dream writer's bar!

In those first two months, I also did side trips to some truly incredible places, of which Starogard Gdański was my clear favourite. This was an old town in a region known as Kociewie and within a few days of being there, I had made a lot of new friends already. I was out in the bars and cafes there too, social vulture loyal – Projekt PRL, Browar Stary Rynek, Basement, Małe Piwko, Klub Kawiarnia Szafa and I was writing about it. It was a refreshing and brilliant city, and I have written about Stari G (as I began to call it) many times on my blogs, and indeed it's in my next book. Perhaps one of the clinchers to me staying in Poland was that the local newspaper there, Gazeta Kociewska ran a full feature on me in the printed newspaper and on their website! I was on the front page next to Oktawia Nowacka, an Olympic medal winner. While touring nearby Pelplin, the major of the town shared my post on social media, and again in Tczew, I was featured online on their website. Polish people started to like my blogs on lesser ventured parts of their country. There was no way now that I could leave a country that was giving me such happiness.

The town of Starogard Gdański is also the birthplace of the legendary Kazimierz Deyna, who helped take Poland to an Olympic Gold and Silver Medal, and a Bronze medal at the 1974 World Cup. Deyna has his statue in the local stadium here, and I decided to make this my Polish team of choice. I have watched them many times now, including in a cup final in Malbork. The team was perfect for me to choose on so many levels. Deyna is Poland's George Best. Both ended up in the USA. Both died too early. Klub Piłkarski Starogard Gdański also play in green and white, and their badge in green and white. My favourite colours and also the colours of Northern Ireland. The club also used Gala's "Free From Desire" as their anthem – same anthem for the Northern Ireland fans that summer! It also linked back to my friends Rafał Kowalczyk and Kamil Turula, who support Legia Warszawa. Deyna's statue also sits proudly outside the Legia Stadium in Warszawa, where he is still hero worshipped.

In amidst all the drama of that, I knew I had found a home in Gdańsk and it was an easy decision for me to decide to stay here for 6 more months. After leaving Hong Kong 10 months earlier, splitting up with Panny and trying to relocate to Bishkek, why should I move again? I loved Gdańsk, Gdynia and Sopot. This was the hattrick I had always craved. One afternoon as I sipped a coffee in Józef K bar on Ulica Piwna in Gdańsk, I knew I had finally found a home. I finished the last edits of my book series *Backpacking Centurion* in that bar. I told my friends and family that I loved Gdańsk and was settling here. I found a room in a flat in the Stare Miasto (Old Town).

There were so many more positives here in Gdańsk, which is also close to many beaches. There is an easy seaside escape. It is also close to inland lakes. Plus there is the history. It might be sad and tarnished but it all really happened here. This was once a separate country with its own currency, laws and borders. The short lived "Free city of Danzig", a German occupied era. Solidarność started here. Lech Wałęsa's trade union movement that was a catalyst in the eventual fall of communism all began at Stocznia Gdańska – the shipyard.

Aside from all that, it is a safe and peaceful city. It is easy to live in. There isn't much stress here. Despite all the problems of the past, modern day Gdańsk revels in a new found glory. Like Northern Ireland, Bournemouth, Parramatta, Montevideo, Hong

Kong and Bishkek did to me in the past, Gdańsk endeared me from day one. I simply loved this city.

Still, it was a huge surprise to me that I loved Gdańsk so much, and so quickly and it made me wonder why I had skipped it so many times before. As I make the final edits to his book today, I just moved into my 10th different flat in Poland. Three of them were in Gdańsk, seven of them were in Warszawa. That's a wow! 2022 is also the tenth calendar year that I have been in Poland (2005, 2007, 2015, 2016, 2017, 2018, 2019, 2020, 2021, 2022). Surprisingly, in seven of those years, I can say I live here. I live in Poland. I'm a nomad even when I feel like I live in a country!

In Hong Kong I was in 5 different flats in a 4 year period. In Australia I was really only in one flat, aside from my backpacking, hostelling, camping in my tent and sleeping in my car days. In London, one. In Dartford, one. In Bournemouth eight. So I'm often a nomad even in the same city. I change multitudinously.

Change happens for a reason. I love quotes and I littered this book (and most of my writing) with them. They are a homage and a nod to those who inspired my journey.

"A change would do you good" - Sheryl Crow.

Now that I had a new flat in Gdańsk and a super city to live in, I began to immerse myself quickly into Polish culture and ways. After those backpacking glory days, I had finally found a home.

This might be the last chapter of this particular book, but this was me opening the first chapter of my new life, my new story.

My blog, Northern Irishman in Poland was born before 2016 faded out of view and I was now an Ulsterczyk in Poland. This was only the start of my adventure in Poland. That blog was started for a laugh, almost by accident when I had depression and felt that "Don't Stop Living" had run its course. I was definitely not aware back in December 2016 that I'd end up living in Poland for 5 years, run a successful blog here, write over 500 articles on Poland and work with the tourist boards in a few cities. My experience of teaching English came in very handy too as I could now take Polish adults (who already had decent English) up to a higher level. Everything fell into place and this was my new life. You'll have to wait for the sequel book to follow the next path on my szalony journey.

The quest for that elusive everlasting smile goes on.

Keep dreaming.

Don't stop living.

[The iron curtain already fell]

Wactionary (Wacky Dictionary)

Rough translation guide from Northern Irish and Jonny Blairish intill English:

afforequoted – quoted before.

Alanis Mozzarella – Alanis Morrisette

alightings – getting off public transport a plural amount of times

apparence - noun form of apparent

arrivation – the act of arriving in that place

authoric – of an author

BB – Boys' Brigade

bake – face

bake on ye / look at the state of yer man / see yer bake – you do not look happy

beg – bag

betweenic – of in-between

Bournemouthian – a person from Bournemouth

Bournemouthic – typical of Bournemouth

boverrated – badly over-rated

brave – really good

bate – beaten, lost

belshynic – of Belshina Belarus

bogs – toilets, loos, toalety, WCs

boverrated – highly over-rated

braceically - twice

breath thefter – something that takes your breath away

buck eejit – cultured idiot

buckie – tonic wine (95% of the time it's the brand 'Buckfast')

busticated – broken

byline – the entire line on a football between the two corner flags, except for the goal part, which is called the goal-line

canalic - of canals, example "Bydgoszcz is a canalic city"

carrotic – of Netherlands 1990 football shirt orange

carryout – takeaway alcohol

caser – leather football

charmigator – something that is very charming

countrywise – in terms of countries

craic – banter so it is

crackation – of cracking

crappuccino – a very bad quality cappuccino

Cremola Foam – a popular fizzy drink in Northern Ireland during the 1980s

dandered, a dander, to dander – walked, a walk, to walk at a normal Northern Irish pace

datily – in order of date

Dennis – wise, clever

docken leaf - rumex obtusifolius, a leaf that helps after a nettle sting

down south – Republic of Ireland (even the northern parts of it like Donegal!)

earthful – around planet earth

eejit – idiot

eejitiotic – like an idiot

electionic – resembling an election

enignymity – not knowing what might happen, mystery, enigma

ensuic – what ensued, what came next

feg - cigarette

fillim - movie

fleg – flag

fly nets – no specified goalkeeper doing nets. Anyone can do nets in this example in park football.

footballic – of football

forwardlash – exact opposite of backlash

freelancic – of freelancing, doing it for yourself

frostbit – bitten by frost, freezing, Baltic, very cold

gat shat – got shot, was fired at using a gun

GAWA – Green and White Army, Northern Ireland football fans

geg – funny person, ridiculously funny

gighopper – a person who goes to lots of gigs/concerts, they "hop" to gigs like a grasshopper hops through grass or a groundhopper hops through football grounds

lew – glow (in my past tense – instead of "glowed")

grass – to tell the authorities about something potentially illegal

gunless – without a gun

here's me till im – after that, I said to this man

holdancy – the situation of holding something

hourfall – at that exact moment where that significant thing happens

impulsivic – stronger adjective than impulsive

intill - into

jamember? – do you remember?

Jurassic Park – it's a fillim about dinosaurs

keeperity – the situation of keeping / maintaining something

leet – litre (example – "gimme a swig of yer two leet")

look at the bake on yer man – look at his face

lovein – fake love that I cringe at

lunatical – crazy

madliness - lunatical

marathonic – an adjective used to describe a person who loves marathons

McCrum, McCrums – penalty kicks / pelanty kicks / pelanties / penalties

minoritise – to prioritise the minority

mundanity – the act of being mundane, bland, boring

musicly – musically

nat – not

nets – goals, goalkeeper, keeper

nightness – the feeling that it is at night

Norn Iron – Northern Ireland

off the wheaten craic – a place where there are no other tourists and no airport (the real "off the beaten track")

oopsilon – whoops in an embarrassing way

ourselfs – ourselves (an acceptable poetic plural form)

nuder – more nude, less amount of clothes

peelers – policemen and policewomen, members of the police force

peeler station – police station

pelanty – penalty, McCrum

photy, photies – photo, photos

pociąg – an alternative word for train (taken from Polish)

Portadownczyk – a man from Portadown in Northern Ireland

premath – opposite of aftermath (beforehand)

quare – a lot of, hugely, magically

quare geg – a right laugh/something funny

Quoile – a river in Northern Ireland

radaboutye – how are you?

randomic – random, adjectivicly

repitivity – the act of repeating

ringathon – a ringing session that doesn't have to be 26 rings

saff – south (in a broad London accent)

scory – a mixture of story and score

screamager – it's a song by Therapy?

see him? – look at that guy

shap - shop

shar – shower

singleton and singledom – being single

so it is – no meaning, can be replaced with a blank space, but that would be boring

solitudinal – the only one of that thing

spake – speak, dialect, style

(to) squeal - to tell the authorities about something potentially illegal

stolica – capital city

tap – top

textbookic – of the finest textbook quality as an example within that field *textbookikly* – done by the textbook, the best way that it should have been done

that there – meaningless Northern Irish garbage

themmuns – those people

theseuns – these ones

thingy – that person, you know that person right?

thon – that wee one

till – to

timeclock – clock of your time

townic – of a town

trójmiastic – of trójmiasto, of Tri-city (Gdańsk, Gdynia, Sopot)

Ulsterczyk – Ulsterman, a man from Ulster, often used when talking about myself (Jonny Blair)

Ulsteric – adjective describing 'of Ulster'

Ulsterka – Ulsterwoman, a woman from Ulster

unchaptertitled – that was not the title of the chapter I gave

unhyperbolic – opposite of hyperbolic, not exaggerated

unin – not included in, not in

unstrong – not strong

UTCIAD – Up the Cherries, in all departments! (AFC Bournemouth fan chant)

wacaday, wacadaisical – (copyright of Timmy Mallet) crazy, lunatical

wallfall – the falling of a wall (e.g. Berlin Wall)

wee – term of endearment, often signifying small

whackpacking, whackpacker – to go backpacking in a crazy way, a crazy backpacker

whackwhopping – a more crazy version of whopping

whatcha – what are ya?

whoppaday – crazy low/high amount

wildernistic – of wilderness

worldic – global

ya, ye - you

yearically – by year, including that year, within that year, you can also use this word the same way as daily weekly, monthly, annually

yer Da woulda stuck thatun away – your father would have scored a goal

yer gegging me – you are joking about with me

yer man – that male person

yer woman – that female person

yoghurty – creamy like a yoghurt

yous, youse, yousens – you people

zielonic – green

If there are any other unknown words or phrases that are used in this book, you can email the author Jonny Blair for clarification, as he often uses his own phrases and confuses others with his peculiar use of language.

The Backpacking Journey of Jonny Blair 1980 – 2022

This is a list of all the places that Jonny Blair visited between March 1980 and January 2022. It includes all continents, countries, disputed regions, wacaday republics, exclusion zones, uninhabited islands, unrecognised countries, micronations, metropolises, cities, conurbations, towns, villages, hamlets and those places deemed significant to be on this list. The list may not be 100% complete, but the author has tried to be as complete as was possible. Continents, countries, places and settlements are listed in alphabetic order.

Continents / Large Regions Visited

Africa, Antarctica, Asia, Caribbean, Central America, Europe, Middle East, North America, Oceania, Pacific Islands, South America

Places Visited

On this list Jonny has included everywhere he has been. He has narrowed it down to cities, towns, villages or what he personally deems to be a significant place. These are listed under the same categories as the countries or regions that Jonny personally classes them as belonging in. Those places in brackets mean he was only there in transit (the bus stopped, the train stopped, he changed flights etc.).

Adammia
Jagstonian Plains, Maternia Province, Tytannia Province
Afghanistan
Aybak, Bactra / Bactria, Balkh, Hayratan, Masar e Sharif, Samangan, Tashkurgan
Albania
Paskuqan, Shkodër, Tirana
Algeria
Algiers

Andaman Islands
Corbyn's Cove, Port Blair
Andorra
Andorra La Vella, Escaldes Engordany, Ordino
Angola
Luanda, Panguila, Viana
Antarctica
Admiralty Bay, Aitcho Islands, Barrientos, Cuverville Island,
Deception Island, Drake Passage, Elephant Island, Foyn Harbour,
Gerlache Strait, Jougla Point, Half Moon Island, King George
Island (Henryk Arctowski Polish Antarctic Base), Neko Harbour,
Neptune's Bellows, Neptune's Window, Neumayer Channel,
Petermann Island, Pleneau Island, Port Foster, Port Lockroy
(British Antarctic Base), Telefon Bay, Wiencke Island
Argentina
Beagle Channel, Buenos Aires, Puerto Iguazu, Ushuaia
Armenia
Garni, Geghard, Goght, Goris, Haghpat, Khor Virap, Noravank,
Sanahin, Tatev, Yerevan
Austenasia
Orly, Wrythe
Austria
Anif, Braunau Am Inn, Grodig, Linz, Neumarkt Kostendorf,
Salzburg, Vienna
Australia
Australian Capital Territory – Aranda, Canberra, Casuarina Sands
Bruny Island – Alonnah, Cape Bruny, Lunnawanna
New South Wales - Blackheath, Blacktown, Blue Mountains, Byron
Bay, Cann River, Coffs Harbour, Coolangatta, Driver Reviver,
Emu Plains, Jenolan Caves, Katoomba, Kiama, Narooma, Nowra,
Maclean, Mount Druitt, Newcastle, Ourimbah, Paddy's Rest,
Parramatta, Penrith, Port Macquarie, Ruined Castle, Sydney, Taree,
Three Sisters, Tweed Heads, Ulladulla, Wentworth Falls,
Westmead, Wollongong, Woodford Island

Queensland - Beerburrum, Brisbane, Broadbeach, Glass House Mountains, Logan, North Lakes, Point Danger, Scarborough, Surfer's Paradise

Tasmania - Bagdad, Bangor, Bangor Farm, Batman Bridge, Bishopsbourne, Bothwell, Bruny Island, Campbell Town, Campspur, Carrick, Cataract Gorge, Cole's Beach, Cradle Mountain, Cressy, Devil's Kitchen, Devonport, Dip Falls, Don, Dove Lake, Dubbil Barril, East Sassafras, Forth, Freycinet National Park, Georgetown, Glenorchy, Gordon, Great Lake, Great Oyster Bay, Hellyer Gorge, Hobart, Isle of the Dead, Kettering, Kindred, Lake Leake, Latrobe, Launceston, Lillico, Longford, Lower Landing, Lynchford, Mackintosh Dam, Mawbanna, Moonah, Moriarty, Mount Amos, Nowhere Else, Penguin, Poatina, Port Arthur, Port Sorrell, Queenstown, Remarkable Cave, Rinadeena, Rosebery, Ross, Sheffield, Squeaking Point, Stanley / The Nut, Strahan, Swansea, Taranna, Teepookanna, Tullah, Turner's Beach, Ulverstone, Wesley Vale, Wineglass Bay, Wrest Point, Zeehan

Victoria - 12 Apostles, 90 Mile Beach, Bairnsdale, Bell's Beach, Brighton, Cann River, Foster, Frankston, Great Ocean Road, Grey River, Kennet River, Lakes Entrance, Leongatha, Lorne, Marlo, Melbourne, Mosquito Hill, Peterborough, Port Campbell, Yarram, Yellow Pinch Dam

Woodford Island - Brushgrove

Azerbaijan

Baku, Balakan, Caspian Sea, James Bond Oil Fields, Lake Masazir, Mud Volcanoes, Qobustan, Quba, Seki, Xinaliq, Zaqatala

Bahrain

King Fahd Causeway, Manama, Muharraq Island, Oil Field, Riffa, Sitra, Umm al-Na'san

Bangladesh

Chittagong, Dhaka, Uttara

Basque Country / Euskadi

Bilbao, Donostia (San Sebastian)

Bavaria
Munich
Belarus
Bobruisk, Barysaw, Grodno, Minsk
Belize
Actun Tunichil Muknal, Ambergris Caye, Belize City, Belmopan,
Benque Viejo del Carmen, Caye Caulker, Placencia, San Pedro,
Spanish Lookout, Xunantunich
Belgium
Antwerp, Bruges, Brussels, Eupen, Ghent, Kettenis, Saint Ghislain
Benin
Abomey, Cotonou, Ouidah, Porto Novo
Bolivia
Arbol de Pietra, Atacama Desert, Cementario Des Trens, Colchani,
Desaguadero, Gorilla Mountain, Incahuasi / Isla Del Pescado,
Laguna Canapa, Laguna Colorada, Laguna Verde, La Paz, Oruro,
Potosi, San Cristobal, San Juan de Rosario, Santa Cruz de La
Sierra, Uyuni
Borneo (see separate country sections for Malaysia, Brunei
Darussalam and Indonesia)
Bosnia
Sarajevo
Bosnia-Herzegovina
Neum, Mostar, Sarajevo
Botswana
Chobe, Gaborone, Kasane, Kazungula, Tlokweng
Brazil
Belem, Belo Horizonte, Fortaleza, Foz Do Iguacu, Juquitiba,
Macapa, Oiapoque, Olinda, Recife, Rio De Janeiro, São Paulo
Brunei Darussalam
Bandar Seri Bagawan, Kampong Ayer, Muara, Serasa
Bulgaria
Gorna Oryakhovitsa, Gyueshevo, Plovdiv, Sofia, Veliko Tarnovo

Burundi
Bujumbura, Lake Tanganyika
Cambodia
Angkor Thom, Angkor Wat, Baphuon, Bayon, Chau Say Tevoda,
Phnom Penh, Poipet, Preah Dak, Siem Reap, Thommanon,
Trapeang Kreal
Canada
Niagara, Toronto, Winnipeg
Catalonia
Barcelona, (Andorra Border)
Channel Islands (also listed individually)
Guernsey, Herm, Jersey, Lihou Island, Little Sark, Sark
Chernobyl Exclusion Zone
Chernobyl Town, Duga Tower, Dytyatky, Kopachi, Pripyat,
Reactor Number 4
Chile
Cape Horn, Hito Cajun, Santiago
China (incomplete)
Anhui Province – Huangshan, Nanping, Yuliang
Beijing - Badaling, Beijing, Forbidden City, Great Wall of China,
Tiananmen Square
Chongqing - Chongqing, Foreigner Street, Yangtze River
Guangdong Province – Chikan, Da Lang, Danxiashan, Dongguan,
Guangzhou, Jin Jiang Village, Kaiping, Majianlong, Mount Daxia,
Ruishi Lou, Shaoguan, Shenzhen, Window of the World, Yao Tang,
Zhuhai, Zili
Guangxi Province - Baisha, Guilin, Li River, Yangshuo
Hunan Province – Changsha
Jiangsu Province - Pingjianglu, Suzhou
Jiangxi Province - Jiangling, Jingdezhen, Likeng Little Likeng,
Nanchang, Sanqing Shan, Shangrao, Wangkou, Wuyuan,
Xiaoqi, Yushan

Fujian Province - Gaobei Hamlet, Gu Lang Yu, Hong Keng, Shancheng, Ta Pa Tsune, Taxia Village, Tian Luo Keng, Xiamen, Yongding
Shanghai – Shanghai
Liaoning Province – Dandong
Yunnan Province - Gejiu, Gum Guy, Jianshui, Jinjiang Waterfalls, Jin Ji Cun, Kunming, Lijiang, Luoping, Nansha, Screw Tin (Yellow Fields), Shilin Stone Forest, Shuhe, Shangri La (Zhongdian), Tiger Leaping Gorge, Upper Trail Hike, Yuanyang Rice Terraces, Xingjie Zhen
Zhejiang Province - Hangzhou, West Lake

Christiania
Freetown Christiania (inside Copenhagen, Denmark)

Colombia
Bogota, Chia, Cucuta, (Duitama), Guasca, Guatavita, Santa Ana Alta, Sopo

Costa Rica
Alajuela, Cacao, Grecia, Penas Blancas, San Jose

Croatia
Dubrovnik, Split, Zagreb

Cyprus
Larnaca, Limassol, Nicosia, Tseri

Czechia / Czech Republic (see also Wallachia)
(Decin), Olomouc, Ostrava, Prague

Democratic Republic of Congo
Bukavu, Kahuzi-Biega National Park

Denmark
Copenhagen, Helsingor

Don't Stop Living
http://dontstopliving.net/

Druze People
Isfiya Village (inside Israel)

East Timor
Atauro Island - Beloi, Vila

Mainland - Cape Fatucama, Dili
Ecuador
Ciudad Mitad del Mundo, Quito
Egypt
Cairo, Giza, Memphis, Pyramids, River Nile, Saqqara, Sphinx
El Salvador
Anguiatu, Barra de Santiago, Chalchuapa, Joya de Ceren, Las
Chinamas, Mangrove Forests, Nejapa, Puerta del Diablo, San
Andres, San Salvador, Santa Ana, Sonsonate, Tazumal
England (incomplete)
Aldershot, Alnwick, Bath, Bideford, Birkenhead, Birmingham,
Blackburn, Blackpool, Blandford Forum, Boscombe,
Bournemouth, Brighton, Bristol, Burnley, Bury, Carlisle,
Carshalton, Cheltenham, Christchurch, Colchester, Crawley,
Crayford, Dartford, Derby, Doncaster, Dorchester, Durdle Door,
Eastbourne, Eton, Exeter, Fleetwood, Forest of Dean, Gatwick,
Gillingham, Gloucester, Gosport, Gravesend, Heathrow, Hereford,
Kings Somborne, Lake District, Lancaster, Leeds, Lee On Solent,
(Leicester), Liverpool, London, Loughborough, Luton, Lymington,
Lytham St. Anne's, Manchester, Mansfield, Milton Keynes,
Newcastle Upon Tyne, New Forest, Newhaven, Nottingham,
Oxford, Pease Pottage, Poole, Portsmouth, Preston, Rochester,
Salisbury, Sheffield, Southampton, Southend, Southsea, Stansted,
Stoke-on-Trent, Stonehenge, Sunderland, Torquay, Truro,
Wakefield, Wallasey, Watford Gap, Weston-super-Mare,
Weymouth, Winchester, Windsor, Woking, Worksop, Woughton
Isle of Wight - Cowes, Newport, The Needles, Yarmouth
Islands - Brownsea Island, Portland
Estonia
Parnu, Tallinn
Ethiopia
Addis Ababa, Asbe Teferi, Dire Dawa, Harar
Faroe Islands
Bordoy - Klaksvik, Norddepil

Fugloy – Hattarvik, Kirkja
Eysturoy – Gjogv
Streymoy - Kirkjubour, Saksun, Torshavn
Svinoy – Svinoy
Vagar - Bour, Gasadalur, Lake Sorvagsvatn, Midvagur,
Sorvagur, Vatnsoyrar
Vidoy – Hvannasund
Fiji
Viti Levu – Nadi, Namaka
Finland
Helsinki, Järvenpää, Suomenlinna
France
Avignon, Campeigne, Cherbourg, Dieppe, Epinay Sur Seine, La
Roche Sur Yon, Lyon, Marseille, Nantes, Nice, Paris, Saint-Gilles-
Croix-de-Vie, St. Jean de Monts, St. Malo
French Guyana
Cayenne, G.S.C., Iracoubo, Kourou, Organabo, Sinnamary, St.
Georges de L'oyapock, St. Laurent du Maroni
Frestonia
Freston Road, Bramley Road (inside London, England)
Gambia
Bakau, Banjul, Barra, Brufut, Kololi, Serrakunda
Georgia
Batumi, Davit Gareja, Gergeti, Gori, Kazbegi, Lagodekhi,
Sighnaghi, Tbilisi, Uplistsikhe / Up Something
Germany
Bah Harzburg, Berlin, Bremen, Dresden, Frankfurt, Hamburg,
Hannover, Leipzig, Magdeburg, Marburg, Munich, Nuremberg,
Oker, Osterweddingen, Romkerhall, Simbach Am Inn, (Trier)
Gibraltar
Europa Point, Gibraltar City, Top of the Rock
Gorno Badakhshan
Kalai Khum, Khorog, Vanj

Greece
Mainland - Athens
Rhodes - Afandou, Faliraki, Rhodes Town
Guatemala
Anguiatu, Antigua, Coban, El Florida, El Rancho de San Agustín, Flores, Guatemala City, Huehuetenango, Indian's Nose Hike, Lago Atitlan, La Mesilla, Lanquin, Melchor de Mencos, Nuevo Valle, Panajachel, Quetzaltenango / Xela, Rio Hondo, San Marcos La Laguna, San Pedro La Laguna, Santa Clara La Laguna, Semuc Champey, Valle Nuevo, Volcan Santa Maria, Volcan Tajumulco
Guernsey
L'Eree, Lihou Island, St. Peter Port
Guyana
Bartica, Corriverton, Falmouth, Georgetown, Kaieteur Falls, Molson Creek, Parika, Sloth Island
Herm
Manor Village, The Common, The Peak
Herzegovina
Mostar, Neum
Honduras
Copan Ruinas, El Florida, El Guasaule, La Ceiba, Puerto Cortes, Rio Cangrejal, San Pedro Sula, Tegucigalpa, Utila
Hong Kong (incomplete)
Hong Kong Island - Aberdeen, Admiralty, Causeway Bay, Central, Chai Wan, North Point, Sheung Wan, Stanley, The Peak, Wan Chai
Kowloon – Austin, Cheung Sha Wan, Diamond Hill, Hung Hom, Jordan, Kowloon Bay, Kowloon Tong, Kwun Tong, Lai Chi Kok, Lam Tin, Mong Kok, Olympic, Prince Edward, San Po Kong, Tai Kok Shui, Tsim Sha Tsui, Yau Ma Tei, Yau Tong
New Territories - Fan Ling, Kwai Fong, Lok Ma Chau, Lo Wu, Sai Kung, Sha Tin, Sheung Shui, Tsuen Wan, Tsueng Kwan O, Yuen Long
Outlying Islands - Lantau Island, Ma Wan/Park Island, Mui Wo, Tai O, Tsing Yi, Tung Chung, Yi O

Hungary
Budapest, Debrecen, Szolnok
Iceland
Blue Lagoon, Geysir, Grindavik, Gullfoss, Keflavik, Kerio Crater, Pingvellir, Reykjavik
India
Delhi - New Delhi
Gujarat - Ahmedabad, Aralaj Vav
Maharashtra – Elephant Island, Mumbai
Goa - Anjuna Beach, Harvali, Mapusa, Vagator, Vagator Beach, Panaji/Panjim
Other - Agra, Anegundi, Chennai, Hampi, Hospet, Karnataka, Mathura, Taj Mahal, Vrindavan
Indonesia
Bali - Denpasar, Kalibukbuk, Lovina, Munduk, Singaraja, Ulun Danu, Ubud
Java - Borobudur, Jakarta, Prambanan, Yogyakarta
Iran
Alamut Valley / Alamut Castle, Bandar e Golmaniyeh, Bayaziye, Bazargan, Chak Chak, Dakmeh, Esfahan, Gazor Khan, Kaluts, Kandovan, Kerman, Khalate Talkh, Kharanaq, Khoor, Lake Orumiye, Mahan, Maku, Marvdasht, Mashhad, Mesr, Nasqh-e Rostam, Orumiye, Osku, Persepolis, Qazvin, Rayen, Sadegh Abad, Salt Flats (near Khoor), Shahr-e Kord, Shiraz, Tabriz, Tarjrish, Tehran, Yaseh Chah, Yazd, Zarad Band
Iraq / Iraqi Kurdistan
Amadiya, Dohuk, Erbil, Sulav, Sulimaniyeh
Other Iraq - Kirkuk, Mosul
Italy
Bergamo, Faenza, Florence, Lido, Milan, Pisa, Rimini, Rome, Treviso, Trieste, Venice
Ivory Coast
Abidjan, Grand Bassam

Japan
Tokyo
Jersey
Les Charrières Malorey, St. Helier
Jordan
Amman, Aqaba, Irbid, Petra, Rum Village, Wadi Musa, Wadi Rum
Kaliningrad
Kaliningrad City, Mamonovo
Karakalpakstan
Nukus
Kashubia
Gdunsk, Gdynia, Kartuzy, Pomlewo, (Wejherowo)
Kazakhstan
Almaty, Ile Alatau, Jibek Joli, Korday, Shymkent, Turkistan
Kenya
El Doret, Lake Nakuru, Maasai Mara National Park, Malaba,
Nairobi, Nakuru, Narok
Kiribati
Tarawa
North Tarawa – Abatao Island, New Jerusalem
South Tarawa –Bairiki, Betio, Bikenibeu, Bonriki, Eita
Kosovo
(Blace), (Kulla), Pristina
Kurdistan (see separate country sections for Iran, Iraq, Syria
and Turkey)
Królestwo Dreamlandu
Dreamopolis (inside Gdynia and Gdańsk, Poland)
Kugelmugel
Kugelmugel (inside Vienna, Austria)
Kuwait
Kuwait City: Sharq, Salmiya
Kyrgyzstan
Ala Archa, Bishkek, Burana Tower, Cholpon Ata, Issy-Kul Lake,
Ruh Ordo, Petroglyphs

Ladonia
Nimis
Lagoan Isles
Baffin's Pond, Beeney St. Georges (inside Portsmouth, England)
Laos
Don Det, Nong Nok Khiang, Pakse, Thanaleng, Vang
Vieng, Vientiane
Latvia
Riga
Lebanon
Beirut
Lesotho
Maseru, Mazenod, Thaba Bosiu
Liechtenstein
Vaduz
Lithuania
Kaunas, Kryziu Kalnas (Hill of Crosses), Siauliai, Trakai,
Uzupis, Vilnius
Luxembourg
Luxembourg City
Lovely
Bow, Eel Pie Island, Leicester Square, Westminster (all within
London, England)
Macau (Macao)
Coloanne, Macau Old Town, Taipa
**Northern Macedonia / North Macedonia (formerly
FYR Macedonia)**
(Blace), Delčevo, Gostivar, (Kulla), Lake Ohrid, Ohrid, Skopje
Malaysia
Batu, Beaufort, Gemas, Kota Kinabalu, Kuala Lumpur, Labuan,
Mamutik Island, Mount Kinabalu, Sapi Island
Malta
Comino Island – Blue Lagoon, Comino, Cominoto
Gozo Island – Ewkija, Mgarr, Victoria

Malta Island –Birkirkara, Cirkewwa, Floriana, Il Birgu (Vittoriosa), Il Mellieha, Luqa, Mdina, Mosta, Paceville, Popeye Village, Rabat, Sliema, St. Julian's, Valletta

Maasai Tribe
Maasai Mara National Park (Kenya), Rabbatt Village (Tanzania)

Marshall Islands
Majuro Atoll – Delap, Djarrit, Eneko Island, Majuro City, Uliga

Mexico
Agua Azul, Ciudad Cuauhtémoc, Mexico City, Misol Ha, Monte Alban, Oaxaca de Juarez, Palenque, San Cristobal de las Casas, Teotihuacán

Moldova
Butuceni, Chişinău, Orheiul Vechi

Monaco
Monte Carlo

Mongolia
Ulaan Baatar

Montenegro
(Budva), Kotor, Nikšić, Podgorica, (Rozaje)

Morocco
(Agadir), Casablanca, Marrakesh

Myanmar
Amarapura, Bagan, Inwa, Mandalay, Sagaing, Yangon

Nagorno Karabakh/Artsakh
Agdam, Askeran, Berdadzor, Gandzasar, Stepanakert, Vank

Namibia
Duesternbrook, Sandwich Harbour, Walvis Bay, Windhoek

Narnia
Aslan, CS Lewis's Wardrobe, Holywood Arches (inside Belfast, Northern Ireland)

Nauru
Aiwo, Anabar, Anetan, Anibare, Arenibek, Arijejen, Arubo, Baiti, Boe, Ewa, Ibwenape, Ijuw, Makwa, Meneng, Nibok, Orro, Ronave, Topside, Waboe, Yangor, Yaren

Netherlands

Amsterdam, Delft, Edam, Madurodam, Noordwijk, (Rotterdam), The Hague, Volendam

New Zealand

North Island - Auckland, Hamilton, Huntly, Mount Manganui, Paeroa, Palmerston North, Papamoa, Rotorua, Taihape, Tamaki Māori Village, Taupo, Taurangi, Waihi, Wellington

South Island - Belfast, Christchurch, Cromwell, Dunedin, Franz Josef Township, Greymouth, Haast, Lake Wanaka, Lawrence, Makarora, Oamaru, Otago Peninsula, Picton, Queenstown, Wanaka

Nicaragua

El Guasaule, Granada, Leon, Managua

North Korea

DMZ, Kaesong, Panmunjom, Pyongyang

Northern Cyprus

Turkish Nicosia

Northern Ireland (incomplete)

Aldergrove, Antrim, Armagh, Ballintoy, Ballyclare, Ballygowan, Ballyhalbert, Ballymena, Ballymoney, Ballyskeagh, Ballywalter, Ballywhiskin, Bangor, Belfast, Benone, Broughshane, Bushmills, Carrick A Rede Rope Bridge, Carrickfergus, Carrowdore, Carryduff, Castlerock, Castlewellan, Cloughy, Coleraine, Comber, Conlig, Craigavad, Craigavon, Crawfordsburn, Crossgar, Dark Hedges, Derry, Donaghadee, Downpatrick, Drumahoe, Dundonald, Dundrum, Dungannon, Dungiven, Dunluce Castle, Eglinton, Galgorm Resort, Ganaway, Giants Causeway, Glengormley, Glenshane Pass, Greyabbey, Greysteel, Groomsport, Helen's Bay, Hillsborough, Holywood, Kearney, Killinchy, Killyleagh, Kircubbin, Kirkistown, Larne, Limavady, Lisburn, Londonderry, Loughgall, Magherafelt, Marino, Middleton, Milford, Millisle, Nendrum, Newcastle, Newry, Newtownabbey, Newtownards, Portadown, Portaferry, Portavogie, Portballintrae, Portbraddon, Portrush, Portstewart, Raffrey, Ringhaddy, Rubane, Scarva,

Seahill, Strabane, Strangford, Tandragee, Templepatrick, Trim Trail, Tullymore, Warrenpoint
Norway
Bergen, Flåm, Fløyen, Gudvangen, Myrdal, Oslo, Rygge (Airport), Voss
Oman
Muscat, Mutrah, Riyam, Ruwi
Panama
Miraflores (Panama Canal), Panama City
Papua New Guinea
Port Moresby
Paraguay
Asuncion, Ciudad del Este, Luque
Peru
Aguas Calientes, Cuzco, Desaguadero, Juliaca, (Lima) *Inca Trail* – Dead Woman's Pass, Hatunchaca, Intipata, Intipunku, Llactapata, Machu Picchu, Miskay, Ollantaytambo, Paqaymayu, Patabamba, Phuyu Pata Marka, Q'Orihuayrachina, Runkurakay, Sayaqmarka, Warmiwanuska, Wayllabamba, Winaywayna
Philippines
Balicasag Island, Bohol Island, Cebu City, Manila City, Panglao Island, Tagbilaran, Virgin Island
Podjistan
Four Gables, Rural Podjistan, The People's Palace
Poland (incomplete)
Auschwitz, Białystok, Białowieża, Biskupiec, Bochnia, Braniewo, Brzeźno, Bydgoszcz, Chałupy, Chorzów, Chodzież, Chotyniec, Częstochowa, Elbląg, Gdańsk, Gdynia, Gliwice, Gniezno, Gręblin, Grotowice, Hel, Jarosław, Kalwaria Zebrzydowska, Katowice, Kętrzyn, Kielce, Kokoszkowy, Kościan, Krajenka, Kraków, Krzyz, Kuklówka – Zarczeczna, Lanckorona, Łeba, Łęczyna, Leszno, Łódź, Łomianki, Łowicz Wałecki, Lubiewo, Lublin, Majdanek, Malbork, Międzyzdroje, Mory, Nieciecza, Nowa Słupia, Nowy Wies, Ojców, Olsztyn, Opole, Pawłowice, Pelplin, Piaseczno, Piła,

Piotrkow Trybunalski, Plock, Poznań, Pruszcz Gdański, Radom, Radymno, Rywałd, Rzeszow, Szczecin, Słowiński National Park, Sopot, Starogard Gdański, Stutthof, Świdnica, Tarnów, Tarnowskie Góry, Tczew, Toruń, Trzcianka, Wałcz, Warszawa, Wilczy Szaniec (Wolfschanze / Wolf's Lair), Władysławowo, Włocławek, Wólka Milanowska, Wrocław, Ząbki, Zakopane, Zakrzewo, Zalipie, Zamość, Zielona Góra, Złotokłos, Złotów.

Polish Antarctica – Henryk Arctowski Base.

Portugal
Alvor, Faro, Lisbon, Portimao, The Algarve

Qatar
Doha

Republic of Ireland
Arklow, Blarney, Cashel, Cork, Donegal, Drogheda, Dublin, Dundalk, Dun Laoghaire, Glaslough, Muff, Rosslare, Wicklow

Romania
Bran, Brasov, Bucharest, Cacica, Campulung Moldovenesc, Humor, Marginea, Moldovita, Suceava, Sucevita

Romkerhall
Kingdom of Romkerhall

Russia
Kaliningrad, Krasnodar, Moscow, Saint Petersburg

Rwanda
Cyangugu / Rusizi, Gitarama, Kigali

San Escobar
San Escobar Embassy (inside Świdnica, Poland), San EscoBAR (inside Warszawa, Poland)

San Marino
San Marino City, Serravale

Sark
Little Sark, Sark, The Avenue, The Seigneurie

Saudi Arabia
Dir'aiyah, Ha'il, Hrabat, Jabal Umm Sanman, Jeddah, Jubbah, Mashar NP, Riyadh, Sand Dunes, Shaqra, Ta'if, Tawarun, Ushaiqer

Scotland
Ayr, Cairnryan, Edinburgh, Glasgow, Gretna, Irvine, Kilmarnock, Stranraer, Troon
Senegal
Dakar, Foundiougne, Karang, Lac Rose, M'Bour, N'Gor Beach
Serbia
Belgrade
Seychelles
Mahe Island – Anse Aux Pins, Anse Royale, Bai Lazare, Beau Vallon, Victoria
Ile Soleil (Island of the Sun)
Singapore
Singapore City
Slovakia
Bratislava, Don Valley
Slovenia
Bled, Lake Bled, Ljubljana, Maribor
Solomon Islands
Guadalcanal - Honiara, US War Memorial Hill
South Africa
Bloemfontein, Cape of Good Hope, Cape Town, Durban, Golela, Groot Marico, Johannesburg, Kopfontein, Montrose, Nelspruit, Pretoria, Robben Island, Simon's Town, Soweto, Sterkfontein
South Korea
DMZ, Imjingak, Incheon, Paju, Panmunjom, Seoul, Suwon
Sovereign Military Order of Malta
Flag Square in Vittoriosa, Private Residence in Fort Saint Angelo
Spain
Basque Country (Euskadi) - Bilbao, Donostia (San Sebastian)
Catalonia – Barcelona
Majorca - Magaluf, Palma
Menorca - Mahon, S'Arenal, San Clemente
Mainland - Alicante, La Linea De La Concepcion, Madrid, Malaga, San Martin, Seville, Torrevieja, Valencia

Sri Lanka
Adam's Peak, Colombo, Dambula, Dellhousie, Galle, Haputale,
Kandy, Kurunegala, Mirissa, Negombo, Pinnawala, Sigiriya,
Tissamaharama, Yala National Park
Suriname
Albina, Concordia Plantations, Marienburg, New Amsterdam,
Nieuw Nickerie, Paramaribo, South Drain, Zanderij
Swaziland / Eswatini
Ezulwini, Lavumisa, Lobamba, Mahlanya, Malkerns Valley,
Mantenga, Manzini
Sweden
Ängelholm, Gothenburg, Helsingborg, Malmö, Solna, Stockholm
Switzerland
Basel, Zurich
Taiwan
Anping, Chiayi, Changhua, Eluanbi, Guanshiling, Hualien,
Kaohsiung, Kenting, Lotus Lake, Shinying / Xinying, Taichung,
Taidong, Tailuga/Taroko Gorge, Tainan, Taipei, Taoyuan,
Tiansiang, Zuoying
Tajikistan
Dushanbe, Hisor, Khorog, Kulob
Tanzania
Arusha, Maasai Mara National Park, N'gorongoro Crater, Rabbatt
Maasai Village, Tarangire National Park, The Serengeti
Thailand
Aranya Prathet, Bangkok, Nong Khai, Udon Thani
Togo
Coco Beach, Lake Togo, Lome, Togoville
Transnistria / Pridnestrovian Moldavian Republic
(Bendery), Tiraspol
Trinidad and Tobago
Piarco, Port of Spain

Tunisia
Carthage, Kairouan, Mahdia, Monastir, Sidi Bou Said, Sousse,
Teboulba, Tunis
Turkey
Adana, Agre, Ankara, Cappadocia, Doğubayazıt / Dog Something,
Goreme, Gurbulak, Istanbul, Kaymakli, Nevşehir, Sumela,
Trabzon, Ürgüp
Turkmenistan
Abdullah-Khan Kala, Anau, Ashgabat, Darvaza Crater, Dashoguz,
Diyar-Bekir, Jerbent, Konye-Urgench, Mary, Merv, Ruhubelent
Uganda
Entebbe, Gatuna, Jinja, Kampala, Lake Victoria, Mbarara, River
Nile Start, Tororo
Ukraine
Lviv, Kiev (see also Chernobyl Exclusion Zone: Chernobyl Town,
Duga Tower, Dytyatky, Kopachi, Pripyat, Reactor Number 4)
United Arab Emirates
Dubai, Sharjah
United Kingdom (see England, Northern Ireland, Scotland
and Wales)
United States of America
Atlanta, (Dallas), Kissimmee, Hollywood, Los Angeles, New York,
Orlando, (Philadelphia), (Pittsburgh), (San Francisco)
Uruguay
Casapueblo, Colonia del Sacramento, (Maldonado), Montevideo,
Punta del Este
Uzbekistan
Bukhara, Denau, Karshi, Khiva, Navoi, Nukus, Samarkand,
Tashkent, Termiz, Urgench
Užupis
Užupis (Zarzecze) (Neighbourhood in Vilnius, Lithuania)
Vatican City State
Saint Paul's Square, Sistine Chapel, Vatican Museums

Venezuela
Caracas, San Antonio del Tachira, San Cristobal
Vietnam
Giang Ta Chai, Halong Bay, Hanoi, Lao Cai, Lao Chai, Sapa,
Ta Van
Wales
Abergavenny, Cardiff, Fishguard, Holyhead, Mardy, Swansea
Wallachia
Hranice, Valašské Meziříčí
Western Sahara
El Aaiún / Laayoune, Foum El-Oued
Zambia
Kazungula, Livingstone, Victoria Falls
Zimbabwe
Kazungula, Victoria Falls City, Victoria Falls

Places I have physically been to but don't count on the list:
(**Mauritania**) (Nouakchott Airport)

Acknowledgements

The author wishes to thank the following people for their help and assistance on this journey around the world, and to Poland. Thanks for being there on my travels and playing a big part in my life.

- My parents Muriel and Joe Blair, who have loved me on every step of my journey.
- My brothers Marko Blair and Danny Blair and my sister Cathy Blair.
- All fellow pupils and members of staff at Kilmaine Primary School where I attended from 1984 - 1991.
- My ex-girlfriend, 44 country together backpacking friend, Panny Yu.
- My best friends in life Rafał Kowalczyk, "Millwall Neil", Michael Whitford, Dan Darch, Austin Sheppard, Sandra Kabasinguzi, Daniel Evans, Lock In Lee Adams, Julia Korcz, Ania Baran, Kamil Turula and Richard "Richboy" Ingram for always being there for me in times of need.
- Authors and Writers Deacon Blake, Stephen Rea, Richard Morgan, Michael Miller, Niall Doherty, Carlo Cretaro, Matt Kepnes, Derek Earl Baron, Gunnar Garfors and Paddy Campbell for inspiring my journey, all people who I have met in real life.
- My backpacking friends Chaz Fitzsimmons, Fifi Rushfield, Russell Sneddon, Natalja Tsumakova and all other honest people who I went backpacking with.
- My Polish backpacking buddy from India, Ilona Skladzien.
- The Polish based bloggers on the "Hello Poland" team.
- Pani Alina Bagińska at Learn Polish in Gdańsk.
- Pani Dorota Maszkiewicz at Klub Dialogu in Warszawa.
- Adela for the cappuccino at Co Jak Co, Poznań.
- All staff at Browar Stary Rynek, Starogard Gdański.
- All staff at Jozef K Bar, Gdańsk.
- All staff at Café Mila / Kawiarnia Mila, Warszawa.

- All Polish media that has featured and promoted me thus far.
- My childhood sweetheart, Claire McKee.
- Kasia's in the Lemon Tree. Yeah Kasia's in the Lemon Tree.
- KP – I miss you.
- Maggie Ivanova, my fine Bulgarian flatmate. Baby blue.
- The Slavic lady who once slept in the bunk bed above me.
- The Hungarian dancer, Noemi Linzenbold.
- Scott Eldo and Daniel Sidebottom at Eldo Design for the book formatting and cover design.
- The Green and White Army, the GAWA, Northern Ireland fans.
- All supporters of AFC Bournemouth.
- All supporters of Glentoran FC.
- Footballers that inspired this book – Kazik Deyna, Zbigniew Boniek, Robert Warzycha, Gerry Armstrong, Pat Jennings, Norman Whiteside, George Best, Teddy Sheringham, Gary McCartney, James Hayter, Eddie Howe, Steve Fletcher, Alan Connell Alan and David Healy.
- Musicians Tim Wheeler, Mark Hamilton, Rick McMurray, Noel Gallagher, Liam Gallagher, Nicky Wire, James Dean Bradfield, Sean Moore and Neil Finn, whose words and songs have inspired me along the way.
- TV Shows that inspired this book – Whatever Happened To The Likely Lads, Only Fools And Horses, Game On, Fawlty Towers.
- All the readers and followers of my one man travel blog, Don't Stop Living.
- All the readers and followers of my Poland based travel blog, Northern Irishman in Poland.
- This book is dedicated to everyone (past, present and future) at Kilmaine Primary School in Bangor, Northern Ireland.

Stay beautiful. Stay young. Stay honest. Stay safe.

Jonny Blair will return.

Do widzenia!

Other Books From Jonny Blair

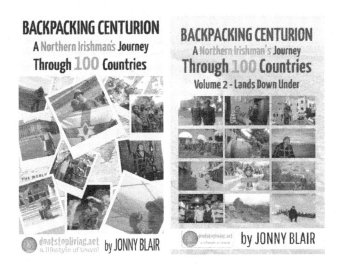

Backpacking Centurion –
A Northern Irishman's Journey Through 100 Countries
Volume 1 – Don't Look Back In Bangor
Volume 2 – Lands Down Under
Volume 3 – Taints and Honours
ChampIAN STEWARTnova – Supporting the Northern Ireland
football team 1980 – 2009

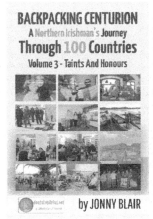